exploring *the* ELEMENTS *of* DESIGN

exploring *the* ELEMENTS *of* DESIGN

Poppy Evans
Mark Thomas

DELMAR
CENGAGE Learning™

Australia Canada Mexico Singapore Spain United Kingdom United States

Exploring the Elements of Design

Poppy Evans and Mark Thomas

Vice President,Technology and Trades ABU:
David Garza

Director of Learning Solutions:
Sandy Clark

Managing Editor:
Larry Main

Senior Acquisitions Editor:
James Gish

Product Manager:
Nicole Bruno

Editorial Assistant:
Sarah Timm

Marketing Director:
Deborah Yarnell

Marketing Manager:
Kevin Rivenburg

Marketing Specialist:
Victoria Ortiz

Director of Production:
Patty Stephan

Production Manager:
Andrew Crouth

Content Project Manager:
Michael Tubbert

Technology Project Manager:
Kevin Smith

For product information and technology assistance, contact us at
Cengage Learning Customer & Sales Support, 1-800-354-9706

For permission to use material from this text or product,
submit all requests online at **cengage.com/permissions**
Further permissions questions can be emailed to
permissionrequest@cengage.com

Library of Congress Control Number: 2007012902

ISBN-13: 978-1-4180-3855-7

ISBN-10: 1-4180-3855-5

Delmar Cengage Learning
5 Maxwell Drive
Clifton Park, NY 12065-2919
USA

Cengage Learning products are represented in Canada by Nelson Education, Ltd.

For your lifelong learning solutions, visit **delmar.cengage.com**

Visit our corporate website at **www.cengage.com**

Notice to the Reader

Publisher does not warrant or guarantee any of the products described herein or perform any independent analysis in connection with any of the product information contained herein. Publisher does not assume, and expressly disclaims, any obligation to obtain and include information other than that provided to it by the manufacturer. The reader is expressly warned to consider and adopt all safety precautions that might be indicated by the activities described herein and to avoid all potential hazards. By following the instructions contained herein, the reader willingly assumes all risks in connection with such instructions. The publisher makes no representations or warranties of any kind, including but not limited to, the warranties of fitness for particular purpose or merchantability, nor are any such representations implied with respect to the material set forth herein, and the publisher takes no responsibility with respect to such material. The publisher shall not be liable for any special, consequential, or exemplary damages resulting, in whole or part, from the readers' use of, or reliance upon, this material.

Printed in Canada
4 5 6 7 11 10 09

M. T. Dedicated with love to mom and dad.
And to brother Greg, uncle Dick, and Art Bargees,
my fishing buddies who help me make sense of it all.

P. E. Dedicated with all my love to Mom, Dad, Evan and Rob.

contents

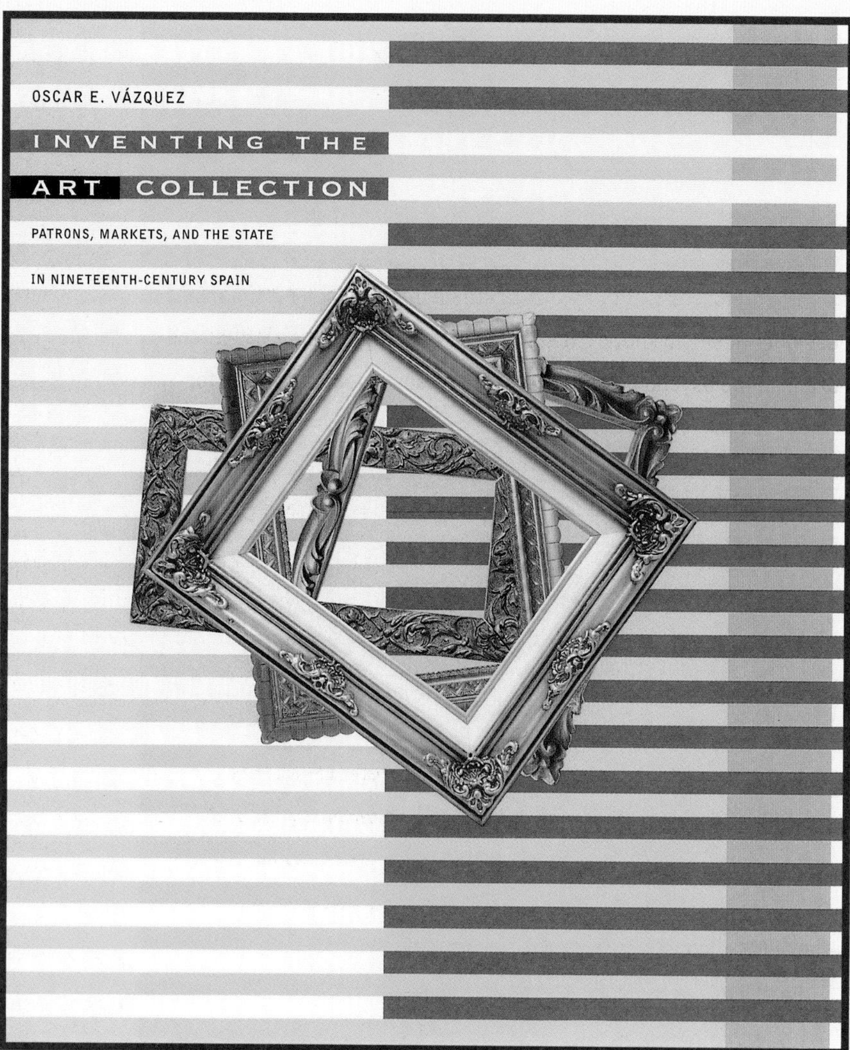
OSCAR E. VÁZQUEZ
INVENTING THE
ART COLLECTION
PATRONS, MARKETS, AND THE STATE
IN NINETEENTH-CENTURY SPAIN

preface

preface

INTENDED AUDIENCE

Understanding how design elements and principles work together to create effective communication is at the core of what every graphic designer needs to know. *Exploring the Elements of Design* is intended to teach visual fundamentals and examine the psychology and visual processes that are the basis for visual communication. This text explains design fundamentals and how they work in the context of the design industry, supported by custom diagrams and examples from professionals in the field. Additional chapter content includes the use of color in design, design research methods, media and design, type basics, and professional profiles. *Exploring the Elements of Design* may be used by introductory- to intermediate-level design majors and non-design professionals who need a primer of design essentials.

BACKGROUND

Exploring the Elements of Design is an attempt to bridge the gap between the theoretical and the practical. Design has traditionally been taught as basic theory supported with visual examples that demonstrate these fundamentals in their simplest form. This approach has led to textbooks filled with diagrammatic examples and projects that engage students in design decisions that are limited to simple shapes, linear elements, and colors. Although these methods work well for introducing rudimentary material, students often have a problem making the leap from visual basics to more complex projects in the professional realm. This text combines diagrams with professional examples to demonstrate how design fundamentals are put to effective use in the real world.

TEXTBOOK ORGANIZATION

This book is structured so that students are introduced to design fundamentals at the beginning of the book and progressively work their way step-by-step through an understanding of design processes, strategies, and professional preparation.

In Chapter 1, students learn about how design works as a visual language built on fundamental principles and elements. The primary principles of unity, variety, hierarchy, and proportion are explained as they affect a design composition as a whole. Scale, balance, rhythm, repetition, and proximity are presented as support principles that govern internal design relationships within a composition. The design elements of shape, space, line, size, color, texture, and typography are also introduced as compositional content.

Chapter 2 addresses typography's role in design and familiarizes students with basic terms and measurement systems. Students also learn how to select typefaces appropriate to a project's design and communication goals and use type effectively in a design composition.

In Chapter 3, students develop an understanding of imagery's role in design. This chapter explains how symbols, logos, and trademarks function as an aspect of image representation. Students also learn how to choose appropriate imagery and make the most of it in a design composition.

Color's role in design is explored in Chapter 4. Students learn about how color is perceived and processed by the eye and brain, and they are introduced to basic color terminology. Color systems and color psychology are explored, as well as strategies for choosing effective color schemes and using color effectively in a composition.

Chapter 5 presents a discussion of the origin of design in nature and the constructed environment as sources for inspiration. It also addresses graphic devices and techniques that support visual relationships and organization. The psychological effect of design is also explored, as well as how design can best be used in support of a communication goal.

Chapter 6 discusses the basis of design research methods and design processes. Connections are made between design problem solving and visual thinking to the fields of psychology and semiotics. A variety of research tools are presented to help establish informed design strategies.

Media options for communication artists are discussed in Chapter 7. Students learn about how technological advancements have affected media development and how design has adapted to new media.

Chapter 8 addresses career opportunities. An overview of the industry and career options is included, as well as advice on self promotion, portfolio preparation, and interviewing strategies.

FEATURES

The following list provides some of the salient features of the text:

- Objectives clearly state the learning goals of each chapter.
- Contemporary examples of graphic design from leading design firms are given.
- Color visuals are used to explain and analyze design fundamentals in graphic and verbal terms.
- The elements of design—line, shape and texture, color, size, and value—are defined and examined.
- The principles of design—unity, variety, hierarchy, proportion, scale, balance, rhythm, repetition, and proximity—are reviewed and explained.
- How typography and imagery can be used successfully in design is explored.
- Research strategies that provide an informed basis for design decisions.
- Profiles of successful graphic designers are included, along with their important industry advice and inspiration.
- Articles by leading professionals in the field give valuable insight into the creative process.
- Review questions and in depth assignments reinforce material presented in each chapter.

INSTRUCTOR'S GUIDE ON CD-ROM

This electronic manual was developed to assist instructors in planning and implementing their instructional programs. It includes sample syllabi for using this book in either an 11 or 15 week course.

It provides answers to the review questions found in the text, tips for assessing completed exercises assigned in the book, and a list of additional resources. It also includes PowerPoint slides that highlight main topics and provide a framework for classroom discussion.

ISBN 1-4018-3287-3

ABOUT THE AUTHORS

Poppy Evans is an award-winning writer and graphic designer with over twenty years of experience in the design industry. She is currently an assistant professor in the Communication Arts department at the Art Academy of Cincinnati. A former art director for an international trade magazine and managing editor for *HOW,* an influential design magazine, Evans is an authoritative voice in design education.

She has written thirteen books on print production and graphic design including *Exploring Publication Design*, and frequently writes articles for a variety of design publications, including *HOW* magazine where she serves as contributing editor. A former education chair and AIGA board member, Evans holds a B.F. A. in Fine Arts from the University of Cincinnati.

Mark Thomas is Professor and Chair of the Communication Arts Department at the Art Academy of Cincinnati where he has been teaching for 20 years. He has developed courses in design research methods, illustration, design systems and a thesis program for communication arts. He is also a graphic designer, illustrator, and published author. He has designed numerous exhibitions, catalogues and posters for graphic designers, fine artists and illustrators including Anita Kunz, Marshall Arisman, Loren Long, Malcolm Grear, Edward Potthast and Kevin T. Kelly. Mr. Thomas holds a National Parent Center Seal of Approval for educational board game design. He also holds a U.S. patent for an educational color demonstration device and method used for teaching color theory. He has an M.F.A. and an A.B.D. in Design Education from the University of Cincinnati and is a board member of AIGA Cincinnati.

ACKNOWLEDGMENTS

Much thanks to Glenn Rand for introducing us to James Gish at Delmar Learning. Our appreciation to the following professionals for their support and expertise: Christian Moore, Rob Ruben, Wayne Williams, Rebecca Seeman, Gary Gaffney, Paige Williams, and Flavia Bastos.

The work and insightful voices of these professionals will forever resonate in our practice of designing and teaching: Lawrence Goodridge, Malcolm Greer, Hermine Feinstein (*in memoriam*), Gregory Wolfe, Roy R. Behrens, Dennis Puhalla, and Noel Martin.

Thanks to our Delmar Learning team of professionals who offered support, ideas, guidance, and trusted us to write the book we believed in: Jim Gish, senior acquisitions editor; Sarah Timm, editorial assistant; Benj Gleeksman, content project manager; and Jack Pendleton, art director.

A special thanks to Nicole Bruno, our product manager, for her support, patience, and trust.

Finally, to the many talented and accomplished designers, illustrators, and artists whose works appear throughout this book, our sincere thanks.

Delmar Learning and the authors would also like to thank Sherrie Geitgey VCT Instructor at Northwest State Community College for her valuable suggestions and technical expertise.

QUESTIONS AND FEEDBACK

Delmar Learning and the authors welcome your questions and feedback. If you have suggestions that you think others would benefit from, please let us know, and we will try to include them in the next edition.

To send us your questions and/or feedback, you can contact the publisher at: Delmar Learning Executive Woods 5 Maxwell Drive Clifton Park, NY 12065 Attn: Graphic Arts Team 800-998-7498 Or the authors at: Art Academy of Cincinnati 1212 Jackson St., Cincinnati, OH 45202, 513-562-8777 Poppy Evans: poppy@one.net Mark Thomas: merj@fuse.net

1 DEFINING *the Language of* DESIGN

objectives

Understand design as a visual language that is built on fundamental principles and elements.

Explain how the primary principles of unity, variety, hierarchy, dominance, proportion, and balance affect the design composition as a whole.

Explain how the supporting principles of scale, emphasis, rhythm, movement, proximity, and repetition affect internal relationships of the elements within a design composition.

Describe the uses of the design elements shape, space, line, size, color, texture, and typography as compositional content.

introduction

Design is a visual language that is built on fundamental principles and elements. The principles are the organizational rules used in conjunction with the elements to create order and visual interest. The principles are presented as two related sets: primary and secondary (or support). The primary principles affect the design as a whole. Secondary, or support, principles affect the internal relationships of the elements. Principles can be thought of as the unseen forces that create interaction between the elements. The elements of design constitute the content of a graphic design composition. The elements are seen and exist on the surface or picture plane of a composition.

Each of the principles and elements is defined and discussed. Accompanying analysis using professional examples is provided, as well as illustrated diagrams.

PRINCIPLES AND ELEMENTS OF DESIGN

The human psyche seeks harmony and resolution in everyday life. You use your senses of touch, smell, hearing, taste, and sight to perceive and navigate in the world. When you perceive that your living or work environments have become too disorderly, you are motivated to organize them so you can again function productively. You see disorder and act to reorganize or rearrange it. On a basic level, the activity of designing is a form of visual organization. The more familiar you are with the environment you want to change, the more manageable is the task of changing it.

Graphic design is the art of arranging pictographic and typographic elements to create effective communication. It is a complex discipline that requires skillful and sensitive use of the eyes for navigating; the hands for crafting; the left brain for analytic reasoning and logic; and the right brain for creative, intuitive thinking. Directing those functions of the mind and body is a demanding human activity. In fact, research in higher education ranks studying visual arts second behind attending medical school in overall demand of the learner. Design is not a collection of formulas that, if followed and applied, ensures effective results. Design is a fluid process that is guided by the designer's sense of intuition, reason, and aesthetic judgment.

To manage the process, successful designers have learned that fundamental principles can be used to guide their creative design decisions. The principles provide a structure for combining the common elements of design in a composition by serving as the relationship between the parts or design elements involved. You may find it helpful to use familiar analogies when thinking about the elements of design; for example, the ingredients in a recipe, the parts of a machine, or the materials needed to build a house. Individually, those components have limited use. But when skillfully combined, they work together to form something useful. When a measure of creativity is added, the result can be not only useful but also pleasing to the senses. Design works in a similar way.

You can understand how design works by first defining an inventory of principles and elements of design. Then you can see why those principles and elements work by examining examples of design that emphasize a particular principle or element. Many lists of principles and elements of visual organization are widely acknowledged and have been written about in books on art and design theory. Most of those principles and elements are universal to any of the visual arts. The principles are often grouped together, suggesting that they have an equal role or are of equal importance. However, some principles have a more dominant function, whereas others serve a supporting role. The principles have been organized here as primary and supporting to help you see their function and relationship. In any given design, one principle can be emphasized over another.

Primary principles *affect the design as a whole* and include the following:

- **Unity**
- **Variety**
- **Hierarchy**
- **Dominance**
- **Proportion**
- **Balance**

Support principles *affect the internal relationships of a design* and include the following:

- **Scale**
- **Emphasis**
- **Rhythm**
- **Movement**
- **Proximity**
- **Repetition**

There are also visual relationships that function as variations or forms of the principles just mentioned. They also will be discussed in this chapter as they are widely used in education and the industry. Those visual relationships include **economy**, **tension**, **direction**, **density**, **harmony**, **discord**, **focal point**, **theme**, and **motif**. The elements of design include shape, space, line, size, color, contrast, pattern, texture, and typography. Typography is included as an element because in addition to having verbal meaning, it also functions in design in the same manner as shape and line.

Primary Principles

Through the study and practice of making works of design, you will become more familiar with the processes and strategies that govern it. A working knowledge of the principles and elements of design provides a foundation for managing design decisions. Keep in mind that the principles and elements are interrelated. You will see how in the discussion of each.

Unity and Variety

In the eye and mind of a viewer of any designed image, the viewer needs to be able to understand what he or she is seeing. An objective of any design plan is to create a sense of unity through the organization of the compositional parts. **Unity** is an overriding principle that is served by all others (Visual 1–1). Unity is the control of variety. Often the content used in a design varies in kind and can include different typefaces, graphic elements, photographs, or illustrations.

visual | 1–1 |

In this range of merchandise from the San Francisco Museum of Modern Art, unity is achieved in several ways. The logo's individual letterforms are strong identifiers that are repeated on each item. The consistent use of a distinctive, saturated color palette also unifies each product. Changing the scale of the logo elements to accommodate the changing size of each souvenir item is a fresh, bold approach to variety. The horizontal bands on the bags mimic the banding effect of the logo applied to other items, and the bands create a layering effect that adds depth. The result is a variety of merchandise applications that tie-in with each other and make a unified presentation. *(Logo and merchandise design by Michael Osborne Design)*

A complementary principle to unity, **variety** is necessary to create visual interest. Managing variety is the art of balancing visual contrasts. It is combining elements that do not appear, on the surface, to have much in common. Unusual combinations of elements directed at the message often are used in the most inventive and successful designs. However, too much variety or random use of it can cause confusion (see Visual 1–2a and Visual 1–2b).

visual | 1–2a |

At a glance, the design seems colorful and lively. But a closer examination reveals that this design is struggling for identity and unity. The photograph of a fall landscape captures a rich, delicate patchwork of color that serves as a backdrop for type and graphic elements. Competing with the photo are three different typefaces as well as two different uses of icons. Although the colors in the border frame relate to the photograph, they overpower the delicate quality of the image. Too much variety has created a dysfunctional design.

visual | 1–2b |

This solution uses two styles of the same typeface, creating a subtle and more unified statement in keeping with the photograph. The green rule implies the word *in* and minimizes clutter. Eliminating the graphic icons also gives the photograph more visibility. A full color border has been replaced by a color rule at the top and bottom of the design. That implied border opens up the photo, making it look as though it could continue beyond the left and right edges of the design. Finally, the decorative band at the top, which mimics qualities of the petroglyphs that can be found on the island, has been reduced in size. The color of the band coordinates with that of the type. In this revision, unity is achieved through economy. **Economy** is the idea of distilling the design to its most essential parts while striving to be sensitive to visual relationships. The type, graphic elements, and photograph are now working in concert to enhance and support one another.

Hierarchy and Dominance

An important function of unity in design is managing visual hierarchy in composition. **Hierarchy** refers to an arranged order. **Dominance**, the prevailing influence of one element over another, and **emphasis**, the importance of one element over another, are commonly thought of as principles. But they are more simplistic, related functions of hierarchy. Hierarchy is the established order, importance, and emphasis given to visual elements, from those that are dominant to those that are subordinate. A designer must manage the size, placement, and balance of the elements used so the viewer can read the image and extract the intended meaning. Controlling hierarchy determines the path the viewer's eye takes as the viewer first scans and then studies a design composition.

If you look at any work of design or art repeatedly, you can experience an eye-movement path.

For the first few seconds of each viewing, the path is the same. Areas of high contrast, faces, or unusual shapes immediately attract the eye. Once you loop a few times around the dominant elements in a work, you become familiar with them and break away from the familiar elements to consider other features and elements that support the main ones (see Visual 1–3).

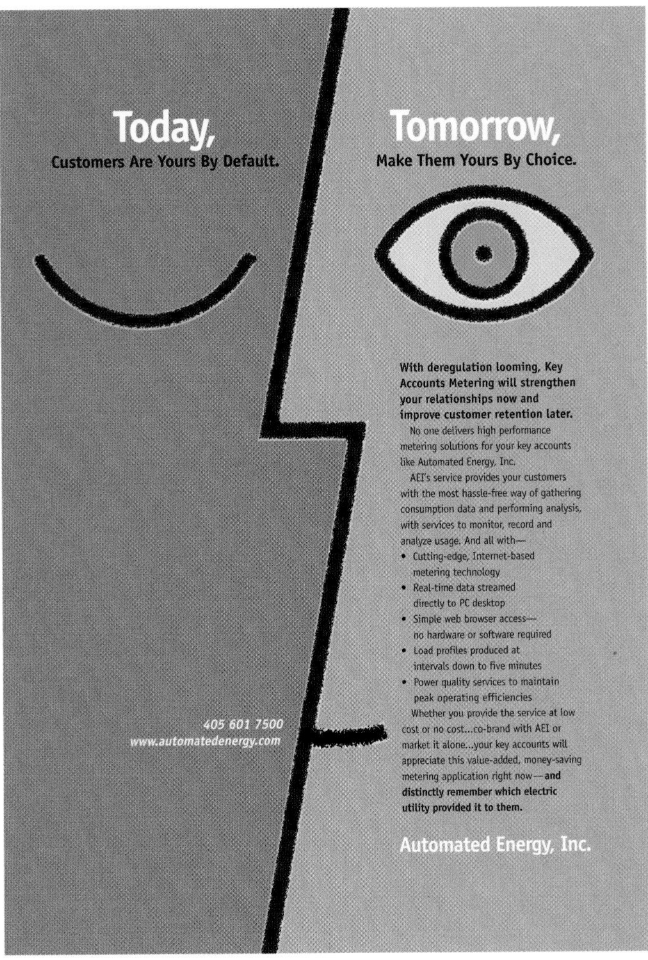

visual 1–3

By determining hierarchy, a designer can control the path a viewer's eye will take when the viewer is scanning a design composition. In the case of the ad, the viewer is first drawn to the prominent open eye and then to the suggestion of a face. The headlines "Today" and "Tomorrow" are the first type elements that are read.

The zigzag vertical line pulls the eye down to the smaller blocks of text. Two clever graphic effects in this image are the dual read of the face from a frontal view to a profile and the completion of the mouth with typographic elements. *(Ad for Automated Energy by Steve Walker)*

Lack of clear visual hierarchy is the reason many designs fail to attract and hold a viewer's attention. It is important to practice the art of critical analysis, or deconstruction of design compositions. A critical analysis begins through examination of the parts of a design to see how they function. That activity can help identify the visual hierarchy and the subsequent eye-movement path. Identifying the most dominant elements in a design, as well as secondary, and other support elements, reveals the meaning in the message. Sharpening that skill will serve your own design.

Bias exists in the way certain cultural groups comprehend visual information, which has an impact on eye-movement tendencies. Designers must be sensitive to viewer partiality with regard to visual orientation, which is influenced primarily by the way written language is read. In Western cultures, people read from left to right and top to bottom. Most Arab and Semitic writing is read from right to left, but numbers are read left to right. Hieroglyphics, pictographic writings that preceded alphabets, are read in different directions. Traditional Chinese calligraphy is read top to bottom and right to left, but modern Chinese newspapers and books are read left to right. Depending on the concept, graphic design can be read from middle to top, from bottom to top, up a side, or down a side. The designer is in control of how a designed image is read by managing visual hierarchy (see Visual 1–4a,Visual 1–4b, and Visual 1–4c).

Proportion

Proportion refers to the size relationships within a composition. Those relationships serve as a transparent, underlying structure for the surface design. The outer dimensions determine the format of a two-dimensional design and are its most basic proportion. A square, a vertical rectangle, and a horizontal rectangle are all formats with unique proportions that affect particular qualities of a design (see Visual 1–5a, Visual 1–5b, and Visual 1–5c). The outer proportions or dimensions of a design have an important relationship to the internal divisions and alignments. As shown in Visual 1–5a, Visual 1–5b, and Visual 1–5c, outer dimensions affect the orientation of the viewer and are often dictated by the nature of the design venue.

Designers and illustrators must work with numerous proportional formats. Books and posters tend to be vertical in orientation, CD covers are square, billboards are horizontal, and three-dimensional surface graphics can assume many forms. Whether the format proportions are a given or are determined by the designer, they are one of the first important considerations in a design plan.

The relationship between outer dimensions and internal divisions can provide a system for managing design decisions. Some proportional systems have been used for centuries in architecture, art, and design. Those systems are based on ratios—a comparison of one set of sizes or quantities with another. Although ratios are commonly expressed in mathematical terms, they also can be expressed as visual relationships. The golden section is a ratio that dates back to ancient Greeks. Its proportional **harmony** possesses both aesthetic beauty and structural integrity.

The ratio of the golden mean (expressed mathematically as 1:1.618) is used to construct the golden rectangle and is the same ratio found in the structure of plants and other life-forms. The spiral order of leaves growing from a branch, the seed pattern in the center of a sunflower, and the spiral of a nautilus shell can all be expressed in terms of the golden ratio. Building a golden rectangle using the ratio requires no calculations. The rectangle is constructed using a series of

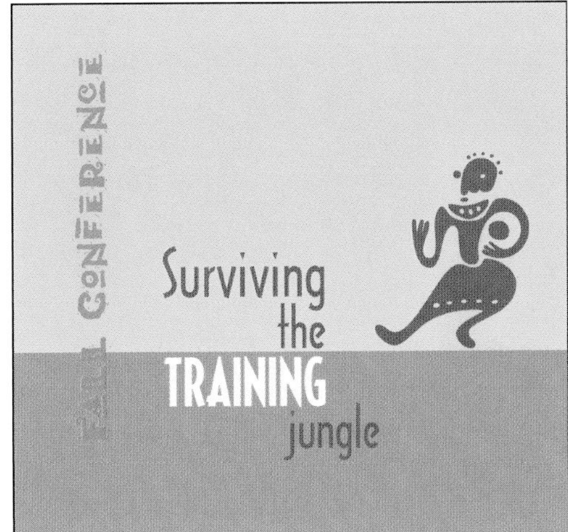

(a)

(b)

(c)

visual | 1-4a to c |

It's sometimes helpful to think of design elements as actors on a stage, with the designer determining which element will lead and which elements will support the lead. The examples are composed of three major players: the primary message or headline, "Surviving the Training Jungle"; a supporting illustration; and a qualifying tagline, "Fall Conference." In Visual 1–4a, all three elements are equal.

Changing the **direction** of the tagline adds a directional element and gangs the typographic information. The resulting pockets of negative space give the illustration room to interact with the type and background. The image in Visual 1–4b places emphasis on the illustration. Its size dominates the typographic information, presenting bold curved-shape edges that frame the headline. The composition seems balanced with the visual placed just to the right of center and the "rag" left shape of the type used to mirror the right side of the visual. In Visual 1–4c, the headline dominates the communication message. The illustration functions as an accent element. The design employs an expected hierarchy that reads from the top down. The varying sizes of the elements in each of the compositions create a unique visual tension between the elements. **Tension** can be thought of as a balanced relationship between opposing elements or the interplay between elements.

extended relationships as described in Visual 1–6a. Those relationships possess a strong aesthetic harmony, because the internal proportions relate in scale to the proportions of the original square and its extensions. The golden section can be extended to construct the golden rectangle, which was used by the Greeks as the basis for much of their architecture, including the Parthenon

(a)

(b)

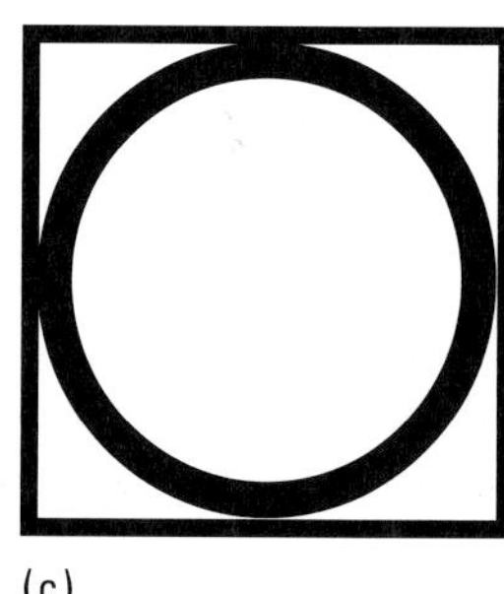
(c)

visual | 1–5a to c |

One of the first decisions a designer makes is to determine a design composition's overall dimensions. Because the internal relationships of the design composition depend on the proportions of the outer dimensions, the overall dimension should not be an arbitrary decision. The shape of a design format also possesses associative meaning. (a) A vertical rectangle in contemporary Western culture is associated with architectural metaphors such as a building, a window, or a door.

A vertical rectangle also can relate to the proportions of a standing human form. Magazines, books, print ads, and most poster designs use the rising presence that a vertical rectangle offers. (b) A horizontal rectangle (center) has a long-standing association with the landscape. In contemporary culture, movie screens, computer monitors, and televisions all make use of this panoramic format. (c) A square configuration offers a stable, neutral format that allows the designer, illustrator, or photographer to influence the overall composition by controlling the relationship of internal elements. The square can be a difficult format in which to design because it does not offer the proportional shift of a rectangle. The square has a proportional relationship to the circle and equilateral triangle. Those three shapes are considered primary shapes.

(see Visual 1–6b). Renaissance artists used the golden rectangle to create overall harmony and balance in works of painting and drawing, and contemporary graphic designers use the rectangle as a format for print and digital media (see Visual 1–6c and Visual 1–6d).

Balance

Balance is the visual distribution of elements in a composition. There are two types of visual balance: symmetric and asymmetric. In symmetric balance, elements are arranged the same or very similarly on either side of a central axis. The elements appear to be projecting a mirror image, like a landscape projected in a still lake (see Visual 1–8a and Visual 1–8b). Symmetry also occurs as the halves of a circle and equilateral and isosceles triangles.

Asymmetric balance, sometimes referred to as dynamic symmetry, is the art of creating balance using uneven numbers, sizes, or kinds of elements. In the visual arts, dynamic symmetry is achieved when the relationship between negative and positive space and form and counterform is managed (see Visual 1–9).

Physical balance is a functional demand of three-dimensional design. Physical balance can be achieved with a base, as in a bottle of cologne, a lamp, or a computer monitor. It also can be designed through the use of legs or pods to support the central form, as in a chair, a coatrack, or an easel.

Support Principles

As stated, the support principles affect the interaction between elements and sometimes have a relationship with a primary principle. Scale and proportion are examples of support principles that have a direct relationship to a primary principle. Support principles help to establish visual organization in a composition.

None of the support or primary principles exist alone. In any composition, multiple principles are at work. However, you will see that in the arrangements of graphic elements, successful design tends to stress the use of one or two support principles.

Scale

Proportion and scale are related principles. Proportion refers to the size relationships of the design elements in a composition as an aspect of the space they occupy in a design composition as a whole. **Scale** refers to size comparisons of the internal parts of a composition, or a size relationship in the comparison of one design element to another. Size, distance, and configuration often are compared in the natural and constructed worlds. Comparisons based on a known constant provide a familiar orientation. The profile of a towering building or the mass of a mountain on the horizon can be difficult to judge in terms of size. However, when juxtaposed with a human figure, an automobile, or an animal, it becomes easy to establish a familiar comparison of size. Scale can be used to create variety and emphasis in a design and help establish visual hierarchy (see Visual 1–7).

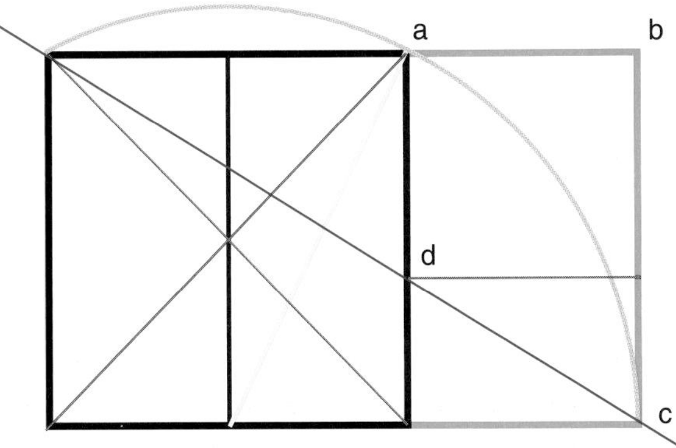

visual 1–6a

The Golden Rectangle. You can construct a golden rectangle by starting with a square. Find the center of the square by drawing intersecting lines through opposite corners, as shown in the gray *X*. From there, draw a vertical line through the intersecting point of the *X*. Place the point of a compass where the centerline intersects the base of the square and scribe an arc that intersects the top right corner of the square (Point a) and extends to the square's baseline.

Complete the rectangle by extending the square to the point where the arc meets the baseline (Points b and c). You can form a second golden rectangle by drawing a diagonal line (shown in red) that extends across opposite corners of the rectangle and drawing a horizontal line from the point where that line intersects the original square (Point d). The second rectangle and its parts are proportional to the original rectangle and corresponding parts.

visual | 1-6b |

The ancient Greeks found the proportions of the golden rectangle of great use in architectural design. Its proportions served them in the building of the Parthenon, contributing structural integrity in columns used to provided support for the entablature and pediment. The golden rectangle also possesses aesthetic beauty in the overall proportional relationships of all of the architectural components. The spacing of the columns related to their height and width and the relationship of the column height to the distributed number of columns and the supported entablature fit into two golden rectangles that share a common square.

visual | 1-6c |

Today designers find the proportions of the golden rectangle useful for organizing and arranging elements in a composition, as in the design of this page from an ad campaign for Growzone.com. The intersecting construction lines used to build the golden rectangle identify critical alignments and placement points in the layout. The random or casual arrangement was actually carefully planned. *(Design by Erbe Design)*

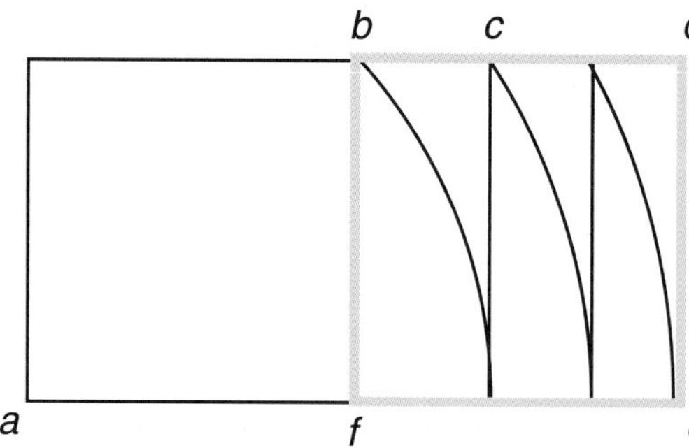

visual | 1-6d |

The dynamic rectangle, although not as elegant as the golden rectangle, also serves as a proportional device for organizing design elements. To construct it, begin with a square. Place a compass point in the corner of the square (Point a) and scribe an arc that intersects the opposite corner (Point b) down to the baseline of the rectangle. Draw a vertical line up to Point c and extend the rectangle. Continue by placing the compass point at Point a and scribe an arc through Point c. Extend the rectangle again. When you continue out to three extensions, you construct a new square. Extend out eight extensions to construct a third square.

Emphasis

Elements in some designs have an arrangement that is evenly distributed over the surface. The elements create a **pattern** that gives equal importance to each element, as shown in the background area of Visual 1–11. Textile designs such as quilts, rugs, tapestry, and fashion often rely on a repeated arrangement, or **motif**, that is perceived as an overall pattern.

However, many designs use a point or points of visual interest that attract the viewer's eye, giving prominence to an element or to an arrangement of the elements. Emphasis is the use of a **focal point** to stress certain elements or to give special attention to an element. Without emphasis, the viewer's eye would wander around a design composition, with no purpose or direction. Emphasis can be achieved in a variety of ways: through size variation (see Visual 1–12), color (see Visual 1–7), visual weight, density, or boldness, such as the bold black and patterned edge created in Visual 1–11 or the shape and placement of the *R* in Visual 1–10a.

Each of those examples results in a different kind of **contrast**: contrast of size, light and dark, color, shape or texture, and contrast of weight or density. They all function to create emphasis. Also notice in the examples that surrounding elements provide alignment or context for emphasis of the prominent elements.

visual | 1–7 |

The known constant in this image is established with human scale. The graphic simplification of the subject matter offers no textural or modeling detail as spatial cues. However, you can estimate the size of the trees and the crashing jet based on the presence of the human figures. Overlapping perspective and the cropping of the figures compress the space and help to balance the action that takes place in the background. The panoramic proportions of the image and the animated treatment of the content give this satiric social commentary a cinematic scale. *("Suburban Blight," Acrylic painting by Kevin T. Kelly)*

(a)

(b)

visual | 1–8a and b |

Two types of symmetrical balance are represented in these compositions. (a) The annual report cover is a bilateral composition where, if an imaginary axis were drawn down the center, one side would mirror the other. (b) The clock design is an example of radial symmetry where elements are arranged and are equally balanced as though they were spokes on a wheel. *(Annual report designed by Cahan Associates; clock designed by Evenson Design Group)*

visual | 1–9 |

In this poster design, asymmetrical balance is achieved by counterbalancing roughly equivalent amounts of positive and negative space, or form and counterform. In this case, the handgun, which dominates the upper left portion of the poster, is counterbalanced by the negative space, or white area, to the right and below the handgun. The two main areas of white "background," or negative space, are activated by their shapes. While those areas are not physically equivalent, they work together as shapes in a complementary relationship. *(Poster design by Post Typography)*

Rhythm and Movement

The term *rhythm* is associated most often with music, defined as an alternating occurrence of sounds and silence.

Rhythm in the visual realm can be described the same way. When you replace sound and silence with form and space, the same description works for graphic design (see Visual 1–10a and Visual 1–10b). Creating a rhythm with visual elements is the choreography of graphic design. This choreography is the implied **movement** of the elements as manifested through the eye of the viewer. Rhythm gives shape to the movement in a composition. In Visual 1–10a, rhythm is articulated through the descending size of the letters in each word. The subsequent movement takes the eye back into space on a curved trajectory in the word *Moon* and in a horizontal direction in the word *Rufe*. The line element offers a quiet contrasting rhythm.

In a sense, rhythm and movement are transparent to the design. They exist in an implied sense defined through the arrangement and configuration (varying line shape, size, and color) of graphic elements. Rhythm dictates the form of the arrangement, giving movement and natural flow to related elements in the composition.

Rhythms can be regular and static (see Visual 1–11) or pulsating and full of exaggerated gesture (see Visual 1–12).

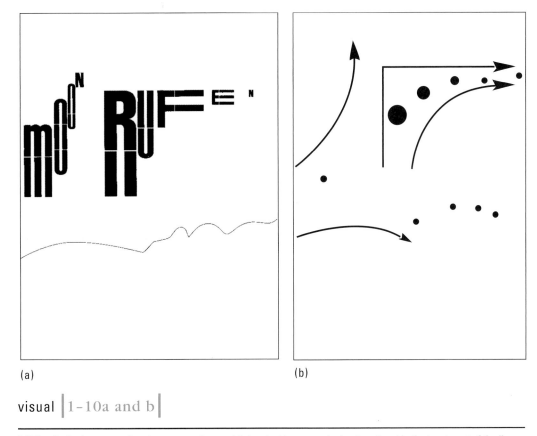

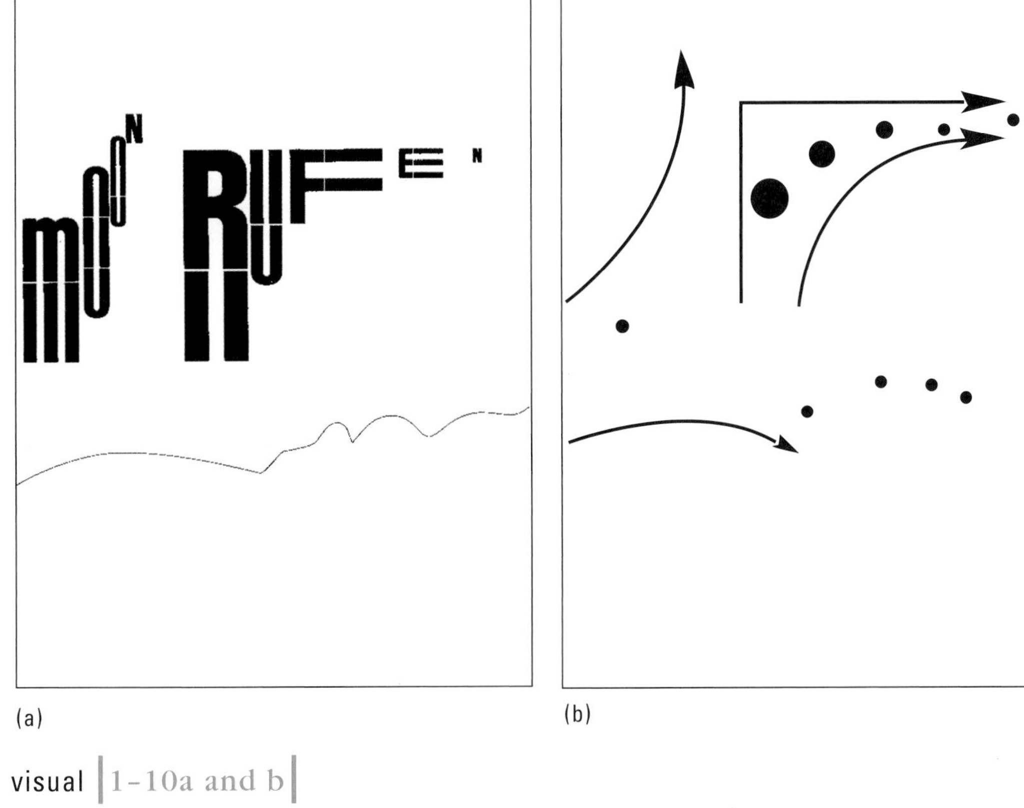

(a) (b)

visual | 1–10a and b |

(a) The rhythmic pattern that the typography establishes in this poster design is echoed in the treatment of the line below it. (b) A diagrammatic breakdown gives a more basic representation of this rhythm. *(Poster design by Wolfgang Weingart)*

visual | 1-11 |

In this turn-of-the-century poster, a regular rhythmic pattern is established to provide a backdrop for the typographic information. Each of the three areas—the solid black rectangle, the graphic background, and the type block—has differing **density**, which creates visual contrast, depth, and visual tension. *(Poster design by Joseff Hoffmann)*

visual | 1-12 |

In this poster, scale and color shifting creates a pulsating effect. Placing the units on the diagonal results in a dynamic rhythm that moves in and out of space. S and Z configurations were used as compositional devices to create dynamic diagonal movement and structure. (*Poster design by Max Bill)*

Proximity and Repetition

One of the most critical decisions a designer makes is where to place design elements. **Proximity** is the position and space given to the placement of elements in a composition. Proximity determines the placement of elements together and apart from one another. Controlling the relative size and distance from one element to another, based on common increments or shared attributes, also establishes visual continuity and aesthetic harmony. Proximity functions in two basic ways. First, repetition follows a regular pattern of related or juxtaposed elements (see Visual 1–11). You also can repeat elements that vary in size or other attributes. The diagonal squares in Visual 1–12 are related by shape, differ in size, and repeat in a varied manner to create both variety and unity. Second, counterpoint placement of elements is a dynamic arrangement of differing elements. In fact, most design is the art of achieving unity with a variety of different typographic and pictorial elements.

Designers look for ways to align images, text, and other graphic elements based on common attributes. Grid systems play an important role in determining placement, whether the message calls for regularity or for counterpoints to create visual interest (see Visual 1–13 and Visual 1–14). A discussion of grid systems is presented in Chapter 2.

visual | 1–13 |

With its *g* placed strategically in the bottom left portion of the circle, the asymmetrically balanced Gymboree logo demonstrates the importance of placement. Centering the *g* within the circle would have resulted in a static, predictable composition.

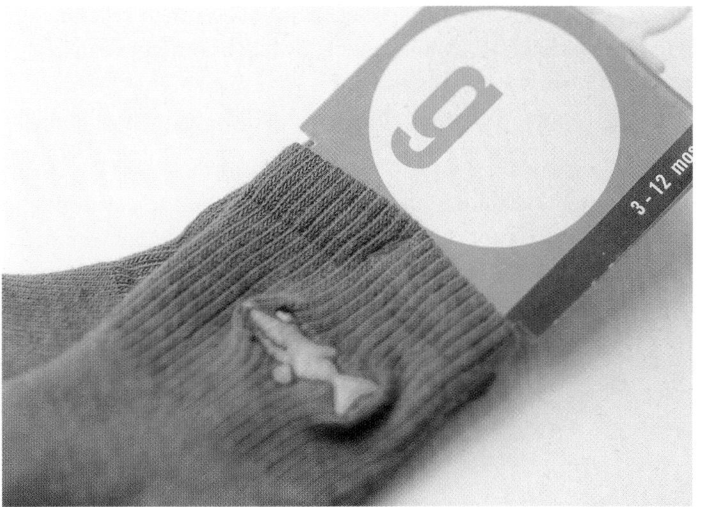

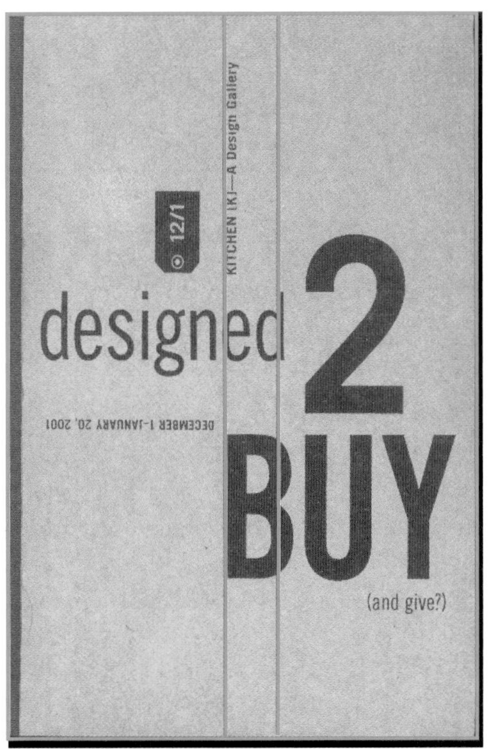

visual | 1–14 |

A grid (shown in blue) serves as the underlying placement guide for the graphic elements on the cover and interior pages of this publication. From there, the alignment of common edges such as the number 2 and letter *U* on the cover, as well as other shared attributes, guided the designers in their design decisions. *(Brochure design by Kinetik Communication Graphics Inc.)*

The space between two or more elements affects their relationship. As they move together, a visual **tension** can result. When they touch, new hybrid shapes can form. And at some point, as they move apart, they can become disassociated with one another (see Visual 1–15). You can think of design as a conversation in which the elements talk to each other. The conversation can be quiet and understated, or it can be loud and chaotic.

The resulting dialogue is affected profoundly by the positioning of the design elements and their number in the composition. Proximity groupings can create patterns, a sense of rhythm, or other relationships that elicit a response from the viewer. Keep in mind that the conversation must be in support of the communication goal or message (see Visual 1–16a, Visual 1–16b, and Visual 1–16c).

As a general rule, varied proximity of elements can result in a visual tension that brings dynamic interest to a composition. Equal and regular spacing between graphic elements of similar size can result in a static, uniform composition.

visual 1–15

This illustration from a book about aliens demonstrates how important the space between two design elements can be. Notice how the background becomes activated and new shapes are formed as the alien ship approaches the car. *(Image by Morris Creative)*

(a)

(b)

(c)

visual | 1-16a to c |

In these three designs, size, color, and orientation of each design element is the same for each composition. However, changing the position of the elements changes their relationship and the resulting conversation. In Visual 1–16a, the elements are independent of each other, but each is touching the edge of the composition. In this somewhat aloof conversation, the shape in the middle is trying to bridge the gap between the letter *t* and the chevron shape. Visual 1–16b brings the elements together, touching in a precarious grouping where the elements are dependent on each other in this curious balancing act. The resulting conversation is playful and mutually supportive. The elements in Visual 1–16c have been carefully aligned and overlapped to create a new form that has three-dimensional qualities. The full identity of each element is concealed, and each serves the newly created form.

Elements of Design

The elements of design can be thought of as content—the design components. The elements discussed in this chapter are considered formal elements. Formal elements are general and abstract in nature—that is, they do not necessarily describe anything in specific terms. Formal elements can be used to represent or describe specific things. A line can represent a leaf, the human figure has shape, and a bowl of fruit has color. Described elements tend to be identified as what they represent; for example, a person rather than a shape. The elements are the visual vocabulary that gives voice to an image, allowing it to speak to the viewer. Study the vocabulary of elements in Visuals 1–26 and 1–27. Both rely on the use of circular elements, a single word form in black and white, and some shared colors. But the distinctive use of shapes and graphic treatment yield a very different feel and message. Studying the elements in formal, critical terms is helpful in understanding how the elements function as descriptive components in a design composition.

Shape, space, line, texture, and type are tangible elements (i.e., they have a physically defined presence). Color, value, size, and volume are examples of elements that are conditional. They exist as an embellishment or as a way of defining the tangible elements.

Shape and Space

Shape can be defined as a figure or form. In two-dimensional design, shapes possess width and length. When shapes possess volume, they move into the realm of three dimensions and are better described as mass. In either dimension, the configuration of the shape or mass determines its meaning. For example, a shape constructed of soft, curved edges can be described as sensual; a shape constructed of angular edges and points can be considered crystalline. Shape configurations can be described on a basic level as geometric or organic (see Visual 1–17a and Visual 1–17b).

Other ways of describing the overall configuration of shapes include figurative, mechanical, or natural.

Shapes must reflect the intent of the message. If your message is one of tranquil feelings, the use of harsh angular shapes would confuse the viewer. A sense of tranquility is more likely to be instilled by the use of flowing organic shapes.

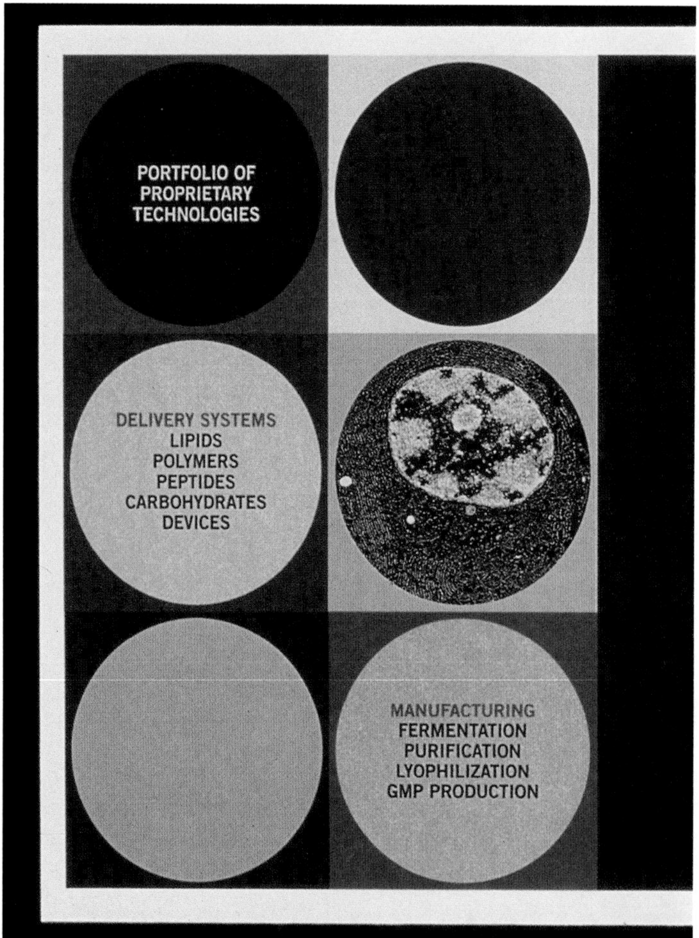

visual | 1–17a |

Shape is often used in support of a message. Within this annual report, Cahan & Associates uses geometric shapes and the circular motif of a microscopic view as a visual metaphor for genetic engineering.

visual | 1–17b |

The organic quality of the shapes, lines, and letterforms in this bakery's logo supports the natural ingredients and organic quality of its baked goods. *(Design by Morris Creative)*

Shapes exist as figures in or on a ground (background or space). Shapes are generally considered positive figures that displace space. The relationship of figure and ground—positive/shape, negative/space—is a fundamental association. But in a curious way, space around figures has shape too. To orchestrate a harmonic balance of the parts of a design, it is critical to achieve a sensitive relationship between the shapes of the design and the configuration of the space around the shapes. Experienced designers know the importance of paying equal attention to the shape of figures and the shape of their surrounding space or ground.

In the most fundamental terms, space is an area activated by the other elements. Graphic design is a discipline concerned with the arrangement of elements in a given space. Artists tend to focus attention on the photograph, letterforms, or illustrated subjects in their design. But to present those graphic elements in a dynamic and visually purposeful way, artists also must design the space around the elements. When a line or shape element is introduced into an area of space, it is said that the space is activated. Activating space can be attained subtly or overtly using line or shape (see Visual 1–18).

visual | 1–18 |

Amidst the arrangement of large-scale shapes, the soft curved line projects a quiet influence as it activates the area within the green plane. The color reversal in the two enclosed areas in the *m* activates the background, creating a figure-ground reversal. The shapes change their position in space depending on how you view them. The line is a constant. It curls into the composition from the right edge, establishing itself in the foreground.

Beyond the formal considerations of space as an element, artists can create a particular kind of space for the viewer to experience. There are four ways that space can function, which you will examine next.

Actual space is the area that the design physically occupies. Some designs do not attempt to transform the actual space, but live in and on the space provided, as shown in Visual 1–30. The arrow shapes and typography exist on the physical surface and occupy the space with respect to the rectangular edges.

Pictorial space is the manipulation of a flat surface to create the sense of depth, movement, or direction. The depth in Visual 1–26 is created through the use of overlapping perspective and is relatively compressed. A much deeper space is achieved in Visual 1–27 using linear perspective and diminishing size. Pictorial space relies on illusory devices that fool the viewer's eye.

Psychological space presents an arrangement that influences the viewer's mind. Neither of the designed spaces in Visual 1–28 and Visual 1–29 represent spaces that potentially exist. Each in its own way, however, presents a space that evokes a strong feeling. In the Weingart poster, the space is activated with a flurry of torn shapes, saturated color, scratched textures, and unique letterforms. The space presents an energy that can be associated with the excitement of learning. The space in the Carroll illustration is a kind of montage of soft dreamlike images that evoke an unsettling feeling. Carroll combines individual figures, the distant skyline and architectural forms, and scratched spirals and curves in his illustration. But he wants viewers to assemble their meaning. The result is a haunting feeling of desperation that is enhanced by the psychological space he creates.

Physical space is the expanse of a three-dimensional area. Three-dimensional or environmental design must consider the function of space or environment and the aesthetics of designing within it. An example of the function of space is when design interfaces with the constructed environment. A signage system in an airport, the designed relationship of the parts of a coffeemaker, or the inherent restrictions imposed by a retail space on the design of a display or signage are examples of space function. How design visually interacts with space is an aesthetic concern.

Line

In formal terms, a **line** is the moving path of a point. The path determines the quality and character of the resulting line. The path can be straight, it can meander and curve across itself, or it can follow the precise arc of a circle segment. The resulting lines from those point paths give a specific character and meaning to a line. Another aspect of line quality is determined by the tool that makes it; for example, the sketched quality of a charcoal pencil line, the precision of a line drawn with a digital pen tool, or the organic quality of a line brushed with ink (see Visual 1–19).

Lines of type can take the form of any configuration of a drawn line (see Visual 1–20).

Another way to think of line is the idea of line as edge. A good example is a horizon line that exists as the line distinguishing land from sky. An edge line can exist along the side of any straight or curved shape or as the result of shapes sharing the same edge. You can see an example of line as edge in Visual 1–18.

Line also can be implied, meaning it exists as the result of an alignment of shapes, edges, or even points. Implying the existence of a line in that way can be very engaging for the viewer. Implying lines also activates the compositional space (see Visual 1–21).

Line functions in a variety of ways in design and art. Line can serve as the contour of an object or a human figure. It can exist purely to serve itself as a graphic element used to separate information, lead the eye in a particular direction, or imply alignment. The three straight lines used in Visual 1–2b function that way. The zigzag line in the same example functions symbolically, representing the style of mark making used by native cultures. Line also can become texture or pattern. The quality of a line can communicate the nature of what is being described; for example, delicate, precise, angular, architectural, mechanical, anatomical, fluid, or awkward.

visual | 1–19 |

Lines can have different qualities depending on the tool used to create them. Shown here are three examples of lines drawn with (from left to right) charcoal, a brush, and a digital pen tool. Note the different characteristics of each. The charcoal line can be described as rough and gritty, the brush stroke line seems loose and casual, and the digitally drawn line is clean and precise.

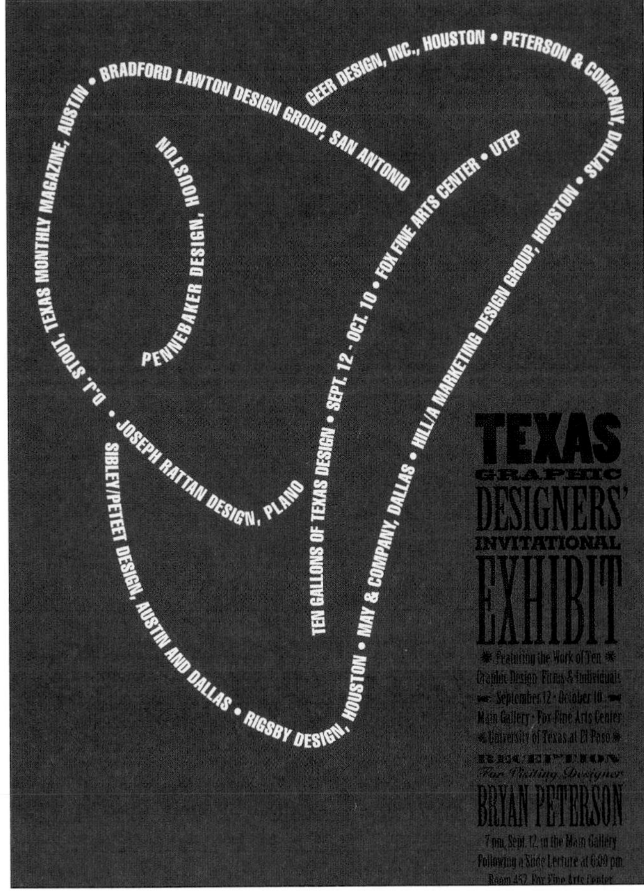

visual | 1–20 |

Type also can be used in a linear way to describe a shape or form, as it does in this poster promoting a Texas design exhibition. The result is playful and has a memorable graphic impact. *(Poster design by Mithoff Advertising)*

THE DESIGNER AT WORK

"Try to work for a company that does good work. If this is impossible, force yourself to do personal projects that you feel good about."

—Stefan Sagmeister

stefan sagmeister

Stefan Sagmeister's work is characterized by innovative and unusual concepts. Many of his design solutions incorporate interactivity, controversial subject matter, and a visual surprise.

His approach is perhaps best exemplified by *Made You Look*, a monograph of his work that was published in 2001. Designed by Sagmeister and his staff, the book incorporates many of the optical tricks and surprises and the interactivity of the designer's CD packaging. In fact, the book's cover, when placed in its red slipcase, portrays what appears to be a photograph of a friendly German shepherd. When the slipcase is removed, the dog's sweet countenance changes to reveal a vicious alter ego, foaming at the mouth.

A native of Austria, Sagmeister received his master of fine arts in graphic design from the University of Applied Arts in Vienna. He came to the United States as a Fulbright Scholar in the late 1980s, receiving his master's degree from Pratt Institute in 1990.

After working in the early 1990s at M&Co. under the mentorship of designer Tibor Kalman, he formed New York City-based Sagmeister Inc. in 1993. Since then, Sagmeister has become best known for designing graphics and CD packaging for popular recording artists such as The Rolling Stones, Pat Metheny, Aerosmith, and Lou Reed. In addition to winning many international design awards, Sagmeister has been nominated four times for the recording industry's Grammy award.

In addition to running a successful design studio, Sagmeister teaches at New York City's School for Visual Arts. He says that his students often inspire him, but they also can be his toughest critics. He was encouraged when a young designer responded positively to his book. "She said that after she read the book she wanted to do a lot of work. That's exactly how I felt when I was a student and I read a book I enjoyed," says Sagmeister. "I was very flattered."

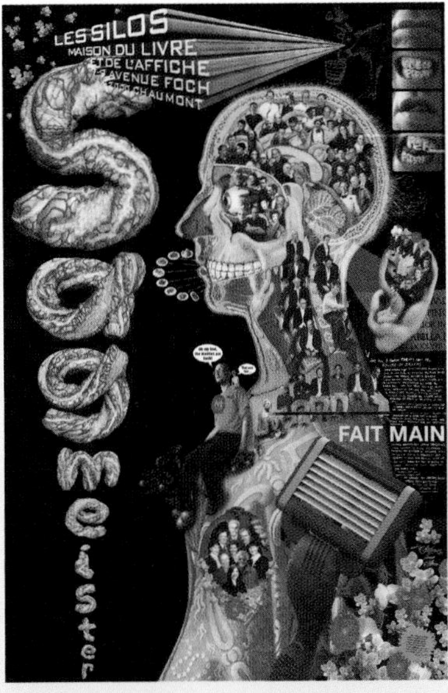

Another poster promoting design exhibitions in Japan features a before photograph of Sagmeister at 178 pounds and a second, after bingeing, in which he is 25 pounds heavier.

Sagmeister has developed a reputation for taking risks in his work, an aspect that is evident in these poster designs. A poster for an exhibition of his firm's design work in France features illustrations of people who have influenced his design. All of the images were hand-painted by artists catering to tourists in New York City's Central Park.

visual | 1–21 |

In this poster, there are a number of implied linear relationships. Some exist through an alignment of shapes and letterforms. Others exist through alignment of end points. Study the poster and see how many implied line relationships you can find. *(Poster design by Josh Higgins Design)*

Size

Size serves scale and proportion. **Size** refers to the physical dimensions of an element or format. Determining the size of a typeface or a photograph or the dimensions of a poster or display is a basic decision that needs to be made within the context of the overall design objective. For some design venues such as CD packaging, magazines, billboards, and Web sites, size is a given. Where and how they will be viewed is a determinant of size. In packaging applications, the size of the product determines the size of the package (see Visual 1–22).

In other situations, the designer may determine the size of a work. Most design is first consumed through the eyes and then manipulated by hand. Books, magazines, other publications, and packaging and product design are good examples. In those instances, size is a function of portability and hand-eye manipulation. In other situations, viewing the message from a distance dictates the venue's size (see Visual 1–23). Even when size is open for consideration, designers are forced to work creatively within externally imposed constraints. A savvy designer uses the comparison of sizes (scale and proportion) to control how the viewer perceives relative size (see Visual 1–24).

visual 1–22

The intimate ritual of applying and wearing fine perfume is intensified in the design of this container and package. The diminutive size creates a precious quality, meant to be handled by fingers rather than hands. The small size allows the product to be easily portable. *(Design by Sayles Graphic Design)*

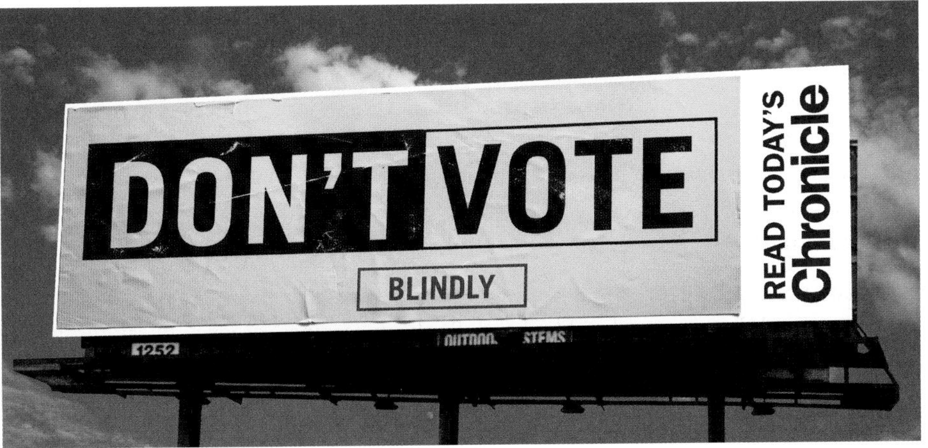

visual | 1-23 |

Designed to be viewed at a distance, the large scale of a billboard does not necessarily mean more room for more information. Billboards usually contain relatively little text and imagery because they need to deliver a message that passing motorists and pedestrians can perceive at a glance. Enhancing the readability of the message is an effective graphic device of using high-contrast colors to reverse the type out of the background. *(Billboard design by Rives Carlberg)*

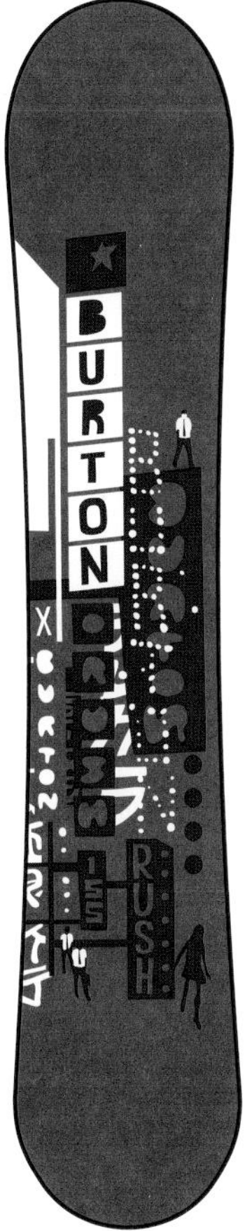

visual | 1-24 |

These snowboard designs use scale change and proportion to create variations on the theme of city nightlife. In the example on the left, the type and overlapping shapes create a sense of proportion with a human scale. The middle example uses a diminishing scale to create a sense of perspective and motion. At right, cropping and changing the size of type establishes a scale that seems larger than the physical space it occupies. *(Snowboard design by Jager Di Paola Kemp)*

Color

Color describes the intrinsic hues found in light and pigment. Hues are distinguished in common discourse by names such as maroon, olive, and ochre. In industry, numerous systems have been designed to categorize, name, and classify color for various applications. As an element, color heightens the emotional and psychological dimensions of any visual image.

Colors carry cultural meaning that communicates immediately without the aid of words or pictures (see Visual 1–25).

Color also can convey an attitude or a mood. Color enhances compositional space by controlling color contrasts. Color can have a role in supporting all of the visual principles and can be applied to the other elements (see Visual 1–26). It can help create emphasis and variety, support an established hierarchy, and activate shapes and space. Chapter 4 addresses color and value and their use in design.

visual |1–25|

Color can support a seasonal message, as it does in this exhibition invitation card. The biannual October exhibition was moved from a gallery located in a park setting toan urban venue. A sienna earth tone color was used in the word "of" and in selected graphic elements to support a fall motif. The grid placed in a black"field" symbolize the urban setting as it contrasts to the shapes and colors of fall leaves. *(Invitation card design by Mark A. Thomas)*

visual |1–26|

Color can be used to manage hierarchy by establishing position in space, as in this restaurant signage where the brightly colored lime jumps forward in space even though it is considerably smaller than the orange directly behind it. *(Restaurant signage design by Sibley/Peteet)*

Texture

Texture refers to the quality and characteristic of a surface. Texture can be tactile and visual. Like color, texture cannot function as a design element on its own. It enhances the other elements, relying on shape and space to exist (see Visual 1–27).

Texture provides designers with an opportunity to create variety and depth in a composition and helps differentiate figure from ground when a design is complexly layered (see Visual 1–28).

Lines of text, painted surfaces, applications of dry media such as pencil or charcoal, or actual surfaces photographed or digitally scanned replicate actual texture but function as visual texture. Illustrators and photographers often make images that simulate real texture (see Visual 1–29).

There are instances in design in which texture is a tactile experience. Perhaps the most common example is the feel of paper surfaces within magazines and books or the paper used for business cards and letters as well as on packaging and other products that are designed to be handled. The paper surface specified by the designer plays an important role in the way the user interacts with the product. A variety of materials such as paper, plastic, metal, glass, and wood play an important role in determining the perception of quality and the function of the design. Texture can be arranged using its direction to create a pattern. Patterns of texture can be arranged to achieve visual tension and movement.

visual | 1–27 |

Combining drawn line and shape elements with the clean lines and shapes in the radial designs results in a rich contrast of visual texture. These motifs were successfully used to communicate the rich Mideastern flavor of the music within this compact disc packaging. *(Package design by Sagmeister Inc.)*

visual | 1-28 |

In this poster, a sense of dimension is created by adding layers of different textured shapes that camouflage the type forms. The effect creates a delay in the reading of the information. Textures and shapes create unity through variety in a visually active design. *(Poster design by Wolfgang Weingart)*

visual | 1-29 |

Artist Jim Carroll's illustration technique combines photography, layers of type, and painted and scratchboard surfaces to create rich textural imagery.

Typography

Typographic forms are elements unique to communication design because they play a dual role. On a formal level, they function as shape, texture, point, and line (see Visual 1–30). But, of course, typographic forms also contain verbal meaning. Word forms must communicate a verbal message as well as function effectively as graphic elements in a composition.

When typographic elements are managed only with regard to their verbal meaning, the design can lack visual impact. When type is manipulated with a treatment that enhances its message, that message is perceived on a sensory as well as an intellectual level (see Visual 1–31).

In primary and secondary school, you related to typography as words in books that contained information for you to learn. You write letters to make words, sentences, and paragraphs that express your thoughts and ideas. That information is usually presented in horizontal lines that are stacked in columns that are arranged on a sequence of pages. After years of relating to type in that way, it is understandably challenging to think of type as a visual form that can assume other configurations. Exercises that provide an opportunity to work with type in unusual and creative ways help reorient your thinking toward type as a potentially dynamic element in design composition. A further discussion of typography will be presented in Chapter 2.

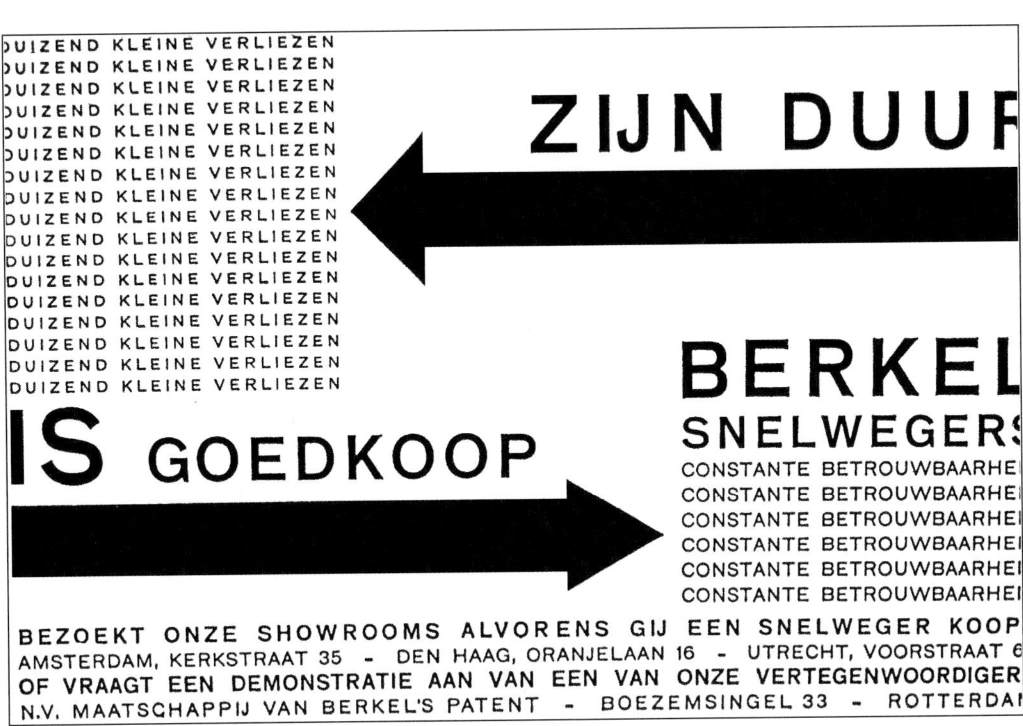

visual 1–30

Blocks of text can create a textural quality. Changing the size and spacing of type changes the look of the textures in the design. *(Ad design by Paul Schuitema)*

visual | 1-31 |

This comparison illustrates two treatments of the same word, with dramatic differences. In the example at the top, the word *ITCH* is understood primarily by reading its verbal meaning. Beneath it, the same word is rendered with textural lines that communicate visually what the word says verbally. The verbal meaning "scratch the itch" is enhanced with a visual embellishment.

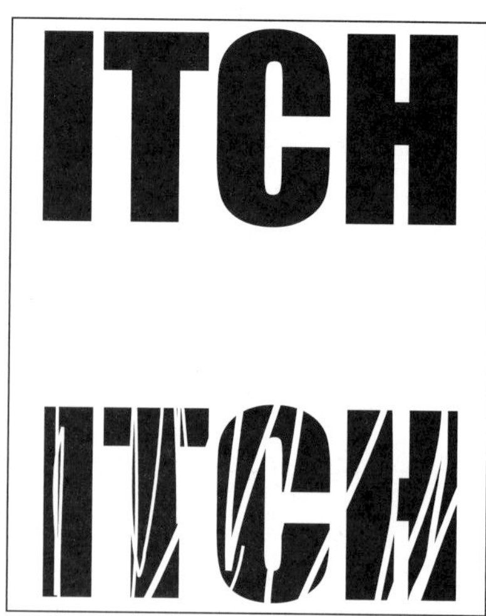

SUMMARY

The principles and elements of design function as a visual vocabulary. And in that sense, learning to use them is like learning a new language. It can be overwhelming to understand how to use all of them in your own designs. Study them individually at first and gradually learn to combine them in more complex ways. Also helpful is to study the work of contemporary designers and design through the twentieth century and contemporary design from the twenty-first century.

The exercises for this chapter stress one or two main principles, limiting the elements used to solve them. Once you have mastered the vocabulary of any language, you can communicate in that tongue. The visual language is complex and fluid. It is fluid because it is influenced by cultural, social, and technological change. Using visual language is an ongoing learning process, but the principles and elements do not change. When you have gained a working knowledge of them, you possess the means to powerful communication.

ANATOMY OF CHAPTER PROJECT

Each project is presented with a Project Title, Objectives, Description, Limitations and Materials, Critique Discussion Points, Vocabulary, References and Resources, and Evaluation Criteria. Read the project carefully so you understand what it is asking you to do. Refer to the objectives as you proceed to solve the problem. Research the artist references, using books and Internet searches to see how professionals and masters have worked with similar creative concerns. The work of these professionals and masters is not, of course, solutions to any of the projects, but rather opportunities to see how design principles and elements are at work in professional examples. You also should be attentive to each project's use of materials and media. Practice with them before you use them to execute the project. Finally, explore possible solutions in preliminary studies. Doing so will allow you to work with ideas without the commitment and pressure of producing a finished product.

projects

Project Title Line Study Grid

Objectives

Gain control of hand-eye coordination in drawing

Work with control of line quality in a variety of tools

Work with a simple grid system to produce a composition

Engage in a process of visual decision-making to create a design

Work with variety and contrast

Description

Draw a series of line sets of equal line length (approximately 2½ inches long and 2½ inches wide) and equal interval from each other. Change the interval from tight to loose as you practice your control in each set. Generate 15 to 20 sets.

Cut the sets into 2-inch squares and arrange 9 of them in a 9-unit grid. Strive for a variety of texture and value as you create this arrangement. Also explore variation in the character and quality of the lines as you draw them.

Drawing is a critical skill for all designers. This type of drawing can be used as a warm-up for brainstorm sketching or design drawing.

Limitations and Materials

Use a quality drawing paper or bristol board. Draw with fine to heavyweight markers, an ebony pencil, medium to soft charcoal pencil, and graphite sticks. Adhere the final 2-inch squares to a two-ply bristol board. Mount the final grid composition on a gray board with a 3-inch border.

Critique Discussion Points

How does the process serve the final design?

What different types of contrast did you achieve?

What role does texture play in the design?

How would you assess your control in the drawing?

Vocabulary

line, grid, composition, variety, contrast

References and Resources

Brice Marden, Willem DeKooning, Robert Motherwell, Jasper Johns, Louise Fishman, Eva Hesse, Louisa Chase, Franz Kline, Jackson Pollack, Susan Hauptman, Cy Twombly, Jean-Michel Basquiat, Stuart Davis, David Carson, Bradbury Thompson, Stephan Sagmeister, Louise Fili, Ryan McGuinness

Evaluation Criteria

Source Work and Research

Concept Development

Design/Composition

Craft/Execution

Project Title Interrupted Line Studies

Objectives

Work with basic relationships of line and space

Expand critical visual judgment skills

Improve hand skills by using a studio knife and a straightedge, measuring, and cutting

Translate verbal criteria into visual form

Work with simple figure/ground relationships in a nonobjective design

Description

Develop a series of five line studies that are spaced and arranged according to the following criteria:

1. Black and white are equal in a regularly spaced interval.
2. Black is constant to itself and white varies dramatically in an alternate spacing interval.
3. Black constantly increases, and white remains constant to itself.
4. Black increases as white decreases in width.
5. Black and white increase constantly but at different rates.

Limitations and Materials

Use vertical parallel lines and use no more than seven lines per study.

Use black paper to cut strips (lines) and arrange them vertically on a white 5- by 5-inch piece of cover stock. Use a glue stick or rubber cement as an adhesive. Finish the studies by mounting them on a gray board with a 3-inch border.

Critique Discussion Points

Identify the figure/ground relationship in each study.

Identify any illusory effects caused by the high-contrast relationships.

What does each study describe or evoke?

Vocabulary

space, figure/ground, contrast, illusory, nonobjective, vertical, parallel

References and Resources

Brice Marden, Robert Motherwell, Louise Fishman, Eva Hesse, Louisa Chase, Franz Kline, Susan Hauptman, Cy Twombly, Jean-Michel Basquiat, Stuart Davis, Frank Stella, Bradbury Thompson, Lance Wyman, Malcolm Greer

Evaluation Criteria

Source Work and Research

Achievement of Criteria

Design/Composition

Craft/Execution

Project Title Letter Form Grid

Objectives

Make compositional decisions using letterforms as design elements

Study type as shape

Work with a variety of high-contrast visual relationships

Manage a variety of figure/ground relationships in the same composition

Prepare for the Line, Leaf, Letter exercise

Description

Produce a composition comprised of nine smaller letterform compositions. Begin by generating 20 to 25 black and white studies that are 3 inches by 3 inches, using a variety of single letterforms. Variety is the key—variety of typefaces, scale changes, figure/ground relationships, orientation, and proximity in the small compositions. Cut the small studies carefully into 3-inch squares. Create a new, larger composition using nine of the small studies arranged in a nine-unit grid, three studies across by three studies down. Work to create overall continuity (unity) and rhythm from one unit to the next.

Hint: Partially obscure the identity of some of the letterforms by cropping, rotating, or reversing them within the small compositions. That will offer variety and visual interest.

Limitations and Materials

Generate type from a computer or photocopy type from printed sources. For the final design, use clean, good-quality laser prints or photocopies. Use a studio knife and metal straightedge to cut small studies. Glue the nine studies in a square grid arrangement on two- or four-ply bristol board and mount to a piece of gray board with a 3-inch border.

Critique Discussion Points

Describe the kind of rhythm and eye movement created in the arrangement.

How does the use of negative space complement the arrangement of the letterforms?

Can you identify a point or points of emphasis? Explain.

What qualities does the composition communicate?

Vocabulary

variety, cropping, orientation, proximity, rhythm, eye movement, emphasis, negative space

References and Resources

Paul Rand, Piet Zwart, Bradbury Thompson, Neville Brody, Paula Sher, Herbert Bayer, Theo van Doesburg, Beatrice Ward, Carol Twombly, Kathleen Tinkel

Evaluation Criteria

Source Work and Research

Achievement of Criteria

Design/Composition

Craft/Execution

Project Title Line, Leaf, Letter

Objectives

Work with an exploration of the design principles

Manage design decisions using basic elements from the designer's toolbox

Establish a hierarchy of elements that achieves unity

Explore visual relationships based on closure, balance, and proximity

Description

Using a line, a leaf, and a letter, produce two contrasting compositions. You also may use up to three planes or divisions in the background. Decide beforehand how the two compositions will contrast by exploring various ideas. Do a group think session to explore visual possibilities. Use a notebook or journal to make note of the visual contrasts that you discussed and what possibilities you would like to explore for your own solution.

Work with the following issues as you explore solutions:

Scale changes between the line, letter, and leaf

Complementary or contrasting qualities in the compared compositions

Quality and character of the letter you chose

Effect of natural color

Control and management of visual hierarchy/dominance, proximity, scale, and closure

Limitations and Materials

Use any source of paper that is neutral in color (newspaper, cover stock, or other solid printed paper) for the planes. You can cut the line and the letter from source material, or you can create the line in drawing media. You can generate the letter from a computer or cut it from an existing source. You might want to press the leaf with an iron to flatten it. Work with an image area of 10 inches by 10 inches on two- or four-ply bristol board. Rubber cement works well as an adhesive, but a glue stick or high-quality adhesive paste is a good low-toxic option. Lay a clean sheet of paper over the design and roll a printer's brayer over the surface to press the paper to the adhesive. Trim the design and mount it on a piece of gray board with a 3-inch border. Depending on the color scheme in the design, black or white board may be better for mounting.

Critique Discussion Points

Which of the primary principles is dominant?

What is the function and relationship of the formal elements?

How did you manage the contrast concept in the compositions?

Discuss the form and function of line in the compositions.

Vocabulary

hierarchy, closure, balance, proximity, scale, dominance, two- or four-ply bristol board, brayer

References and Resources

Wolfgang Weingart, David Carson, Piet Zwart, Laszlo Maholy-Nagy, Josef Albers, Neville Brody, Bradbury Thompson, Robert Motherwell, Ben Nicholson, Jean Arp, Georges Braque, Jean Miro, Andy Goldsworthy

Evaluation Criteria

Source Work and Research

Concept Development

Design/Composition

Craft/Execution

In Review

1. Which of the primary principles controls variety?
2. What is the distinction between proportion and scale?
3. What is the distinction between how the primary and support principles function?
4. What is the purpose of formal elements?
5. Which of the elements is unique to graphic design?
6. Which two elements can exist only in support of or as an enhancement to the other elements?
7. Discuss various forms that line can take.

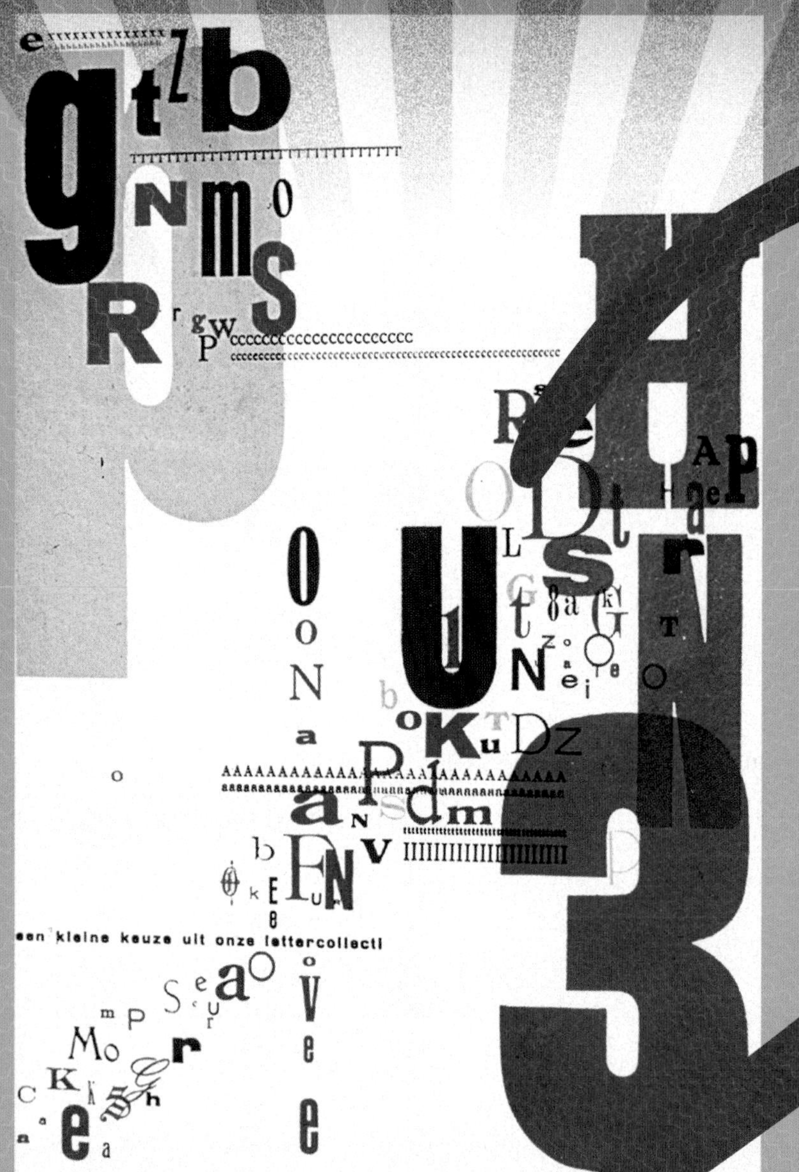

2 TYPOGRAPHY *in* DESIGN

objectives

Define typographic terms and explain measurement systems.

Explore how to select typefaces appropriate to a project's design and communication goals.

Explore ways that type can lend expression to a design.

Examine harmonious combinations of type with imagery and other design elements.

Explore how to use type judiciously when legibility is a factor.

introduction

You are surrounded by type. Everyday you encounter it on billboards, in newspapers and magazines, on the Web, and in your mailbox. Although type allows you to communicate complicated messages to other people, there is no guarantee that the intended audience will notice, read, or respond to its content.

In fact, when you think about it, relatively few printed messages with which you are bombarded on a daily basis hit their mark and make a memorable impression. To a large extent, people's perception and comprehension of the printed word are influenced by how it is presented. Designers who know how to use type effectively use it to enhance text—to engage an audience and create visual appeal while communicating the intended message in a clear and compelling manner.

Using type effectively requires an understanding of its communication and visual possibilities. Chapter 1 introduced some of those aspects by discussing how type can function as more than just a means of communicating content. Type can work to satisfy several design objectives at once, serving as text to be read and as a means of adding expression to a message while simultaneously functioning as a composition element.

Some features of working with type addressed in Chapter 1 included how styling type or handling it in a certain way can enhance the meaning of a word or phrase. By presenting examples that demonstrated how typographic forms function as shape, line, or texture, Chapter 1 also showed how type works as a design element. This chapter discusses those aspects in more detail by examining additional examples and other ways where type works to support content and composition.

Because a knowledge of basic typographic terms and measurements is essential to understanding and working with type, this chapter also introduces basic terminology and the rules that govern how designers work with type.

DESIGN AND TYPOGRAPHY

In a design composition, type works as a design element, just as shape, line, color, and texture serve as design elements. So all of the principles that guide decision making in a design composition also apply to typography. How to style type, what typeface to use, and what size and color the type should be are all dictated by the primary principles of hierarchy and dominance, unity and variety, balance, and proportion. The secondary principles of scale, emphasis, rhythm, movement, proximity, and repetition apply as well.

When designers begin a project, they are given a message (typically verbal content) to communicate. The designer's job is to determine what kind of typographic form this content will assume and how it will be handled relative to the other elements in the composition.

Hierarchy

Many designers find it helpful to start by determining the hierarchy, or most important element, in a composition. From there, they organize type and other elements around that focal point. Often the quality of an image, nature of the message, or overall concept determines whether imagery or type will play the leading role in a design composition.

Imagery and type should be combined in a synergistic manner. It is up to the designer to determine what the hierarchy and balance between those as well as other design elements will be.

The designer also manages the treatment and placement of the elements in a way that controls how the viewer's eye will travel from image to text and loop around a design composition. Even if the most prominent element in a composition is a photograph or another image, type still needs to be organized and assigned a hierarchical role so the viewer is led through a design composition in a way that supports the message's intent and its ability to be understood and that allows the viewer to take in all of the design's visual information (see Visual 2–1).

When typographic hierarchy is assigned, the most important part of the verbal content or message is given the most prominence. When you examine a Web or printed page that is composed entirely of type, you can see how the headlines assume a predominant role and how subheads and other smaller text play a secondary or subordinate role in a design composition. Depending on the vehicle, the verbal content receiving the most prominence could be a headline, title, compelling sentence, word, or phrase. Once the viewer is hooked, the most prominent content is followed by information of secondary or supplementary importance (see Visual 2–2).

As with other design elements, size, color, and surrounding negative space all affect the degree of prominence a typographic focal point will assume. Relative size or scale is often used to control hierarchy in a design composition. Words, phrases, or sentences that are larger than surrounding text will be more dominant. Type that is a different color than that of surrounding text or its background also will assume prominence by standing out in contrast. Type, even if it is small, will stand out if it is surrounded by large amounts of negative space (see Visual 2–3).

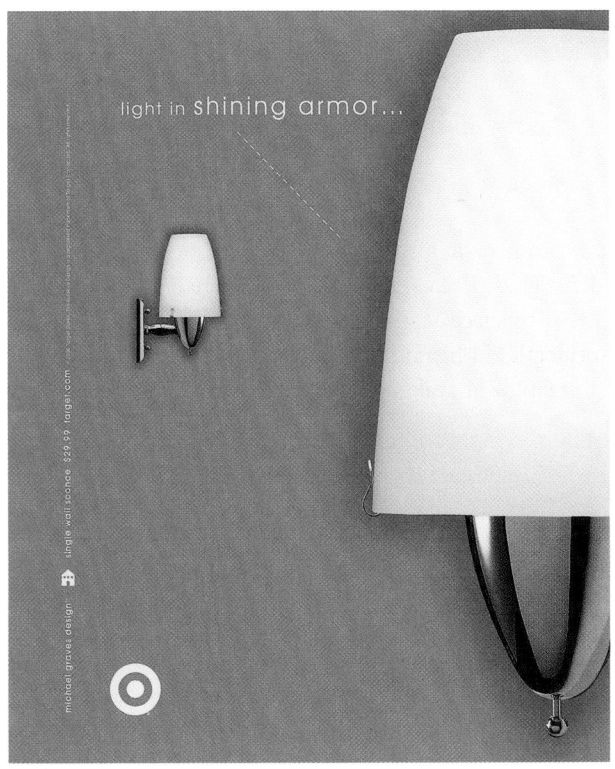

visual |2–1|

This ad for Target uses type as a linear element to guide the viewer's eye from the large lamp at the right, across the top of the ad, and down the left side so the eye loops around the entire composition, taking in all of its visual components. *(Design by Design Guys)*

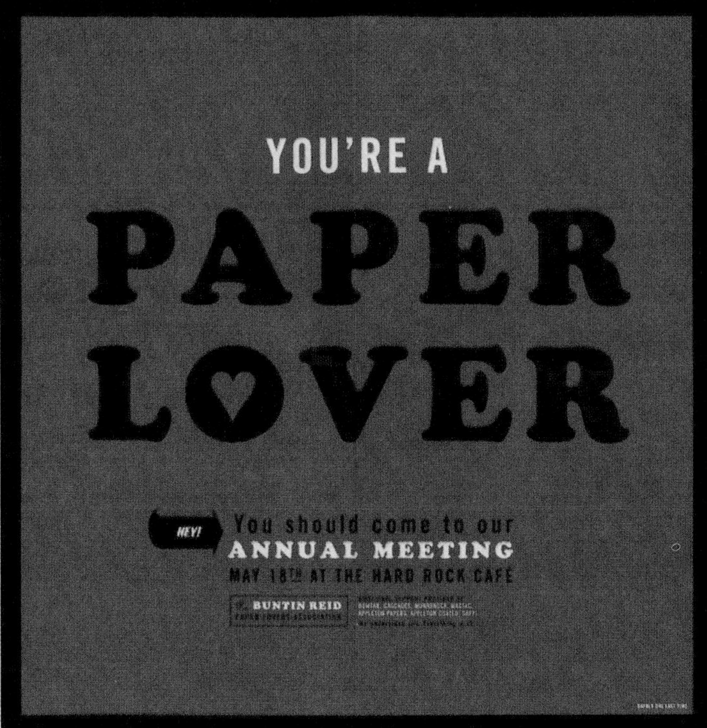

visual |2–2|

In this show invitation, a clear hierarchy is established with the size and prominence of the type. To catch the viewer's attention, the words *PAPER LOVER* are largest and most prominent. From there, the viewer's eye is drawn to supplementary information. *(Design by Kolegram, Gatineau)*

Balance

After hierarchy has been assigned, balance determines the visual distribution of type and how it will appear in relation to the other visual elements in a design composition. As you learned in Chapter 1, there are two types of visual balance: symmetric and asymmetric. Type in symmetric balance is arranged so that it is equally distributed on either side of a central axis. Asymmetric balance is achieved when type is distributed unevenly on a page so that positive and negative space are in balance (see Visual 2–4).

Use of Type to Create Theme and Variation

The design principles of unity and variety also apply to type. Type can play an important role in unifying a composition or creating variety within it. When various visual elements need to be incorporated into a cohesive visual scheme, using the same typeface helps to create unity. That can be an important factor in magazine and brochure design where visual continuity needs to be established over many pages. Applying a single typeface family ensures a rhythm as well as theme and variation (see Visual 2–5).

Although using a single typeface family in a design is a foolproof way of achieving typographic harmony, in some instances, too much of the same thing can result in a design that is repetitive and boring. Sometimes a mix of typefaces is more appropriate to the theme or message of a design and may be necessary to achieving graphic interest, or an even richer sense of theme and variation. However, care should be taken to combine typefaces in a way that is harmonious and appropriate to the message or theme (see Visual 2–6).

visual 2–3

Even though the type in this example is quite small, the surrounding negative space draws your attention to it. The small type gets noticed because it stands alone in a sea of black.

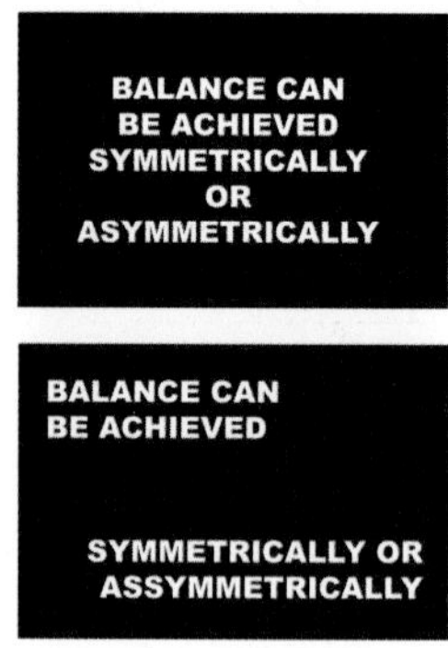

visual 2–4

In these examples, the type size and format of the rectangle are identical. However, the top example shows a symmetric arrangement where type is equally distributed on either side of a central axis. The bottom example demonstrates how an asymmetric arrangement balances positive and negative space.

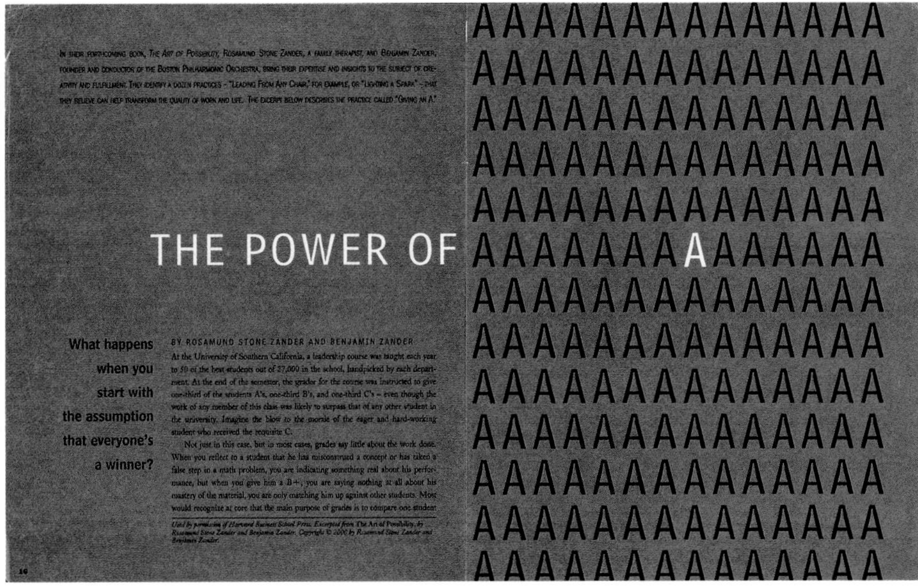

In their forthcoming book, *The Art of Possibility*, Rosamund Stone Zander, a family therapist, and Benjamin Zander, founder and conductor of the Boston Philharmonic Orchestra, bring their expertise and insights to the subject of creativity and fulfillment. They identify a dozen practices – "Leading From Any Chair," for example, or "Lighting a Spark" – that they believe can help transform the quality of work and life. The excerpt below describes the practice called "Giving an A."

THE POWER OF A

What happens when you start with the assumption that everyone's a winner?

BY ROSAMUND STONE ZANDER AND BENJAMIN ZANDER

At the University of Southern California, a leadership course was taught each year to 50 of the best students out of 27,000 in the school, handpicked by each department. At the end of the semester, the grader for the course was instructed to give one-third of the students A's, one-third B's, and one-third C's – even though the work of any member of this class was likely to surpass that of any other student in the university. Imagine the blow to the morale of the eager and hard-working student who received the requisite C.

Not just in this case, but in most cases, grades say little about the work done. When you reflect to a student that he has misconstrued a concept or has taken a false step in a math problem, you are indicating something real about his performance, but when you give him a B+, you are saying nothing at all about his mastery of the material, you are only matching him up against other students. Most would recognize at core that the main purpose of grades is to compare one student

Used by permission of Harvard Business School Press. Excerpted from The Art of Possibility, by Rosamund Stone Zander and Benjamin Zander. Copyright © 2000 by Rosamund Stone Zander and Benjamin Zander.

visual |2-5|

Varying weights of the font Bell Centennial add variety and interest to this magazine spread. Rhythm and repetition also play an important role in the success of the design. *(Design by Keith A. Webb, Boston Globe Magazine)*

visual |2-6|

A mix of typefaces lends character and a festive look to this poster promoting a casino. Although in this case the combination is effective, mixing several typefaces in this manner requires an expert eye. *(Design by Eleven Inc.)*

Mixing Typefaces Effectively

The trick to mixing typefaces is to make the difference look obvious and purposeful by using opposites—typefaces that have different but complementary typeface characteristics or that are radically different. In the top example shown in Visual 2–7, a sans serif typeface (Arial Black) is contrasted with a serif typeface (Garamond). The second example contrasts two versions of the same typeface (Modula). Setting one word in extra bold all caps and the other in all lowercase provides visual interest and variation. The third example contrasts a delicate, feminine typeface set in upper- and lowercase (Centaur) with a more masculine typeface (Arial Black) set in all caps. Avoid combinations that use similar typefaces, such as the pairing shown in the bottom example of Frutiger and Helvetica. Mixing typefaces that are close but not quite alike can have a disturbing effect on viewers who sense, rather than see, the subtle disagreements.

TYPE
LOGIC

TYPE logic

Type
LOGIC

TYPE
LOGIC

visual 2-7

Proportional Systems and the Grid

When considering proportional relationships within a composition, it is useful to think of type as a design element that is aligned or confined to columns within a grid. As discussed in Chapter 1, a grid is a modular compositional structure made of vertical and horizontal lines that divide a composition into a proportional format. In design compositions that conform to a page, the proportional grids typically consist of columns of type. The negative area of space surrounding the columns of type is called the margin area.

An underlying grid structure helps to maintain clarity, legibility, balance, and unity—aspects that are especially important in publication design where consistency needs to be established over many pages. In addition to serving as a unifying element and a means of organizing text and visuals, a grid automatically sets up a system that creates blocks of text that can be easily arranged as elements in a composition (see Visual 2–8).

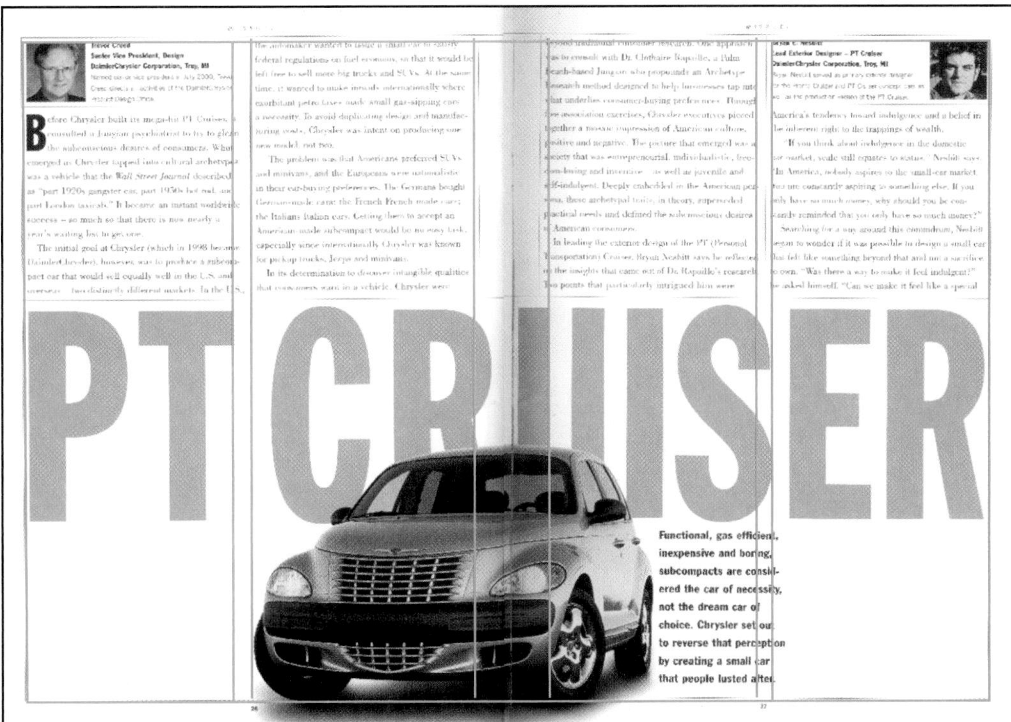

visual 2–8

The underlying structure for this spread is a two-column grid. All of the spread's text is aligned to this format as well as its photos. (*Page layout from @ issue: Design by Kit Hinrichs, Pentagram)*

Type Alignment

Arranging type so that it conforms to a grid requires aligning it to the imaginary axes that form the grid structure. Arranging or styling type that way is called *type alignment*. Type alignment options that designers frequently use are as follows:

- Flush left/ragged right—text or lines of type aligned to a left vertical axis that is uneven on the right side
- Flush right/ragged left—text or lines of type aligned to a right vertical axis that is uneven on the left side
- Justified—text or lines of type aligned to both left and right sides
- Centered—text or lines of type centered on a central vertical axis (see Visual 2–9)

TYPE AS A DESIGN ELEMENT

As you learned in Chapter 1, type functions as a design element, adding shape, line, pattern, or texture in a design composition, as well as verbal content.

Type as Line

When type is produced on a computer or by other means, it takes the form of a linear set of characters (letters in the alphabet, numerals, and punctuation marks) that are read from left to right in Western culture. As a result, designers often rely on individual lines of type to function as linear elements in a design composition. When a line of type works as a linear element, it can be used to guide a viewer's eye through a composition or to connect elements in a composition by the linear direction it assumes. Lines of type can be straight or curvilinear depending on how they need to function in a design (see Visual 2–10).

visual 2–9

Type can be timeless
or trendy. It can express
a mood or an attitude.

Flush left, rag right

Type can be timeless
or trendy. It can express
a mood or an attitude.

Flush right, rag left

Type can be timeless
or trendy. It can express
a mood or an attitude.

Centered

Type can be timeless
or trendy. It can express
a mood or an attitude.

Justified

visual 2–10

Type does double duty in this ad, providing content and serving as a link between the graduate and the cap she has tossed in the air. *(Design by Clarity Coverdale Fury)*

Type as Shape

Typographic forms also can serve as shapes in a design composition. The letterforms of a well-designed typeface have an inherent beauty and a sense of balance and proportion that can be exploited in a design composition, often adding interesting positive and negative relationships to the design. Enlarged letterforms or numerals can serve as the basis for a dynamic composition (see Visual 2–11).

In addition to the shapes that occur when letterforms are enlarged, blocks of smaller type called text also create shapes in a design composition. Text type can be formatted to rectangular columns and be made to conform to more contrived shapes that support a design composition's communication message or content theme (see Visual 2–12).

visual 2–11

In this CD design, the letterforms of the names and the negatives space between them are all that is necessary to create a dynamic composition. *(Rage CD design by Aimee Macauley, Sony Music Creative Services)*

Visual 2–12

Type is formatted to suggest the shape of a vase in this poster design. *(Poster design by Elaine Manglicmot, Henderson Bromstead Art Co.)*

Type as Texture

Just as large-scale type and letterforms and blocks or columns of text serve as shapes in a composition, small-scale type lends textural richness to a composition. The perception of texture is largely controlled by the weight or variety of weights of the typefaces used and the degree of negative space interjected into the text through line or letter spacing as well as layering (see Visual 2–13).

Again, contrast, balance, and scale and the manipulation of graphic space to create illusion dictate how type is handled relative to other design elements in a composition. It is possible to use type alone to create an exciting composition where all of those factors come into play. Exploiting these aspects can yield results with a timeless quality. (see Visual 2–14)

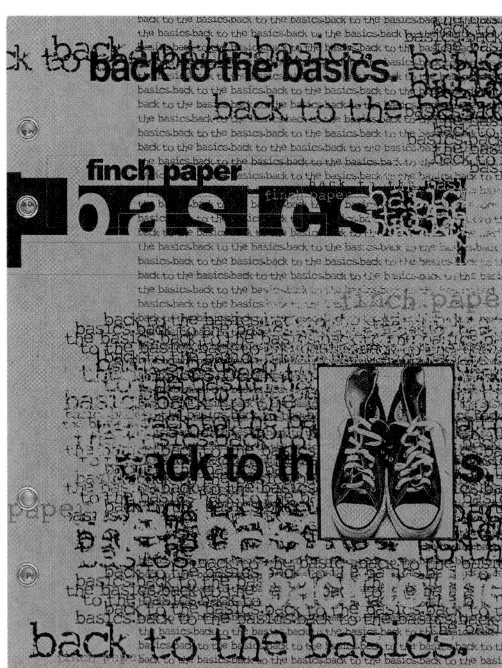

visual 2-13

A variety of sizes and weights and layering create typographic texture in this cover for a paper promotion. *(Design by Robert DeLuke, Finch Paper)*

visual 2-14

This page from a type specimen book, design by Piet Zwart in 1930, demonstrates how type alone can be scaled, colored, and arranged to create a sense of depth and movement in a dynamic composition. The results look just as fresh by today's design standards,as they did when this page was first created.

TYPOGRAPHIC CONVENTIONS

Type is measured and described in a language that is unique to the world of the printed word. In fact, many of the typographic terms and conventions in use today have their roots in the days of Gutenberg, when type was set in metal. Because designers, graphic arts professionals, and the equipment and computer programs they use employ this unique terminology and measurement system, it is important to understand their meaning. To start, typographic nomenclature can be divided into two categories: terms that identify type and typographic forms and terms associated with sizing and adjusting type.

Terms That Identify Type and Typographic Forms

character—Individual letterforms, numerals, punctuation marks, and other units that are part of a font.

letterform—The particular style and form of each individual letter in an alphabet.

lowercase—Smaller letters, as opposed to capital letters, of a type font (a, b, c, etc.).

typeface—The design of a single set of letterforms, numerals, and punctuation marks unified by consistent visual properties. Typeface designs are identified by name, such as Helvetica and Garamond.

type family—A range of style variations based on a single typeface design (see Visual 2–15).

type font—A complete set of letterforms (uppercase and lowercase), numerals, and punctuation marks in a particular typeface that allows for typesetting by keystroke on a computer or another means of typographic composition.

type style—Modifications in a typeface that create design variety while maintaining the visual character of the typeface. These include variations in weight (light, medium, or bold), width (condensed or extended), or angle (italic or slanted versus roman or upright).

uppercase—Capital or larger letters of a type font (A, B, C, etc.) (see Visual 2–16).

Terms Associated with Sizing and Adjusting Type

line length—The horizontal length of a line of type, traditionally measured in picas, but also in inches.

point size—A unit for measuring the height of type and vertical distance between lines of type (see Visual 2–17).

Helvetica Medium

Helvetica Bold

Helvetica Bold Italic

Helvetica Narrow

Helvetica Extended

visual |2-15|

In a type family such as Helvetica, style variations based on the design include (from top to bottom) medium, bold, bold italic, narrow, and extended versions.

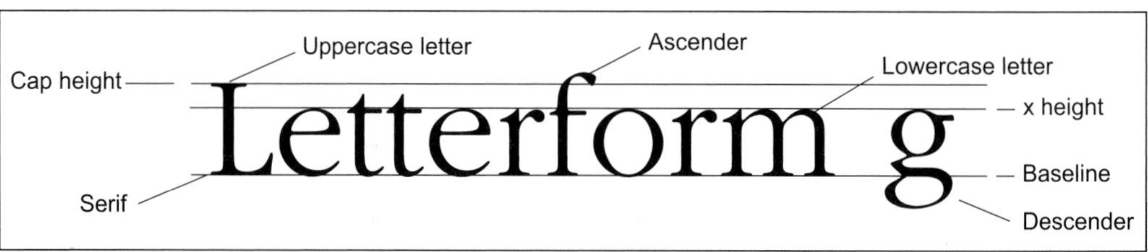

visual |2-16|

Terms associated with letterforms include *uppercase* (which describes capital letters) and *lowercase* (used to describe small letters). The height of a typeface's lowercase letters is called its *x-height. Ascender* refers to the parts of a lowercase letterform that ascend the typeface's x-height, and *descender* refers to the parts of a letter that fall below the baseline.

Type size: 21 points

Leading: 24 points

Type can be timeless or trendy.
It can express a mood or an attitude.
It can function as shape or line in a
composition, or as pattern or texture.

Line length: 28 picas

72 point E 48 point E 24 point E 18 point E 12 point E

visual |2-17|

Points are used to measure the height of type and leading, the vertical distance between lines of type. The horizontal length of a line of type is measured in picas or inches.

LETTER SPACING

L E T T E R   S P A C I N G

visual 2–18

Letter spacing refers to the distance between characters and words in a line of type.

leading—The amount of space between lines of type, measured in points. The term is derived from metal type where strips of lead were inserted between lines of type (alternative terms: *line spacing* and *interline spacing*) (see Visual 2–17).

letter spacing—The distance between characters in a word or number and between words and punctuation in a line of type (see Visual 2–18).

Typeface Design

In addition to graphic designers, there are designers who specialize in type design. Those typeface designers (also called typographers) design the typefaces that are manufactured as fonts and installed on computers. Those fonts allow designers to set and style type as they choose.

Although many of today's more traditional typefaces have been in use for more than a hundred years, others are fairly recent. Typefaces generally reflect the aesthetics of the era in which they were produced. In fact, many of the typefaces that have been designed and manufactured in recent years reflect today's visual trends (see Visual 2–19).

Selective Letter Spacing

When words are produced as type on a computer, the letter spacing that occurs between letterforms is not always even. That uneveness is usually not noticeable when type is small; however, type often appears uneven in headlines or other large type applications. Seasoned designers know it is their responsibility to manually adjust, or *kern*, the letter spacing in those instances.

That can be especially important in situations where certain letters come together, such as in the before and after examples of the word *WILLOWY* shown in Visual 2–20.

After space is adjusted between the *W*, *I*, and *L* and between the *W* and *Y*, the spacing between the letters appears to be more balanced.

Avant Garde

Suburban

Modula

visual 2–19

Contemporary typefaces include (from top to bottom) Avant Garde, which was designed by Herb Lubalin in the 1970s, and typefaces designed more recently, such as Modula. *(Designed by Suzanna Licko of Emigre)* and Suburban *(Designed by T-26)*

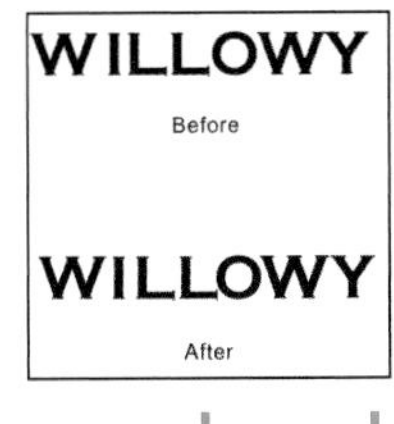

visual 2–20

LEGIBILITY VERSUS EXPRESSION

You probably have noticed that typefaces come in a broad range of styles. Some are easy to read, whereas others present a challenge. Glancing at a newspaper will likely reveal examples of both. Because it is important to get time-sensitive, newsworthy information to readers as quickly as possible, most newspapers use typefaces that are bold, clear, and highly legible for articles and headlines. However, a newspaper's masthead or logotype may be set in a typeface that is not quite as easy to read. In the presentation of a newspaper's name, sometimes it is more important for the typeface to project an attitude or image that readers will associate with the newspaper. When making an impression is important, legibility is often sacrificed for the sake of expression (see Visual 2–21a and Visual 2–21b).

Another factor designers take into consideration when weighing legibility versus expression is the length of the text. In the case of a company or product name, legibility is not such an important factor, because reading a few words at a glance is far less taxing to the eye than reading long passages of text.

"All the News That's Fit to Print"

The New York Times

VOL. CLII . . . . No. 52,541 — Copyright © 2003 The New York Times — FRIDAY, JULY 11, 2003

Questions on Data Cloud Luster of Houston Schools

Unreported Dropouts Are Said to Skew Ratings

By DIANA JEAN SCHEMO

HOUSTON — When Jerroll Tyler, a sophomore at Sharpstown High School here, turned 18, he met the full force of Texas' no-nonsense approach to education. He received an attendance contract, warning that if he missed more than two days of school, he was out permanently. By week's end, Mr. Tyler had caroused his way past the limit.

Months later, when he showed up to take a state math exam needed for graduation, a dean at Sharpstown told him he was no longer enrolled. "I went home, and I never looked back at school again," Mr. Tyler said.

Which was why Mr. Tyler and his mother, Karen Gamble, were shocked to see that Sharpstown High had claimed it had no dropouts at all last year. It reported, instead, that Mr. Tyler had transferred to Southwest High, a charter school he had never even visited. Some 462 other students left the school that year, and Sharpstown claimed not one had dropped out.

Sharpstown was not alone. A recent state audit here, which examined records from 16 middle and high schools, found that more than half of the 5,500 students who left their schools in the 2000-2001 school year should have been declared dropouts but were not. That year, Houston schools reported that only 1.5 percent of its students had dropped out.

The audit — which recommended lowering the ranking of 14 of the 16 schools from the the best to the worst, has been a stunning blow to the Houston school system, the largest and most celebrated district in Texas. Last year, the city won a $1 million prize as best urban district in the country, from the Los Angeles-based Broad Foundation.

The city has also been a pillar of the so-called Texas miracle in education, whose emphasis on grading school performance became the model for the rest of the country under the federal No Child Left Behind Act. It was largely on the strength of his success here that Rod Paige, Houston's former superintendent, followed George W. Bush east to become secretary of education.

Now, some here are questioning whether the miracle may have been smoke and mirrors, at least on the high school level. And they are suggesting that perhaps Houston is a model of how the focus on school accountability can sometimes go wrong, driving administrators to alter data or push students likely to mar a school's profile — through poor attendance or low test scores — out the back door.

"It was Enron accounting," said Joseph Rodriguez, a former employee of the district's office of research and accountability, who is running for an open seat on the Houston school board. "Who are our dropouts? We haven't identified them."

Dr. Paige, who ran the Houston system from 1994 to early 2001, declined to directly address questions about the undercounting of dropouts. Dan Langan, a spokesman, said, "The secretary stands by his record of accomplishment in Texas." Mr. Langan said that "Dr. Paige has a very strong record of success in edu-

Continued on Page A12

Associated Press

Ready for a Grim Anniversary

The bodies of 282 Bosnian Muslims massacred at Srebrenica await burial today, exactly eight years after the killings. At The Hague, the war crimes tribunal is under pressure to conclude its investigation. Page A3.

For 2 Senators With 2 Hats, A Defining Issue Stands Out

By SHERYL GAY STOLBERG

WASHINGTON, July 9 — Now that the Senate has blocked President Bush's plan to cap jury awards in medical malpractice cases, the battle will only intensify during next

text" of the malpractice debate.

Republicans, who have been pressing for tort law changes since long before Dr. Frist and Mr. Edwards joined the Senate, are now using the

WAR'S COST BRINGS DEMOCRATIC ANGER

Lawmakers Voice Surprise at Rising Pentagon Estimate

By DAVID FIRESTONE

(a)

Choice of typography, the layout and organization of information, the paper stock, etc., all contribute to my impression of you as a designer and your design capabilities.

(b)

visual | 2–21a and b

(a) *The New York Times* is a good example of a newspaper that makes use of a simple, easy-to-read typeface for its headlines and fine print. (b) The calligraphic look of *The New York Times* logotype projects a sense of tradition and stability—attributes that are important to the credibility of a newspaper. However, this typography is too decorative to be used as a text typeface. Its lack of legibility becomes apparent when several lines of text are set in Old English, a typeface with a similar look.

Reader-Friendly Type

In addition to selecting (needs to stay—designers need to choose a typeface before then can style it) a legible typeface, other considerations guide designers in sizing and styling type so the typeface is easy to read (see Visual 2–22, Visual 2–23, and Visual 2–24).

IT MAY SEEM AS THOUGH ALL UPPERCASE
OR CAPITAL LETTERS WOULD BE LIKELY
TO CATCH A READER'S ATTENTION, BUT ITS
LACK OF LEGIBILITY IS MORE LIKELY TO ALIENATE
THAN ATTRACT READERS.

It may seem as though all uppercase
or capital letters would be likely
to catch a reader's attention, but its
lack of legibility is more likely to alienate
than attract readers.

visual 2–22

You can see how much easier it is to read this text when it is set in upper- and lowercase. That is because the eye reads words at a glance more easily when upper- and lowercase letters are used. All capital letters are best reserved for short passages of text.

This Can Work for Short Lines of Text

But excessive letterspacing can
cause problems in long passages
of text where word groupings
become harder to separate from
surrounding space.

visual 2–23

Wide letter spacing in short lines of type can create an interesting graphic effect but can affect legibility when applied to a block of text. Adjusting the space between letterforms may be necessary in logo design and other applications that involve large-scale type.

Short lines of text are hard to read, be- cause they create un- necessary hy- phenation and awkward line breaks.	Long lines of text are hard to read because they cause the eye to track back to the beginning of the next line. Readers forced to read long lines of text often find themselves starting to read the line of text they have just read, instead of tracking down to the next line. Sometimes designers compensate for this factor by increasing the amount of leading between lines of text. Although adding space can help the eye to differentiate one line from the next, this option may be impractical when space needs to be saved. To save space and ensure reader-friendly text, set up a column width that allows for no more than fifty characters per line. Above sample set in Garamond 8/10 at 25 picas. Sample at left set in Garamond 18/21 at 10 picas.

visual 2–24

Long lines of text are hard to read, because the eye has difficulty tracking back to the beginning of the next line. Short lines of text are hard to read and often unsightly, because they can result in a great deal of hyphenation and awkward rags in a rag-right configuration. For best legibility, line lengths should be approximately fifty characters long.

WAYS OF CATEGORIZING TYPEFACES

Over many years, designers and others who work with type have developed several ways of breaking down and organizing typefaces into categories based on style and practical application. Because designers need to differentiate between legibility and expression, it is helpful to think of type as falling into two basic categories. In fact, font manufacturers often make this distinction by sorting their typefaces into two groups: text and display.

Text Typefaces

These typefaces are used where legibility is an issue—typically for small print and long passages of text. Text typefaces are easy to read and easy on the eye when a great deal of reading is involved. Newspapers, magazines, and books use text typefaces for the bulk of the content on their pages—this textbook is a good example (see Visual 2–25). Although text typefaces are known for their reader friendliness, they work equally well in large-scale applications.

Display Typefaces

Display typefaces, used when projecting a mood or an attitude is important, are selected for their expressive quality. Display typefaces are typically used for names, logos, titles, headlines, and other short passages of text (see Visual 2–26). Display typefaces come in a wide range of styles, all having a distinctive and unique character or personality. Later in this chapter, you will learn more about how display typefaces can be used expressively. There are very few situations in which a display typeface should be used to set lengthy content. In fact, inappropriate use of a display font as a text application is likely to discourage, not encourage, readers (see Visual 2–27).

Ariel
Garamond
Times New Roman

visual | 2-25

Text typefaces are used for long passages of text and other situations where legibility is a factor.

Old English
Impact
Sand

visual | 2-26

Display typefaces are used when projecting a mood or an attitude is important. Each of these typefaces has an expressive quality.

For the past 18 years, Tippecanoe & Typer Too has designed the Candid Corporation's annual report. And for each of those reports, the design firm has commissioned a fine artist to produce work that supports each report's central theme.

For the past 18 years, Tippecanoe & Typer Too has designed The Candid Corporation's annual report. And for each of those reports, the design firm has commissioned a fine artist to produce work that supports each report's central theme.

visual | 2-27

When you compare a text passage set in Brush Script, a display typeface (top), and Times New Roman, a text typeface (bottom), the importance of choosing a typeface with high legibility becomes apparent.

THE DESIGNER AT WORK

Rich Roat (left)
Andy Cruz (right)

"Andy and I did not build a company on ideas—we built it on hard work and picking the best ideas to execute. Just remember that good design doesn't happen on its own. Take the time to do your research, then take a lot more time to execute your idea, and don't be afraid to do something if it just 'looks cool.' "

—Rich Roat

House Industries is a type foundry, an illustration studio, and a design firm that markets unique fonts and artwork to designers. The firm was established in 1993 by Andy Cruz and Rich Roat. At that time, the business partners had backgrounds in graphic design and had experienced a degree of success with their own design firm, Brand Design. However, Cruz and Roat had an interest in typography and a desire to broaden their business by developing and marketing a line of fonts. They enlisted the help of a friend, Allen Mercer, and initially developed ten fonts that they marketed to designers through catalog mailings. Some of the original typefaces evolved out of hand lettering Cruz and Mercer had done for clients.

The fonts hit the market at a point when computerized design and typography were beginning to take hold and designers were seeking distinctive fonts to load onto their computers. House Industries' catalog and other marketing materials (designed by Cruz, Mercer, and Roat) also did a great job of sparking the imagination of designers by showcasing House fonts in creative and cutting-edge ways. The initial library of ten fonts caught on; and before long, House fonts started to show up on CD packaging, ads, TV commercials, and other high-profile design arenas, further promoting the company's typography and prompting Cruz and Roat to develop additional fonts.

As House Industries grew, the partners increased the size of their staff and added more typefaces to the House font library. Although Cruz and Roat capitalized on the growing need for computer fonts, their typography and extensive use of illustration in their marketing materials manifest their appreciation for hand lettering and traditional media. Over the years, the foundry has gone outside the realm of commercial art to collaborate with those who provided them with endless inspiration, such as hot-rodding legend Ed ("Big Daddy") Roth, who was known for his uniquely sculpted custom car designs.

The foundry's success is largely due to its ability to synthesize bits of culture into practical typography, then effectively market it to the creative community. House Industries has played a prominent role in setting design trends in motion through marketing and promotional materials that continually inspire designers to re-create these looks in their own designs. In recent years, the firm's offerings have expanded into custom illustration and lettering, textile design, and a line of furniture and accessories. House Industries' award-winning typography packaging and merchandise design have been featured in the Smithsonian Institution's Cooper-Hewitt National Design Museum, as well as in countless books and magazines.

FUNHOUSE	PRINTHOUSE	roughthouse	CHOPHOUSE
SCÜBYZHOUSE	BUGHOUSE	BEACHOUSE	DOGHOUSE
RANDUMHOUSE	KATHOUSE	FRATHOUSE	HOUSEPAINT
ROADHOUSE	Housecut	Poolhouse	[illegible]
NUTHOUSE	OutHouse	COFFEEHOUSE	StrawHouse
HouseParty	FUNKHOUSE	CLUBHOUSE	STUNTHOUSE
Birdhouse	Housemaid	COUNTRYHOUSE	Roundhouse
CRACKhouse	Cleanhouse	BRICKHOUSE	HOUSEBROKEN
[illegible]	TREEHOUSE	WAREHOUSE	STAKEHOUSE
MESSYHOUSE	SLOPHOUSE	WHACHOUSE	HOUSEMIX
PLAYHOUSE	FIREHOUSE	BIGHOUSE	Dollhouse
HOUSECOPY	BUBBLEHOUSE	HALFWAY HOUSE	
HOUSEFLY	HOUSESAWCE	[illegible]	

One of House Industries' early font collections included fifty typefaces and a picture font.

House Industries' marketing materials and packaging features fonts inspired by legendary hot-rodder Ed "Big Daddy" Roth.

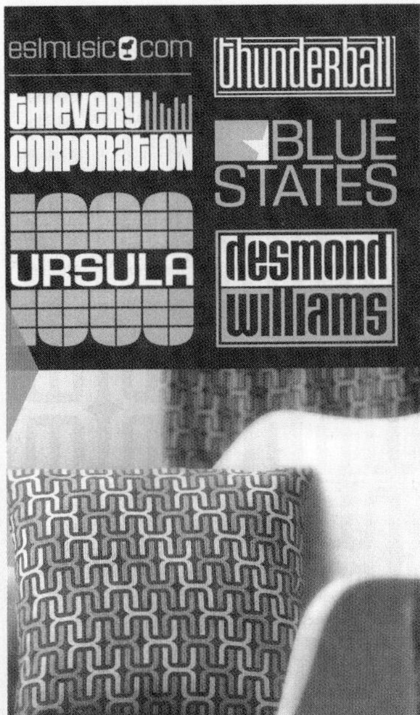

An aesthetic that evolved out of House Industries' House Gothic typefaces has spun off a textile pattern that is available in pillows and other home accessories.

Additional Typeface Classifications

There are literally thousands of typefaces from which to choose. Selecting a typeface from the vast array of possibilities may seem like a daunting task if you do not have a clue as to what distinguishes one typeface from another. Fortunately, there are ways to help designers narrow their selection.

To help in organizing and choosing typefaces, designers and typographers have identified characteristics that typefaces have in common and have grouped the typefaces accordingly. For instance, most text typefaces can be classified as either serif or sans serif. Serif typefaces originated with the Romans, who identified their stone shrines and public buildings with chisel-cut letterforms. To hide the ragged ends of the letterforms, the Romans would cut a short, extra stroke on the ends of their letters. That extra cut was called a serif, a term still in use today.

Sans serif literally means "without serif." These typefaces originated in the early twentieth century in response to the industrial revolution. As a result, sans serif typefaces project a more streamlined and contemporary aesthetic (see Visual 2–28).

Serif Sans serif

visual |2-28|

Serif typefaces such as Garamond (left) are characterized by short strokes, or serifs, at their ends. They tend to convey a traditional look.

Sans serif typefaces such as Helvetica (right) tend to project a more industrial look.

Beyond serif and sans serif typefaces, designers and typographers have traditionally relied on other typeface classifications to help them organize typefaces. Old style, transitional, and modern—those style categories refer specifically to serif typefaces and reflect modifications that have taken place over time from the original Roman or old style serif letterforms (see Visual 2–29).

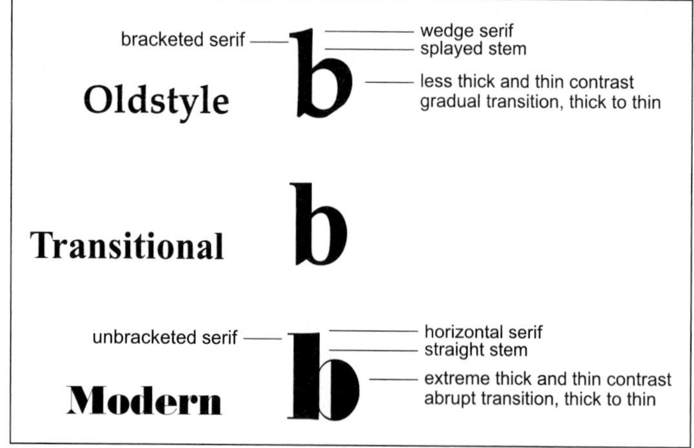

visual |2-29|

Old style typefaces (top) are direct descendants of the chisel-edge Roman letterforms. They are characterized by angled and bracketed serifs and less thick and thin contrast. Examples: Times Roman, Garamond, and Caslon. Modern typefaces (bottom) are a style of Roman type characterized by extreme thick and thin contrast and straight, unbracketed serifs. Examples: Bodoni and Caledonia. Transitional typefaces (center) exhibit characteristics of both modern and old style typefaces. Examples: Baskerville and Century Schoolbook.

Script—These typefaces most resemble handwriting and run the gamut from elegant to casual.

Egyptian/slab serif—These typefaces (also called square serifs) are characterized by heavy, slab-like serifs.

Decorative—Many typefaces, by default, fall into this category. Most are highly stylized and suitable only for display use (see Visual 2–30).

Brush

Zaph Chancery

Serifa

Lubalin Graph

Capone

visual | 2-30 |

Script typefaces such as Brush can resemble hand-painted signage or, in the case of Zaph Chancery, calligraphy.

Egyptian or *slab serif* typefaces such as Serifa and Lubalin Graph are characterized by slablike serifs. Other typefaces that are highly stylized and suitable only for display use fall into the decorative category. These typefaces include period looks such as *Capone*, which resembles typography of the 1930s.

USING TYPE EXPRESSIVELY

As you may recall, typefaces that convey a mood or tone are more likely to be used for company or product names or logotypes. Typefaces that project an attitude are commonly used for headlines of magazine articles and for book and movie titles and entertainment graphics, product packaging, posters, advertising, and other applications where communicating an immediate impression or eliciting an emotional response is important. In those situations, type serves double duty—communicating emotional as well as verbal content.

Typefaces, like people, have character and personality. Typefaces can be exciting or bland. Some are playful, whereas others are serious. The physical characteristics of a typeface have much to do with its character. Typefaces with hard edges tend to project a more serious or industrial mood and look more masculine. Those that are curvilinear, flowing, or organic in form tend to be associated with feminine characteristics (see Visual 2–31).

Looking at signage will reveal many examples of how type works to support a message or a mood (see Visual 2–32a, Visual 2–32b, and Visual 2–32c).

Feminine

Masculine

visual |2-31|

Like people, typefaces have gender characteristics. Some, such as Garamond Italic (top), have a distinctly feminine look, whereas others, such as Arial Black (bottom), appear masculine.

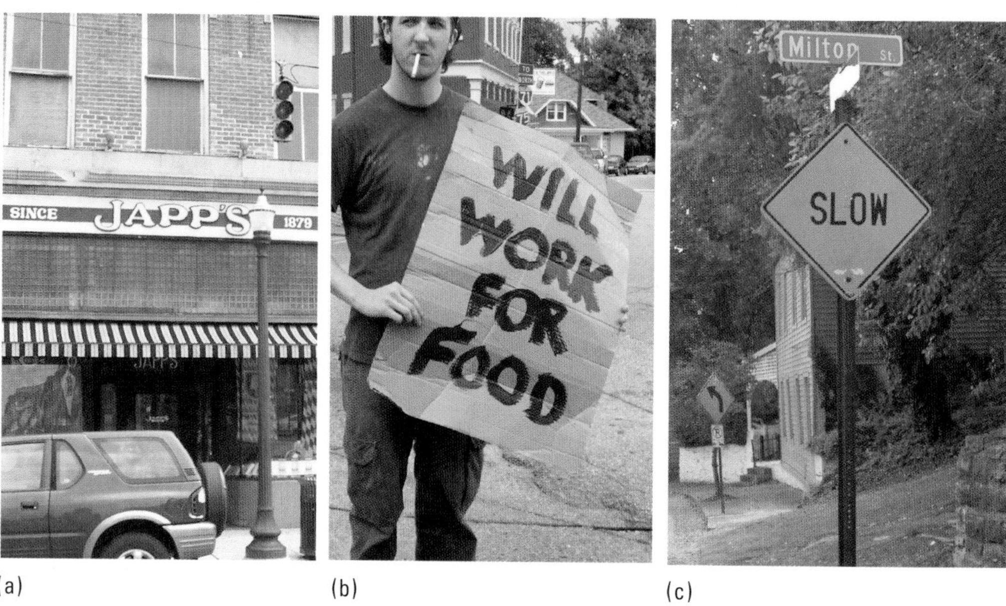

(a) (b) (c)

visual |2-32|

These examples of signage exhibit a range of sensibilities. Many of today's typefaces are based on ones created years ago, such as the typeface appearing on this store front (a). Some typefaces are casual and capture the rawness of a hand-scrawled sign (b). So that they can be easily read and understood, road sign typography is intentionally bland, without emotional content (c).

Typefaces convey period looks as well as an ethnic or cultural sensibilities. They can express a broad range of moods (see Visual 2–33).

Choosing a typeface with an attitude that enhances the message you are trying to convey is one of the most important components of effective typography (see Visual 2–34).

ugly FingerPainted

frilly Calligraphy

grungy *Ornate Script*

visual 2-33

Many typefaces have "voice" and can express a broad range of attitudes and cultural sensibilities. If you want to project a certain attitude or emotion, chances are good that you will find a typeface that captures it.

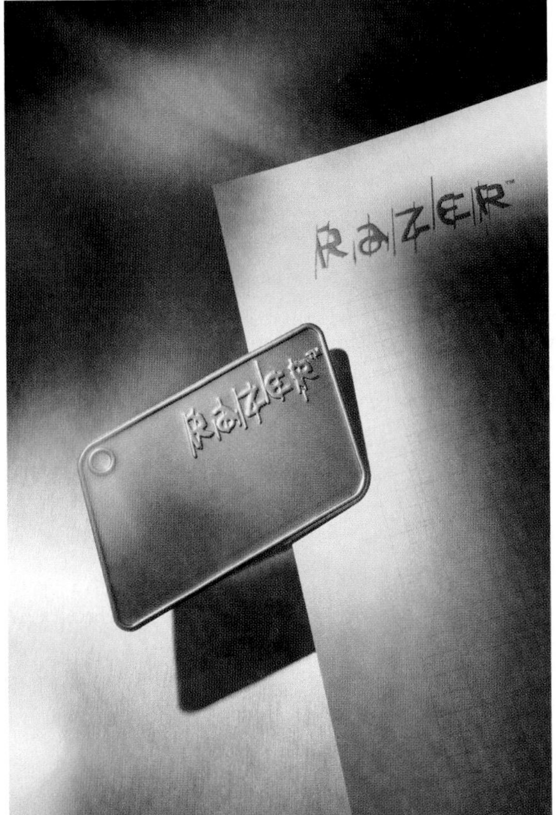

visual 2-34

Razer is the brand name for a highly sensitive computer mouse that is marketed to hard-core gamers. The slashed and degenerated look of the typography used for its logotype suggests an aggressive, cutting-edge attitude appropriate to the product and its market.

Type can be altered to express an attitude or a concept as well. Computers make it easy to configure type so that it suggests an image or a shape (see Visual 2–35).

Type can also be distressed or manipulated to convey movement or motion. It can be layered or otherwise configured to suggest a sense of depth or perspective (see Visual 2–36). Physically manipulating type is one of the easiest and most obvious ways of adding expression (see Visual 2–37).

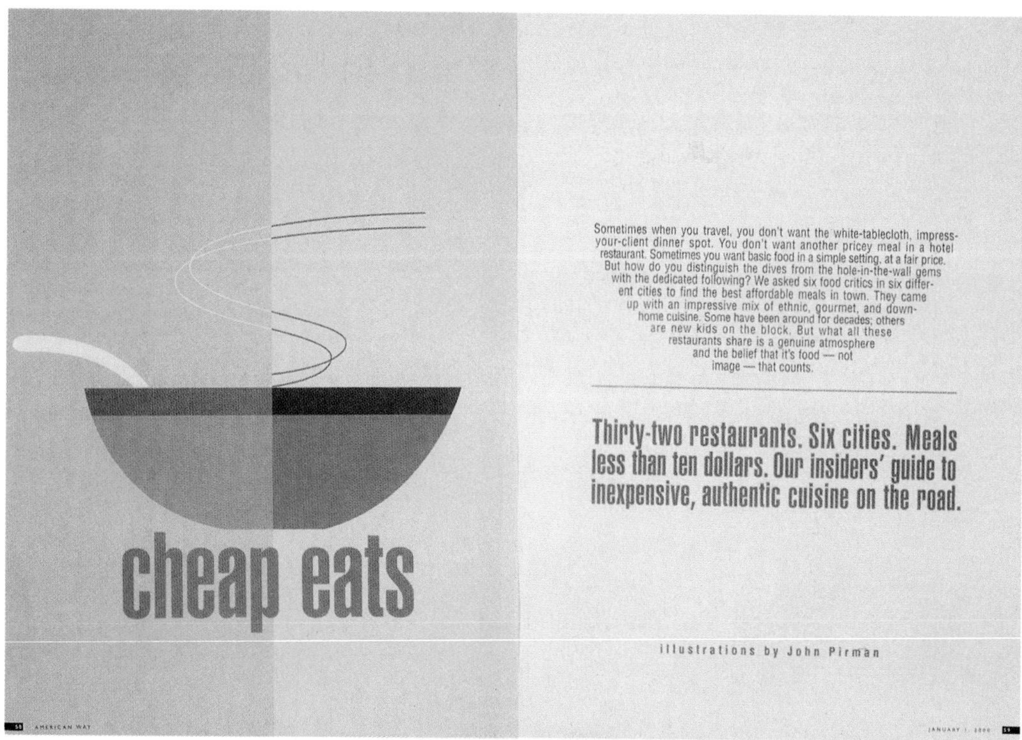

cheap eats

Sometimes when you travel, you don't want the white-tablecloth, impress-your-client dinner spot. You don't want another pricey meal in a hotel restaurant. Sometimes you want basic food in a simple setting, at a fair price. But how do you distinguish the dives from the hole-in-the-wall gems with the dedicated following? We asked six food critics in six different cities to find the best affordable meals in town. They came up with an impressive mix of ethnic, gourmet, and down-home cuisine. Some have been around for decades; others are new kids on the block. But what all these restaurants share is a genuine atmosphere and the belief that it's food — not image — that counts.

Thirty-two restaurants. Six cities. Meals less than ten dollars. Our insiders' guide to inexpensive, authentic cuisine on the road.

illustrations by John Pirman

visual 2-35

This article about dining out on a shoestring uses text formatted in the shape of a half circle to echo the image of the bowl on the opposite page. The formatted text not only reinforces the article's message but also serves as a strong compositional element in the layout of the page. *(Design by Charles Stone and Melanie Fowler, American Airlines Publishing)*

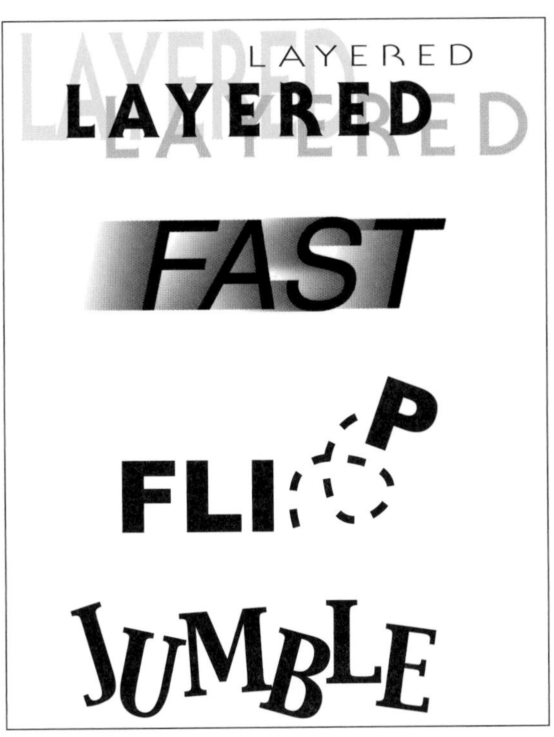

visual |2-36|

In the examples here, the meaning of each word is enhanced through type manipulation. A sense of space and perspective is achieved in the top example by superimposing different sizes and grayed values of the word *layered*. For the word *fast*, a blur filter in a photo editing program was applied to an italicized typeface to achieve a sense of forward motion. Strategic positioning of letterforms was used in the words *flip* and *jumble* to convey an appropriate sense of movement.

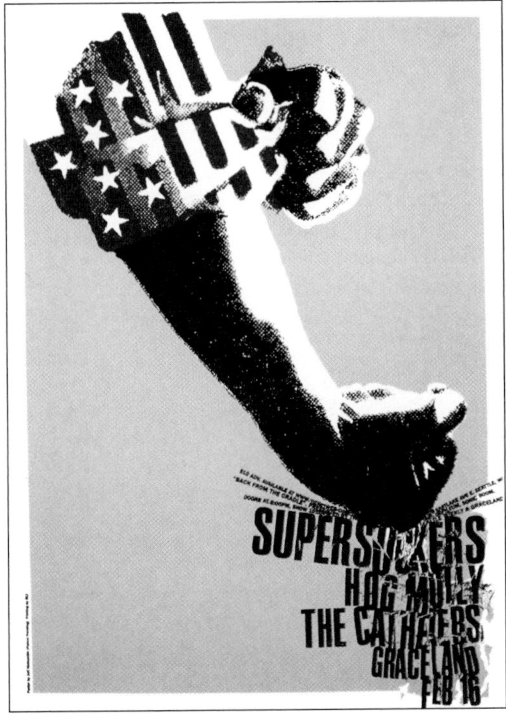

visual |2-37|

Distressing the type on this poster adds clout to the message by helping viewers imagine the potential impact of the fist. *(Design by Jeff Kleinsmith, Patent Pending)*

CASE STUDY: Designing a Logotype

As you learned earlier in this chapter, designers select a typeface to enhance the communication message of a design. In the case of a book title or a headline, an existing typeface usually suffices. However, a company or product name typically needs a more proprietary look. In those cases, a designer is often hired to hand-letter or otherwise develop a logotype that is unique and different from an existing typeface or font.

In the case of Blisscotti frozen desserts, Hornall Anderson Design Works was contracted to develop a logotype that would be clearly legible on packaging and would appeal to the product's audience of upscale consumers. After considerable research, the design firm determined that the aesthetic it needed to develop should project a high-quality, hand-crafted look, a sense of European romance, and simple elegance. In addition, the logotype had to be highly legible and look high-end but approachable.

One of the initial approaches the Hornall Anderson design team explored was pencil sketches of logotype ideas. According to firm's principal Larry Anderson, the renderings were a way of quickly putting down an idea on paper that captured the look and feel of the attitude the team wanted to convey (see Visual 2–38). Other approaches the team explored included letterfoms with obvious embellishments (see Visual 2–39). Computer renderings of logotype ideas also were developed and presented to the client, along with the hand-rendered logotype designs. The design that was ultimately chosen combined the best of all of the examples submitted—high legibility with a hand-crafted look (see Visual 2–40). Additional refinements were made to the final design to produce a logotype with custom letterforms and an even more proprietary look (see Visual 2–40 and Visual 2–41).

visual 2-38

From the onset, the Hornall Anderson team developed ideas that allowed the letter *L* to run beneath the *I* and *SS* as a way of underscoring the word *Bliss* in *Blisscotti.*

visual 2-39

To achieve an old-world sensibility, many of the ideas that were developed incorporated romantic flourishes and other embellishments that gave the logotype a hand-tooled look.

visual |2-40|

Although the type for these concepts was generated on the computer, letter spacing and individual letterforms were tweaked to give the logotype a custom look and feel.

visual |2-41|

The design that was chosen combines a custom-designed *L* with the high legibility of Gotham, a sans serif typeface. Filligree is suggested by the tiny dots that surround the Blisscotti name.

SUMMARY

The role of type in design is communicating content, but type also can add expression to a design and function as a compositional element. To work with type, you need to understand basic type terminology and the typographic systems designers and other graphic arts professionals use when working with and classifying typefaces. Expressive typography can add emotional emphasis to a design's message but may interfere with legibility. When choosing typefaces, designers must make judicious choices between type that is legible and type that is expressive. The role type will play in a design involves determining hierarchy and using type so that it works synchronistically with imagery and other design elements. Type needs to work effectively as an interesting visual element in a design composition by functioning as shape, line, or texture. It can serve as a unifying element in a composition, as well as a means of adding theme and variation.

projects

Project Title Word/Type Mix and Match

Objectives

Practice finding typefaces that support a mood or attitude

Discuss how the physical characteristics of a typeface support its character or mood-conveying attributes

Explain how type can enhance the meaning of a word or phrase

Description

For each of the following words, provide a typeface that expresses its meaning.

stoic

organic

fancy

old-world

casual

Limitations and Materials

notepaper or scrap paper

Critique Discussion Points

Which typeface did you pick for each of the terms?

What physical characteristics of each typeface supported your choice?

How do your choices compare with those of your classmates?

Vocabulary

display type, script, sans serif

References and Resources

Allan Hayley, House Industries, Matthew Carter, Herman Zaph, Edward Benguiat, Herb Lubalin, Zuzana Licko

Project Title Expressive Type and Design

Objectives

Gain practice at selecting typography that enhances meaning

Experiment with type manipulation to enhance meaning

Explore type possibilities by browsing font libraries and other typographic resources

Manage design decisions using basic elements

Practice using type as a compositional design element

Study letterform as a shape

Continue an exploration of design principles

Description

Select a typeface that is expressive of each of the following words and manipulate the typeface to further enhance the meaning of the word.

stodgy

crush

ornate

sludge

Select one of the words you manipulated and incorporate it into a black-and-white design composition that includes shapes or linear elements that support the meaning of the word. Apply the principles you learned in previous chapters, such as repetition, rhythm, and scale, to create a dynamic composition.

Limitations and Materials

Use a computer or magazines or other printed materials to serve as a source for finding type. A computer, a photocopier, or other tools can be used to distress or otherwise manipulate the type. Cutting, painting, or embellishing the type with pen or pencil or other drawing tools is an appropriate means of modifying the type you have chosen if it is used in a way that supports a word's meaning.

Limit your black-and-white design composition to a 10- by 10-inch format. Explore various design possibilities before you settle on a final solution. Use the computer, gouache, or acrylic paints to create your final composition. Incorporate different values of gray, if you like, to create a dynamic composition.

Discussion Points

Of the typefaces you chose, which one does the best job of supporting the meaning of each word?

What physical characteristics does each typeface possess to support the word's meaning?

How was the type manipulated or changed in a way that further supports each word's meaning?

What physical characteristics does the manipulated type possess to support the word's meaning?

How does type function as a design element in the final composition?

Which element in the composition has the most emphasis?

How does the type relate to other elements in the composition?

What design principles are at work in the composition?

Identify the figure/ground relationships in the composition.

Vocabulary

hierarchy, dominance, closure, proximity, scale, figure/ground, script, serif, sans serif

References and Resources

Wolfgang Weingart, David Carson, Neville Brody, Bradbury Thompson, Alex Brodovitch, Otto Storch, Emigre

Project Title Type Collage

Objectives

Discuss how type can function as a purely compositional element

Experiment with type as a design element by using it as a means of creating line, shape, and texture

Work with basic relationships between shape, line, and space

Description

Make three collages composed entirely of black-and-white type using type cut from magazines or other printed materials. Each composition should be well balanced and in a square format.

Compose each design to show how type can function in each of the following roles:

As line

As shape

As texture

Limitations and Materials

Use a 5- by 5-inch piece of cover stock or bristol board for each composition. Limit your selection of type to black and white or values of gray. Use a photocopier or another means of reproducing the type to scale or create multiples of the type you have chosen. Use scissors or a utility knife to cut the type and rubber cement, a glue stick, or another appropriate adhesive to adhere the type to the bristol board. If you want, make a photocopy of each final composition so each is a seamless design.

Discussion Points

How successfully does each composition satisfy the listed objectives?

What physical characteristics (shape and size) of the typography help it function as shape, line, or texture?

How does line function as a composition element?

Where does rhythm, repetition, or pattern occur?

How does type style, leading, or letter spacing affect the texture of type?

Vocabulary

rhythm, repetition, pattern, scale, linear, curvilinear, parallel, text type, display type, serif, sans serif, leading, letter spacing, type style

References and Resources

Emigre, Rudy VanderLans, Piet Zwart, Laszlo Moholy-Nagy, Herbert Bayer

In Review

1. What is the difference between a typeface and a type family?
2. What do the terms uppercase and lowercase mean?
3. What units are used for measuring the height of type and the vertical distance between lines of type?
4. What does the term leading mean?
5. When is it appropriate to use a display typeface? When is it appropriate to use a text typeface?
6. What is the difference between a serif typeface and a sans serif typeface?
7. How does type work to unify a composition?
8. What does the term alignment mean? What types of alignment options are there?

IMAGERY *in* DESIGN

objectives

Explain the differences between symbols, logos, and representational and informational imagery and ways they function in design and communication.

Explain the differences between photographs and illustrations and ways they can be fully exploited to best serve and enhance a communication message.

Explain how iconographic symbols differ from other types of imagery and how they communicate visual information at a glance.

Discuss how logos are designed and how they identify brands in the marketplace.

Examine ways in which identity and wayfinding systems are developed.

Develop a knowledge of the basic types of charts and graphs and the way they put statistical information into a visual context.

introduction

You have no doubt had the experience of thumbing through a magazine and becoming immersed in an article because an arresting photograph or illustration caught your eye. Everyone has had that experience, as well as similar ones such as being drawn to an image on a billboard or poster. Because "a picture is worth a thousand words," designers often use imagery to grab an audience's attention and to establish an immediate connection with the audience.

Representational imagery such as photographs and illustrations do a good job of arousing curiosity, luring a viewer, and eliciting an emotional response. However, a photograph or an illustration is often too complex to serve as an effective means of communicating universally understood information at a quick glance. Airport signage, for instance, guides travelers with simple iconography or symbols that are understood by all individuals, regardless of language or culture.

Simple iconographic symbols called logos also are used in the marketplace to identify products and services. Think of a product brand you have grown to trust. If you are like most consumers, you associate that brand's symbol or logo with quality and consistency. So when you consider purchasing a new product or service, you are more likely to look for one bearing that brand's logo than to choose one with which you are unfamiliar.

In the design process, it is important to distinguish between different image types and to produce or select appropriate imagery for each application. The right image can help you connect and communicate with members of your intended audience, whereas the wrong image can confuse and alienate them.

REPRESENTATIONAL IMAGERY

Think of how a picture of a sunny tropical beach can transcend you into a more relaxed state of mind. That is probably because, on some level, you are experiencing what it is like to be on that beach. Representational images rely on creating the illusion of a reality that exists only in the mind's eye.

When designers want to communicate a mood or affect viewers on an emotional level, nothing speaks more clearly than a photograph or an illustration. In the case of the tropical beach scene, part of the appeal lies in seeing the blue sky, sunny beach, and water and imagining how that feels. Being able to see details such as tropical foliage helps distinguish this beach from one in a more northerly climate. The realism in a representational image is what helps to convince audience members that what they are seeing is or could be within the realm of their experience.

Photography

Because most people assume the camera never lies, photographs are generally regarded as the most credible type of imagery. This visual assumption sets up a situation in which the viewer is likely to accept a photograph as being real, without question—a premise that supports the visual power of photography. Photographs are often used in a photojournalistic way to support newsworthy editorials or to document informative content. They also are used when accuracy or recognition is important (see Visual 3–1).

visual 3–1

In this ad for milk, a photograph of the rock band Kiss ensures that viewers will recognize the band and relate to the ad's message. *(Ad concept and design by Bozell New York; photograph by Annie Leibovitch)*

Food manufacturers and retailers are well aware of how a photograph with strong appetite appeal can prompt a purchase. In fact, the temptation to alter a photograph of a product to enhance its appeal prompted legislation that now requires all food manufacturers to use unaltered product photographs on product packaging.

Practically everyone has had the experience of buying ice cream or a cold drink on a hot day because a photograph of a cool, icy treat made the product seem irresistible. Photographs of food and beverages are often used at point of purchase to promote food products and food service establishments. They also are used in advertising and other promotional venues, such as consumer Web sites (see Visual 3–2).

Photographs also can be extremely effective at eliciting an emotional response or at helping the viewer visualize himself in a specific situation. Photographs are frequently used in advertising to portray scenarios where the viewer can easily identify with the individuals or setting that is depicted (see Visual 3–3).

In addition to advertising, photography is an important component of editorial design, annual reports, corporate literature, and other types of publication design. In those situations, designers often commission commercial photographers, working with them in the creation of photographs that support the designers' design and communication needs. Commercial photographers have years of training and experience when it comes to understanding lighting, composition, and other aspects of the photographic process that are beyond most designers' expertise. Commercial photographers also can offer studio space, professional lighting, and other equipment necessary for producing high-quality results.

Designers often use stock agencies that grant limited rights for the use of their photographs. Stock agencies feature the work of professional photographers and allow potential customers to browse through the agencies' Web sites, searching for the relevant subject matter. When a suitable photograph is found, the customer pays for the image and downloads it from the Web site. Photographs purchased through these agencies are typically contracted for a usage-based fee, typically for one-time use.

visual | 3-2 |

The appetite appeal of these ice cream sandwiches is highlighted on this Web site for Blisscotti frozen desserts. Seeing the real product helps convince the audience of the dessert's cool sweetness. *(Web site design by Hornall Anderson Design Works)*

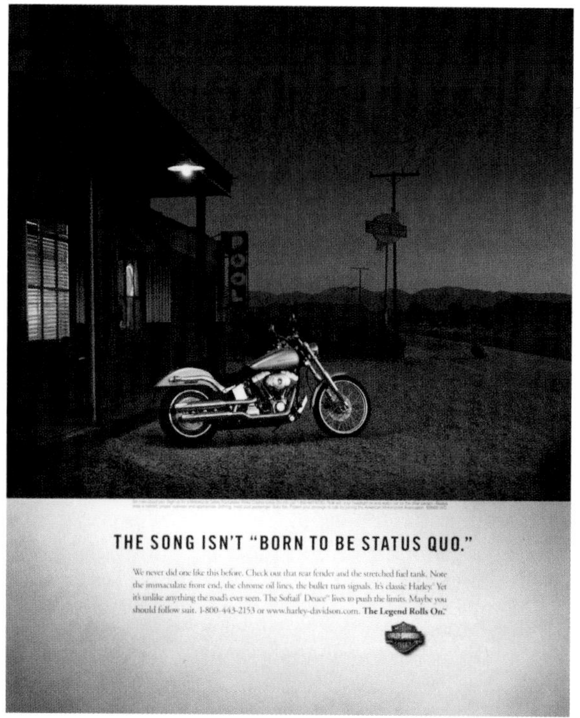

visual 3-3

The realism of photography helps the reader identify with a situation or setting, as well as clearly identifies a product. In this case, the romance of the road calls to those who would like to imagine themselves engaging in the lifestyle of a motorcyclist. *(Ad concept and design by Carmichael Lynch; photographs by Paul Wakefield and Chris Wimpey)*

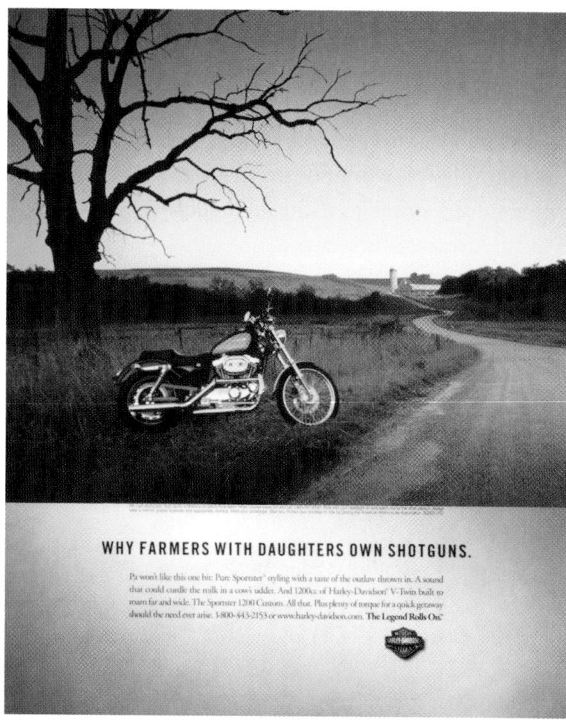

Cropping should take into account the most interesting portion of an image and the shape the final image will assume in a composition. When dealing with human subjects, cropping close on a subject's face puts more focus on the individual as opposed to his clothing, gesture, or activity in which he is engaged (see Visual 3–5a, Visual 3–5b, and Visual 3–5c).

Judicious Cropping

When you are in a position to take your own photographs or commission them from a professional photographer, you have control over how an image is framed and what the composition of the final photograph will be. However, on many occasions, designers must work with supplied photos or make adjustments to their own photographs to produce the best possible image. Beginners often overlook this need, assuming they should use all of a photograph, including its entire background. However, seasoned designers understand that removing portions of a photograph that detract or distract the viewer's attention from its central focal point can draw attention to what is most meaningful about the photograph. Knowing where and how to crop an image involves studying it and singling out its best part (see Visual 3–4a and Visual 3–4b).

(a)

(b)

visual | 3–4a and b |

The original photograph of the flowers can be improved. Its background commands too much attention and can be minimized with some cropping. (b) A tighter crop eliminates the distracting background and puts more focus on the flowers, yielding a more interesting image.

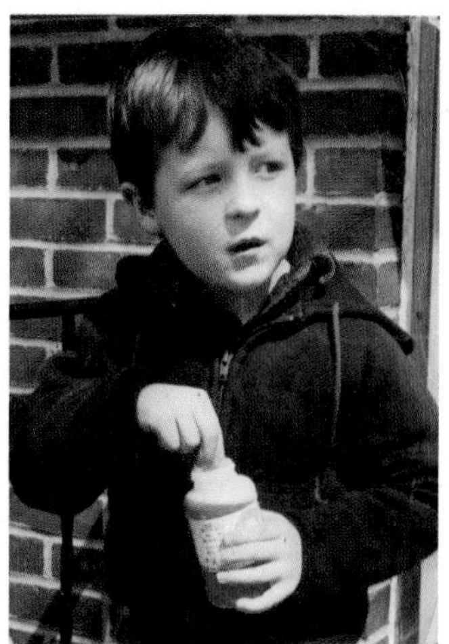
(a)

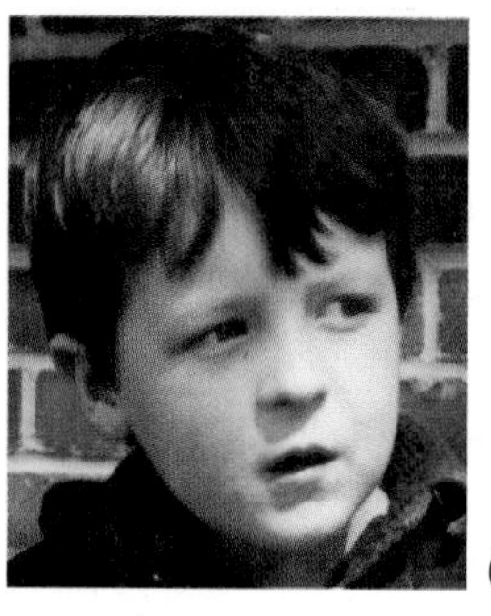
(b)

visual | 3–5a, b, and c |

(a) The original photograph shows a child engaged in an activity. (b) A closer crop puts more emphasis on the face. (c) This crop focuses even more on features. Its horizontal format can assume a different role in a composition than the vertical thrust of the original photograph or the square format in the second version.

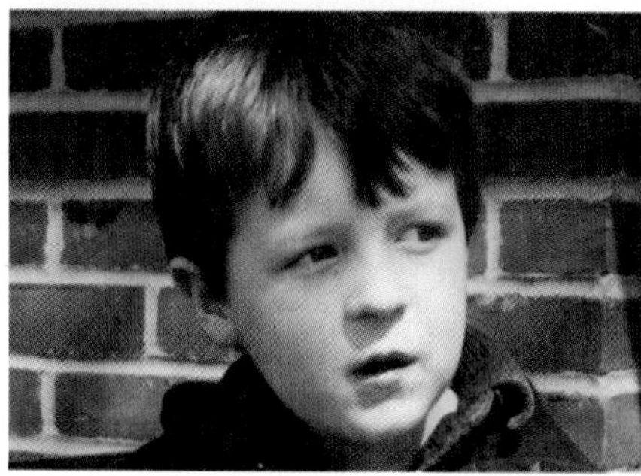
(c)

There may be occasions when a photograph's central image should be featured without any background. Isolating a subject from its background is called *outlining* or *silhouetting*.

This technique may be your only option if the photograph is poorly composed or the background is so distracting that it needs to be removed. Outlining or silhouetting also is appropriate and used frequently when an image works well as a compositional element (see Visual 3–6a and Visual 3–6b).

Choose the Right Photographic Option

Here is an overview of the different options from which to choose when finding, commissioning, or otherwise producing photographic imagery. Each imaging option has its advantages and disadvantages.

Slides and transparencies—Pros: Slides shot with a 35 mm camera and other transparencies offer excellent color reproduction, because they offer greater tonal range than color photographic prints. A good-quality transparency can be enlarged up to about seven times its size, or 700 percent. Cons: Slides and transparencies need to be scanned or digitized to be brought into computerized design and production.

Digital photos—Pros: Digital photographs can be incorporated into the digital production process quickly.

visual 3-6a and b

In this poster, photographs of guitars were isolated from their background so that they appear to be floating in space in the final design. *(Poster design and photography by David Steinbrunner)*

Cons: Although they are an excellent option, inexpensive digital cameras tend to produce unreliable results, particularly where detail and color are concerned.

Photographic prints—Pros: Color and black-and-white prints can be easily examined and evaluated for quality. Because the tonal range in a print is already compressed, they are easier to match on press. Cons: Photographic prints cannot be enlarged much from their original size without losing clarity. They must be scanned or digitized to be brought into computerized design and production.

Use a Photograph That Dictates Its Role in Your Design

A good photograph can communicate an idea with few, if any, words. When a designer starts with a solid image-based concept and commissions a high-quality photograph to support his idea, the results can be powerful (see Visual 3–7).

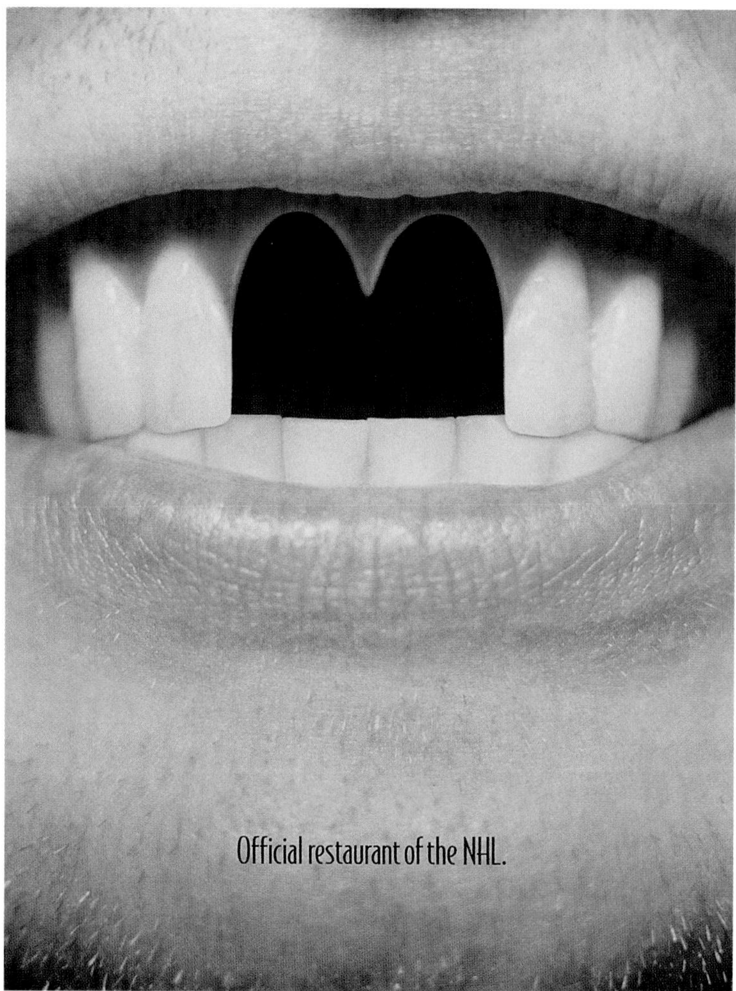
Official restaurant of the NHL.

visual 3-7

Few words are needed to make the point in this ad. The photograph, manipulated to show a toothless gap echoing the shape of McDonald's golden arches, clearly communicates its intended message. *(Design by Palmer Jarvis DDB)*

However, novice designers often try to make a photograph fit their design, rather than working the design around the photograph. Seasoned designers know that the opposite should happen—the composition should be dictated by the quality and size of the photograph. Follow these guidelines when working with photographs:

- Section off the best part of the photo. Use cropping blocks (two L-shaped pieces of paper or card stock) to help determine the best part of the image and then determine how the design will best work with the cropped image.
- Do not try to enlarge a photograph of marginal quality to make it fit your design. The quality of the photograph should determine its size, not the size of the area you have chosen for the photograph in your design.
- Give good photographs the attention they deserve by displaying them prominently in your design. Photographs with strong emotional or aesthetic appeal deserve first-class treatment.

Illustration

The expressive quality of illustrations makes them valuable when a mood or feeling needs to be enhanced. A case in point is romance novels, which for years have depicted posed models on their covers in illustrations, but rarely in photographs. That is because illustration is the more expressive of the two mediums (see Visual 3–8).

The mood projected in an illustration is largely controlled and dictated by the illustration technique as well as the medium. Pen and ink, scratchboard, pastel, gouache, and digital drawing programs are just some of the media possibilities available (see Visual 3–9a, 3–9b, and 3–9c).

Each medium has a unique look and sensibility and, in the hands of different artists, can convey additional nuance and feeling (see Visual 3–10).

visual | 3–8 |

Although the media and rendering technique in this poster illustration promoting a road race make it appear photographic, its unusual lighting, vantage point, and exaggerated perspective have resulted in an image that is more surreal than real. *(Illustration by John Maggard; poster design by Cliff Schwandner)*

(a)

(b)

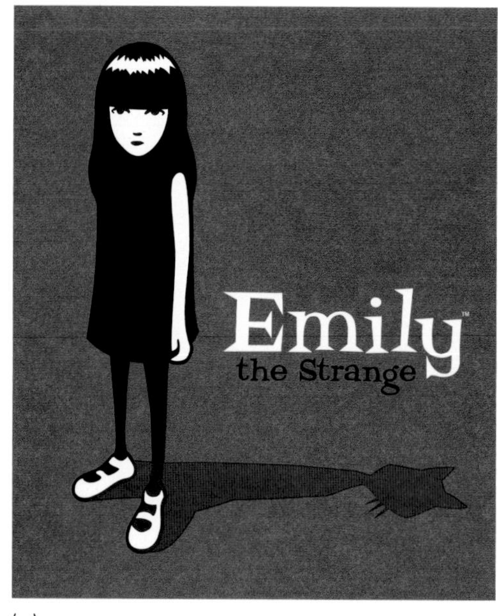

(c)

visual |3-9a, b, and c|

Black-and-white illustrations include a range of media possibilities. Shown here are (a) a scratchboard illustration by Greg Dearth, (b) a charcoal rendering by Mark Lawrence of Gil Schuler Graphic Design, and (c) a digital rendering by Cosmic Debris for Chronicle Books.

(a)

(b)

(c)

visual |3-10|

This series of posters for the French Paper Company demonstrates how different the same individual can look when depicted by different illustrators. Shown are portraits of company president Jerry French created by various staff members of Charles S. Anderson Design.

Illustrations also can help an audience visualize something that cannot be seen or help an audience better understand a complex concept. For instance, medical illustrations give those who study medicine a fuller understanding of how the body works. Diagrammatic illustrations help technicians assemble or maintain complex equipment.

Illustrations, like photographs, are usually chosen or commissioned with output in mind. It is important to select or commission black-and-white media for output in black and white, as opposed to converting a color illustration to black and white.

Sources for Imagery

Many designers generate their own imagery, shooting pictures or creating drawings, paintings, or digital art for their designs. However, if you are not able to generate your own imagery, the following resources are commonly used:

- Royalty-free collections—Collections of illustrations and photographs with no limitations on their usage can be purchased on CD-ROM or downloaded from commercial websites as an inexpensive source of imagery. Their only drawback is that some of the images have a generic look. And because they are available to anyone willing to purchase them, there's always the chance that an image from a royalty-free collection may appear (or may have already appeared) someplace else.
- Stock agencies—These agencies grant limited rights use of their photographs and illustrations for a fee. The drawbacks are similar to royalty-free collections in that there is no guarantee that an image has not or will not appear elsewhere.
- Commissioned—Hiring a photographer or an illustrator will yield an original piece of art. Professional photographs and illustrations typically, but not always, cost more than stock or royalty-free collections.
- Fonts—Some typeface companies offer symbol or picture fonts. These images are very simple and often iconic, so they are legible in small as well as large sizes and typically come in themed collections. They function just like fonts, with each image accessible by a keystroke, and can be purchased the same way that fonts are purchased.
- Found imagery—Small or flat objects such as leaves and coins can be directly scanned and incorporated into designs (see Visual 3–11).

Uncredited illustrations and photographs found in printed materials that are at least seventy-five years old can be used. These images fall into a category called *public domain*, meaning they are no longer protected by copyright (see Visual 3–12).

Image Terminology for Production

Bringing an image into the design and production process requires digitizing or scanning so it can be printed in a way that will result in the best possible reproduction of the original. To determine the best way of scanning an image, it is important to know how prepress houses and scanning manufacturers classify imagery and the terminology they use.

- continuous tone—A photograph or an illustrated image that is composed of a series of gray or color tones with gradations from one tone or color to the next, as opposed to color or tonal areas that are flat and distinct from one another.

visual |3-11|

Small, flat objects such as the buttons shown here can be photographed by placing them on a scanner.

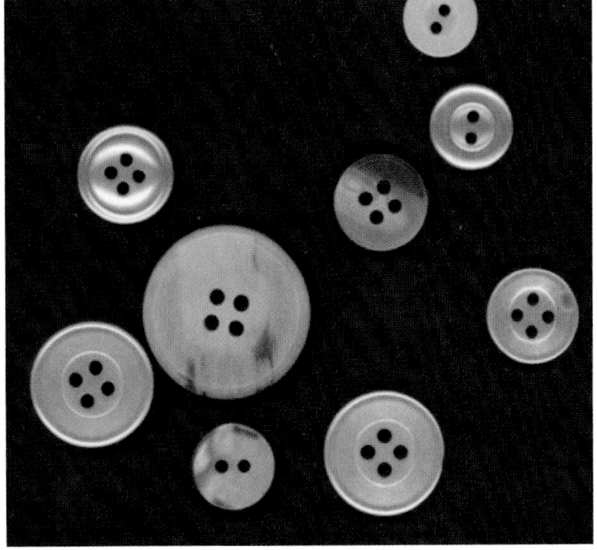

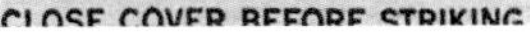

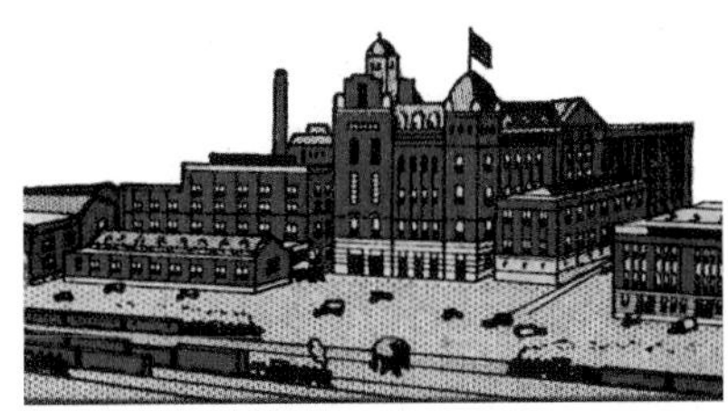

visual |3-12|

Uncredited photographs and illustrations that are at least seventy-five years old, such as the one on this matchbook, are no longer protected by copyright laws and can be freely incorporated into designs and layouts.

- grayscale—A continuous-tone black-and-white image.
- halftone—A method of reproducing a continuous-tone image by photographing it through a fine screen to convert the image into a series of dots. A color image is called a *CMYK halftone*.
- line art—Refers to a black-and-white image that does not have continuous tones, such as a logo, a graphically reduced image, or a pen-and-ink illustration. Also called a *bitmap*.

SYMBOLS AND LOGOS

Because they need to be easily and often universally understood as well as recognizable in both small- and large-scale applications, symbols and logos are images or words that have been stripped down to their simplest form. Understanding how to simplify an image or a series of letterforms and making them symbolic is based on many of the design principles you have already learned. Creating a well-balanced design with pleasing proportions is important, particularly in a logo design, in which the character or essence of a brand or business must be communicated.

Graphically Reducing an Image

Taking an image down to its simplest form while preserving its ability to be recognized is called making a *graphic reduction*. The simplicity and legibility of a graphically reduced image makes it especially suitable for pictograms or logos.

Graphic reduction is a process of image translation. Most often the translation is an edited, simplified version of the original subject. Logos, symbols, marks, pictograms, and ideograms need to be deciphered quickly if they are to communicate successfully. Reducing subjects to their essential parts yields images that fulfill this requirement (see Visual 3–13).

To achieve unity and harmony, the visual attributes of a graphically reduced image must have a structural as well as aesthetic relationship. Through the process of editing and translating, careful consideration must be applied as the subject is drawn and redrawn. Working toward a final graphic translation of the original subject requires visually aligning and tuning the feature parts. Width, length, and sizes of visual attributes can be based on a constant unit of measure.

visual |3–13|

In this example, a photograph of a pencil (left) is converted from a continuous-tone, grayscale image to black-and-white icons. In the process of graphically reducing this image, important attributes were retained, including the pencil's basic shape, the contours of its edges, and its black lead point.

The transformation of a continuous-tone image to a graphic reduction can be accomplished in many ways: describing the contours of an image with an outline, converting the basic form of an object to a silhouette or simple shape, interpreting shadowed contours of a form into a series of shapes, or using a combination of those methods. To successfully reduce an image, the designer should concentrate on emphasizing essential qualities—a process that involves retaining some details of the image while eliminating others. Contours may be converted to simple curves. The designer's role in the process is one of judicious decision maker—deciding what features of an image will go, what will stay, and how the elements that are retained will take on new meaning within a new, more simplified context (see Visual 3–14).

visual |3-14|

A graphic vocabulary based on graphically reduced panda images serves as the basis for this flexible identity system used to promote the UPS shipment of pandas from China to the Atlanta Zoo. The identity was applied to crates, a jet fuselage, and other vehicles. *(Identity design by Deep Design)*

Simple Image Terminology

The following terms will help you differentiate among the different types of simple image applications:

- ideogram/ideograph—A pictorial image or symbol that represents an idea or a concept; for instance, a representation of a lightning bolt to symbolize a thunderstorm warning.
- logo—A logotype or mark or a combination of the two used symbolically to represent a product, brand, company, or group.
- logotype—Letters, words, or a name formed in a distinctive way and used symbolically to represent a product, brand, company, or group.
- mark—A symbol used to represent a product, brand, company, or group.
- pictogram/pictograph—A pictorial image that depicts a simplified representation of an object or activity.
- symbol—A letter or sign that represents an activity, idea, or object that can be used within a cultural or commercial context. Effective symbols are universally understood and transcend language and cultural boundaries.

Logos and Trademarks

If you are shopping for athletic wear, spotting the logo of well-known brand helps you immediately identify the price range and quality of the merchandise. When you are loyal to a brand, you are more likely to look for and buy merchandise bearing that logo. The term *logo* is used describe whatever symbol a company uses to identify its brand in the marketplace.

A logo can be more than a symbol or a mark. As you learned in Chapter 2, a logo can be a distinctive typographic treatment of a company name, called a *logotype*. Or, it can be a combination of a mark and logotype. A logo that includes both offers a degree of versatility. A name and mark work well together, but they can function independently of each other if necessary (see Visual 3–15).

visual |3-15|

This combination of mark and logotype allowed for flexibility in the development of a corporate identity system for the OneWorld Challenge team that competed for America's Cup. The two components work well together on letterhead and packaging but function equally as well independent of each other. *(Identity design by Hornall Anderson Design Works)*

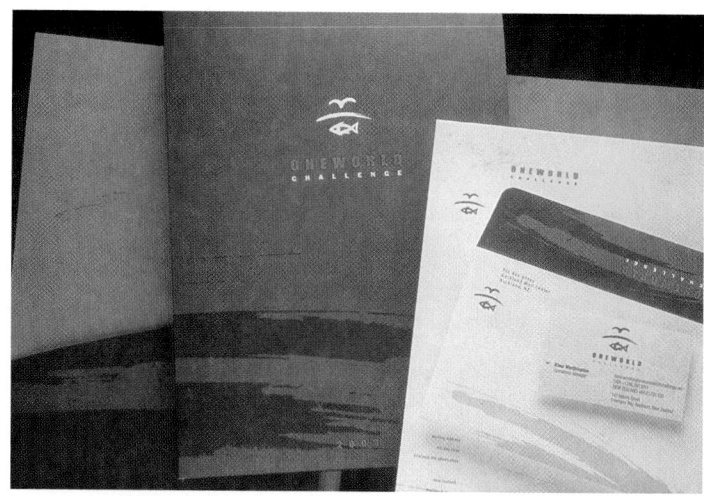

ONEWORLD
AMERICA'S CUP
2003

ONEWORLD
techtv
NEXTEL
ONEWORLD
LINCOLN
SAIC

ONEWORLD
Enhanced H2O
710mL (24oz.)

Manufacturers recognize the importance of consumer loyalty and brand devotion and work hard to develop a logo that captures and communicates the spirit or essence of their brand. If they are successful, their logo is a unique identifying mark that cannot be confused with any other logo. In fact, logos are so important to brand recognition that most manufacturers trademark their brand's logo, a process of legally registering it with the government's trademark registry. When a logo becomes a registered trademark, it is the exclusive property of the trademark holder. No other company can apply that logo to its product or merchandise without suffering legal consequences.

In addition to a design expressing the character of a company or brand, another important factor of a logo's design is its ability to be easily recognized in many applications. Because logos often appear on apparel labels, in newspaper ads, and in other situations where there is little control over the size and color of the logos' reproduction, the design is typically clean and simple so they can be recognized and understood easily regardless of scale or color.

Make Images Part of a Logotype

Logotypes and images are typically paired up so they can work together or apart from each other to identify a firm or an organization. However, images also can take the place of a letterform or become part of a letterform in a logotype, as demonstrated in Visual 3–16. Images also can be incorporated into numerals, as demonstrated in Visual 3–17. Graphically reducing an image to its simplest form makes the melding process between image and letterform or numeral much easier.

visual | 3-16 |

The Kazi Beverage Company logo uses a silhouette of a martini glass to fill in the open area of the *A*. *(Design by Hornall Anderson Design Works)*

visual | 3-17 |

These numerals, representing floors in the American Museum of Natural History, signify where visitors can find areas of interest. The animal forms that are combined with the numerals derive their inspiration from the fossils and scenes that appear on each floor. *(Icon design by Lance Wyman)*

Logos and Identity Systems

Once an organization's logo has been determined, business materials such as stationery, shipping labels, and business cards are designed bearing the logo. Beyond those basic identity needs, most companies have other situations where their logo needs to appear, such as on their Web site, promotional literature, merchandise, packaging, and signage and for vehicle and uniform applications.

Although it may seem as though identity applications would require little more than scaling and positioning a logo, an organization's identity is often based on more than just its logo. A distinctive color palette and typography as well as other identifying elements also may be involved in the identity. To provide a means of applying those elements across a broad range of materials, designers develop what is called an identity system. The overall goal in designing an identity system is to provide a unified presentation based on the image established with the logo. Identity systems are often sophisticated, modular schemes that provide a flexible means of applying recognizable features of a company's identity to a variety of design venues.

The Making of an Olympic Identity

The identity for the 2002 Winter Olympics in Salt Lake City involved developing a sophisticated visual vocabulary that could be flexibly applied in a broad range of venues that included banners, flags, sports equipment, signage, uniforms, interior and exterior architectural graphics, and a variety of vehicle applications.

In 1995, the International Olympic Committee (IOC) awarded the 2002 Olympic Winter Games to Salt Lake City, Utah. In 1997, the Salt Lake Organizing Committee (SLOC) hired Landor Associates, San Francisco, to develop the Salt Lake Olympic brand (Visual 3–18a). A key element of the logo, the "crystal emblem" (Visual 3–18b) was created to symbolize specific aspects of the games: athletic courage and the Olympic flame (Visual 3–18c), Native American cultural heritage (Visual 3–18d), and the Utah landscape with its snowcapped mountains (Visual 3–18e and Visual 3–18f). Landor expanded on the crystal emblem to create a more detailed icon (Visual 3–18g) that was extended into a pattern and cropped (Visual 3–18h) to create a rich and flexible graphic vocabulary.

The SLOC built an internal design team to create the Look of the Games. Bob Finley, Amy Lukas, and Cameron Smith, the Look of the Games in-house design team, developed the graphic guidelines of the Salt Lake 2002 Games. The team developed standards further used within the system, which included the use of color, typography, patterns, and photography. The parts included many elements, such as banners, flags (Visual 3–18i), and uniforms (Visual 3–18j). To create a rich and varied color palette for the identity, the design team expanded on the fire-and-ice theme of the crystal emblem's colors (Visual 3–18k).

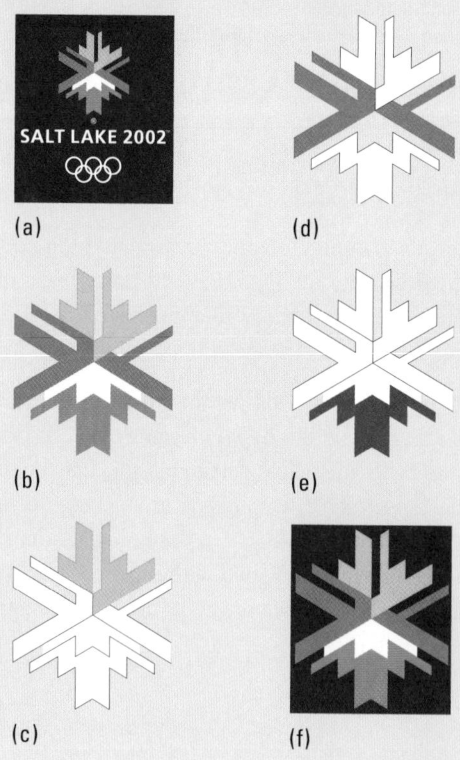

(a) (d)

(b) (e)

(c) (f)

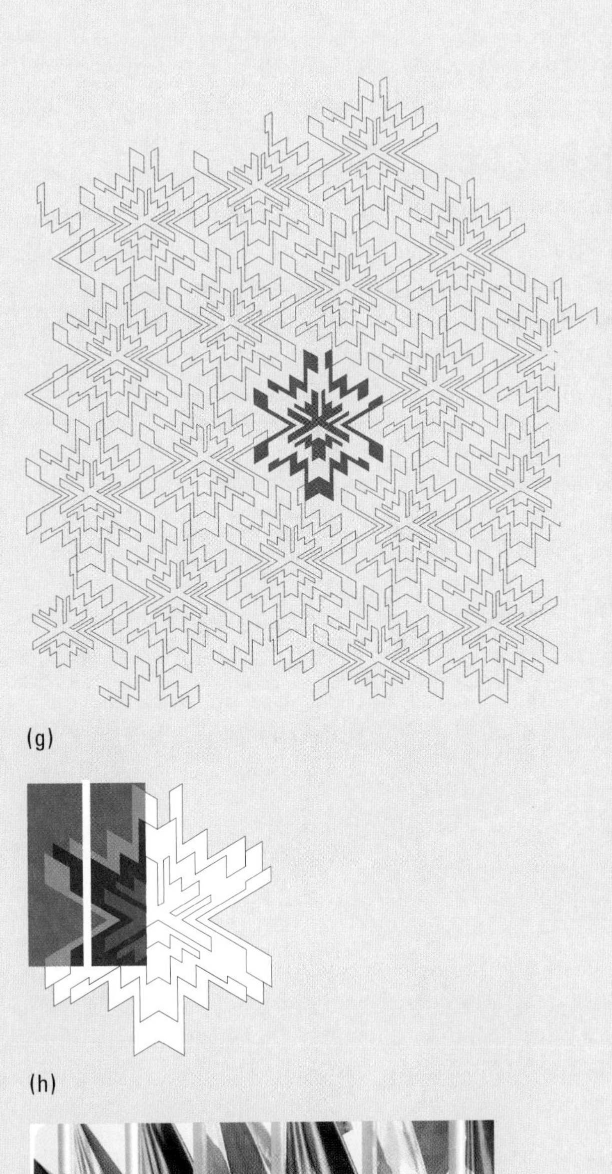

(g)

(h)

(i)

(j)

REDROCK | 704
SUNSET | 165
WILDFIRE | 186
SANDSTONE | 144
SUNSET | 165
AMBER | 1235

MT SHADOW | 2726
TURQUOISE | 312
LAPIS | 2746
DARK TURQ. | 3145
DECO BLUE | 2716
LAKE | 319

(k)

visual |3-18a to k|

To ensure that a company's identity is applied consistently across the board, designers often develop graphics standards manuals to serve as a guide for others in implementing an identity system. With a graphic standards manual, the arrangement and application of the logo in a variety of situations is assured, as is consistency in the use of the identity's colors and typographic requirements.

Stationery and Business Card Design

Any individual or organization doing business needs to produce correspondence on stationery bearing its identity. Business stationery includes important contact information such as the business address, phone and fax numbers, and e-mail and/or Web site address. The business's logo is typically placed at the top of the letterhead, but any arrangement is acceptable as long as enough space is left for the correspondence. The letterhead design should not overpower the message it contains. Because postal regulations limit the amount of space on an envelope that can include a design, an organization's logo, return address, and other identity elements containing imagery or type should be confined to the upper left corner of the envelope.

Business cards are handed out when professionals want to exchange contact information. That is why the name of the individual needs to be featured prominently on the card along with the business name and contact information that appears on the letterhead. The business card should be visually coordinated with the stationery system, using the same typefaces, color palette, and other identity elements to ensure a unified presentation (see Visual 3–19).

Because stationery and business cards are handled and require close inspection, the tactile qualities of the paper that is used play an important role. Many paper companies manufacture paper lines in a variety of textures and colors that include standard letterhead and business card weights as well as coordinated envelopes.

INFORMATIONAL IMAGERY

Informational imagery guides and informs people in situations where words do not do an adequate job. Maps, for instance, help people find their way in unfamiliar situations. Diagrammatic illustrations, such as those used in textbooks, enable people to understand better how things work by showing them what they cannot see or easily visualize. Instructional diagrams often help individuals operate, maintain, assemble, or install complex or unfamiliar equipment or technology.

Beyond those needs, designers are often involved in creating sophisticated wayfinding systems composed of directional symbols and pictograms that can be universally understood. Designers also work with charts, giving informational data visual form so it can be more easily understood. This section discusses each of those design applications in more detail.

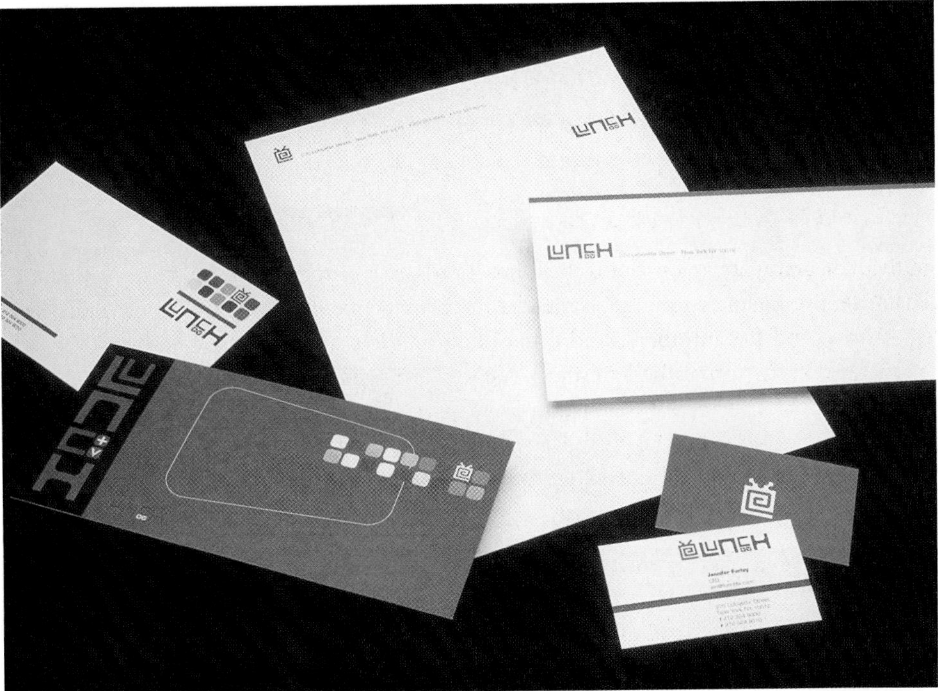

visual | 3-19 |

This suite of business materials for Lunch TV, a television and video production company, features a logotype and mark that work well as a team and independent of each other. Other unifying elements of the Lunch TV identity include a palette of red, blue, and violet hues and round-cornered squares that mimic a television screen. All of the identity elements work together in a modular way that allows for a variety of design options. Even the logotype is modular, with letterforms that work just as well stacked vertically as they do horizontally. *(Design by Stoltze Design)*

Symbols and Wayfinding Systems

If you have ever flown to a destination where you are unfamiliar with the native language, you know how important symbols can be when finding your way around an airport. Signs with pictograms of luggage direct you to the baggage claim area. Other symbols guide you to places where you can exchange money and find ground transportation. And if you are totally confused and need help finding your way around, chances are you will be looking for signs bearing the ? symbol.

Pictograms and symbols convey information that is universally understood. They are especially helpful to anyone navigating unfamiliar territory and are often incorporated into the design of wayfinding systems—a configuration of symbols, typographic applications, and signage that help to guide visitors in parks, airports, museums, and other situations that accommodate a cross-cultural audience. For instance, when developing the symbols and wayfinding system for a zoo, a designer typically becomes involved in developing pictograms that involve reducing an image of an animal species or family to its simplest and most recognizable form and making it part of a visually unified system. Those pictograms are combined with directional symbols such as arrows and are strategically placed at path intersections and other places in the zoo to help guide visitors (see Visual 3–20).

visual |3-20|

Brooklyn's Prospect Park Wildlife Center uses an identity and wayfinding system based on colorful animal cutouts. The animal iconography, which appears on signage throughout the park, helps visitors immediately identify areas of interest. *(Design by Russel Design Associates)*

Designers often need to incorporate a wayfinding system and its symbols as well as other informational graphics into a broader identity scheme so that visitors receive an overall impression that is conveyed in everything they see and experience. For instance, the symbols used to guide visitors in a zoo are more likely to be rendered with a more casual or playful spirit than those used in an airport. A well-coordinated and unified wayfinding system will be stylistically in tune with other aspects of an identity system and will make use of the same color palette.

Charts and Graphs

Nothing seems as boring and can alienate a reader more quickly than a page of statistics.That is where charts can help (seems to add emphasis to leave as two sentences). Charts are more likely to engage a viewer's attention. They also help readers visualize how the numbers look in a more meaningful and visually dynamic way.

Although there are many ways of plotting information, pie charts, bar charts, and graphs are most commonly used. Pie charts demonstrate how a population segment or lump sum can be broken down into portions. Pie charts work well for showing how a group voted or how the group is composed in terms of demographics or opinions, how budget money was allocated, or where funds came from to arrive at a total (see Visual 3–22).

Bar charts work well for comparing data. Whether the data involves sales or snow, bar charts show how things literally stack up when what happened in one defined period is compared with another period. The bars in bar charts can run vertically or horizontally. They are often represented as stacks of coins, as pictograms, or as other symbols (see Visual 3–23).

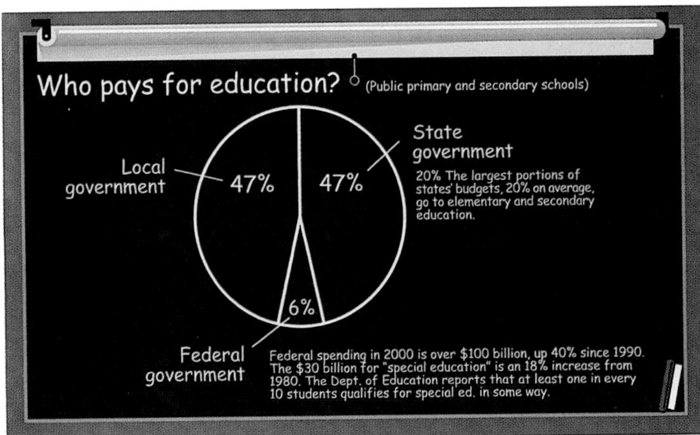

visual |3-22|

Pie charts show how a total is a sum of its parts or how the total can be broken down into portions. This example shows what portion of public education is funded by state, local, and federal governments. *(Design by Nigel Holmes and Meredith Bagby)*

visual |3-23|

Bar charts give a visual representation of how data stacks up on a comparative basis. In this instance, a bar chart is used to plot a decline in gun murders over a five-year period. *(Design by Robert Greenberg)*

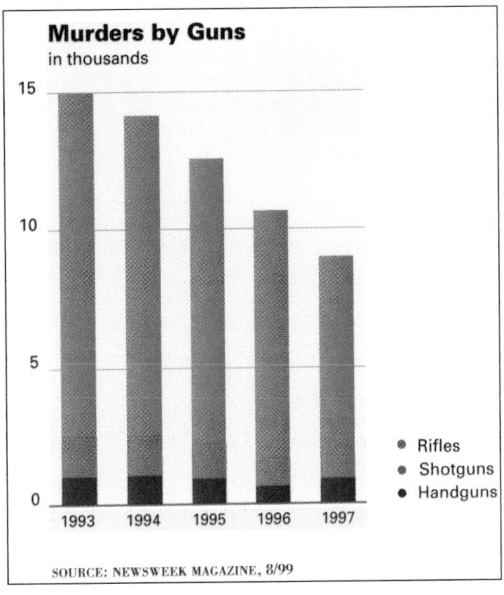

THE DESIGNER AT WORK

If I was ever going to accomplish something as unconventional as drawing pictures for a living, it would be up to nobody in this world but me and it would not happen by goofing around.

—Loren Long

loren long

Two-time Golden Kite award winner and New York Times number one best-selling illustrator Loren Long is an artist straight from the heart of America. Born in Joplin, Missouri, and raised in Lexington, Kentucky, Long is a storyteller in pictures who draws on his roots to depict a soulful American landscape peopled with imaginative characters who take on mythic, even heroic, dimensions.

Long graduated from the University of Kentucky with a BA in Graphic Design/Art Studio and went on to graduate studies at the American Academy of Art in Chicago. For a time, he was an illustrator at the Gibson Greeting Card Company in Cincinnati. He gained recognition as an editorial illustrator for numerous magazines and newspapers in the 1990s, most notably *Forbes*, *Time*, *Atlantic Monthly*, and *Sports Illustrated*. He began illustrating book covers for HarperCollins, Penguin, Houghton Mifflin, and the National Geographic Society.

In 1999, Long was commissioned to paint a grand-scale mural for a restaurant in Lincoln, Nebraska. His has illustrated picture books that include *Mr. Peabody's Apples*, written by Madonna; the classic story *Little Engine That Could*; and *Wind Flyers*. Long has received numerous accolades for what *The New York Times* calls his "muscular style inspired by 1930s W.P.A. murals."

In 2002, the United Nations chose Long's "The Firefighter" to hang with twenty-one other works of art from the

Society of Illustrators' expansive exhibition "The Prevailing Human Spirit." In 2004, the Art Academy of Cincinnati presented a retrospective of Long's picture book work.

Long's work is in the permanent collections of the Cincinnati Art Museum, the U.S. Golf Association's Museum, and Sports Illustrated magazine. In November 2001, his work was included in an exhibition of noteworthy Ohio illustrators at the prestigious Centro-Cultura Recoleta in Buenos Aires.

Long can be found drawing every day at his home near Cincinnati, Ohio, where he lives with family and their Weimaraner, Stella.

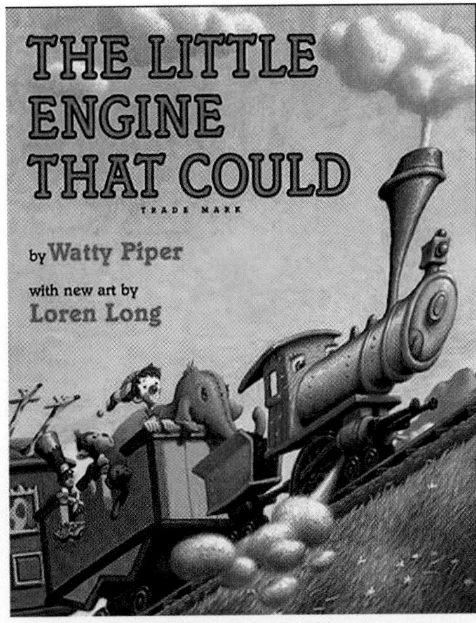

A cover illustration for *The Little Engine That Could*, published by Philomel in 2005.

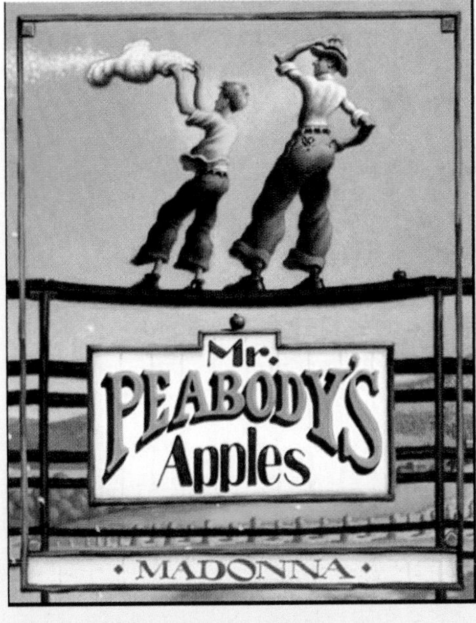

Pop icon Madonna chose Long to illustrate the children's book she authored, *Mr. Peabody's Apples*, published by Callaway Editions.

This illustration, *Babe Ruth: The Called Shot*, was used on the Official World Series Program in 2002.

Graphs do a good job of plotting trends. They are particularly effective when showing dramatic growth or when comparing growth in several areas. They can be dressed up with pictorial representations or can become eye-catching visual additions to a layout when color is applied to their lines (see Visual 3–24).

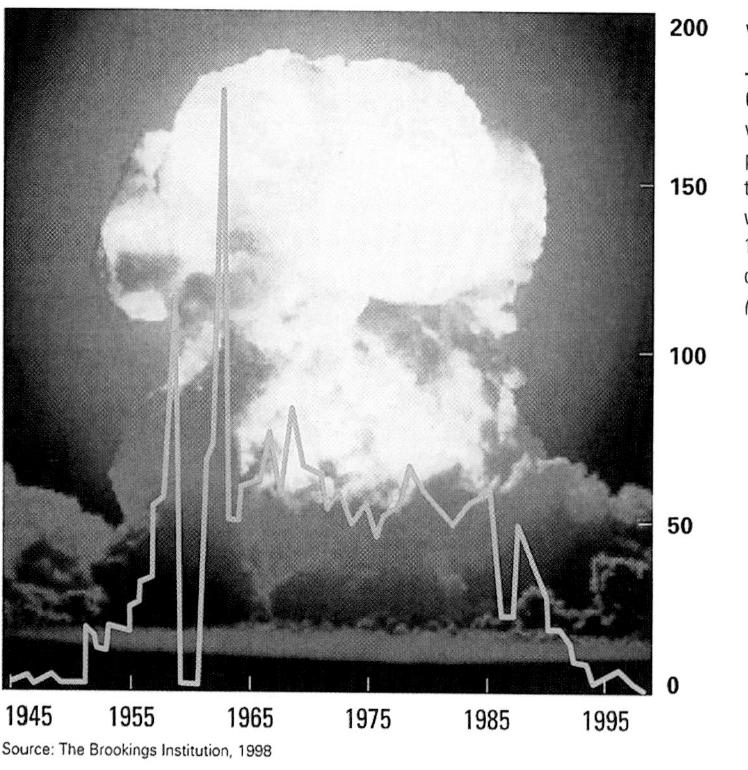

visual 3-24

Graph charts help readers visualize trends. This chart plots, over a fifty-year period, the number of nuclear weapons detonated since 1945 and when most occurrences took place. *(Design by Kit Hinrichs)*

SUMMARY

Representational imagery can enhance a message and helps draw attention to content. It is important to use photographs when recognition, documentation, and accuracy are important. Illustration offers a range of looks and media possibilities and can lend expressiveness to representational imagery. Graphically reduced images, are images that are visually represented in the simplest possible way. They work well as universal symbols and in logo applications and are often used as trademarks for identifying brands. Logos and trademarks are typically extended to a broader context where they serve as part of a visual scheme of coordinated color, typography, and other graphic elements that constitute an identity system. Identity systems are applied to stationery, business materials, products, product packaging, architecture, signage, and other situations that need to display a company's name and identity. Symbols and visual themes also are used in an informative way as environmental graphics that guide individuals who are in unfamiliar situations. Charts and graphs are another means of informative imagery and are used to make statistics more visually engaging.

projects

Project Title Graphic Animal

Objectives

Study from observation to produce a visual analysis

Study the process of form reduction

Demonstrate design drawing ability

Refine and achieve an appropriate level of craft

Apply the use of mechanical tools to produce finished work

Make a connection between graphic reduction and logo/pictographic design

Description

Choose an animal or insect and research its behavior, anatomy, and physical characteristics. Before you begin, do a physical analysis and study of the animal from photographs. Look at it from a variety of viewpoints. Count the number of features and anatomical parts and describe the individual attributes in diagrammatic drawings. Do a series of ten to fifteen studies to refine the composition. Refine and translate a chosen drawing into a final black-and-white study that is a graphic reduction or an object simplification of the original. Keep only the attributes that describe the object.

Limitations and Materials

Produce pencil sketches that are thumbnail or small-scale studies that are confined to an area no larger than 4 inches by 4 inches. Working on tracing paper will allow you to trace over parts of a drawing you like in order to generate refinements. When you arrive at a final drawing, enlarge it on a photocopier so it measures 8 inches by 8 inches. Transfer the final drawing to illustration board with 4H pencil. Ink with fine-point black pens and markers or a ruling pen and black gouache. Touch up your image if necessary with white gouache or acrylic paint. Use a ruler, triangle, and template for precise drawing.

Critique Discussion Points

Does the final simplified image maintain the essence of the original object? Why or why not?

What did you learn about the object from the physical analysis?

What did you find most challenging about this assignment?

What pleases you most about the final image?

Vocabulary

graphic reduction, symbol, icon, pictogram, value, grayscale, continuous tone

References and Resources

Lance Wyman, Ryan McGinness, Malcolm Grear, Luba Lukova, Paul Rand, Oti Aicher

Project Title Name Logo

Objectives

Use typography in a meaningful way

Design a symbol that supports a message

Combine typography and a symbol in a simple icon that is easily read and understood

Demonstrate design drawing ability

Refine and achieve an appropriate level of craft

Combine traditional media with digital and electronic tools to produce finished work

Description

Make a logo of your name. Start by researching typefaces through online type libraries as well as the font library that is already installed on an available computer system. Find several typefaces for your name that you believe convey an attitude appropriate to who you are and combine your name (in one of the typefaces) with a symbol that does the same. Use the technique you learned for graphically reducing an image in the previous project to develop an appropriate symbol. Limiting yourself to black-and-white media, experiment with different ways of combining the symbol and your name using layering, scale changes, and other ways of combining the elements in a harmonious manner. Consider figure/ground relationships with a combination of image and type and apply the design principles you have learned to combine them in a synergistic manner. Keep your design simple so it can be read and understood easily on small- as well as large-scale applications.

Limitations and Materials

Use a computer to generate at least six variations of your name, each time making use of a different typeface or stylistic treatment. You can distort the type on the computer with a drawing or photo editing program or manually distress the type. Use pencils, pens, and black-and-white media as described in the previous project to develop an image icon that can be combined with your name. Use pencil sketches and tracing paper to trace and refine the visual ideas you are developing and combine your image icon with the typographic treatment of your name. Use a photocopier to reduce and enlarge or make copies of the elements of your design. You also may use a scanner to scan your drawings or photocopies and trace over them with a digital drawing program. The computer also is a useful tool for combining type with an icon as well as for further refining your final design.

Critique Discussion Points

How is the typography you used expressive of you and/or your personality?

What physical attributes does the typeface possess that give it its character?

How does the image icon that you chose express you and/or your personality?

What design principles influenced your design decisions when you were combining type with iconography?

What types of refinements did you make to produce the final design?

Vocabulary

typeface, type style, graphic reduction, symbol, icon, pictogram, figure/ground, logo, logotype, synergistic

Project Title Photo Crop

Objectives

Determine which portions of a photograph are worth salvaging and which are not worth saving

Develop a judicious eye for photographic composition

Practice cropping techniques

Description

Find two photographs that can be improved through cropping. Find the best portion of each photograph and crop it so the viewer's eye is redirected to a portion of the photo.

Limitations and Materials

Locate a poorly composed photograph, or one that could be cropped so that attention is drawn to a different portion of the original image. Locate a second photograph of a human or animal subject that contains the head and all or part of the body. Make cropping blocks from two L-shaped pieces cut from black poster board or construction paper. Use a T square to ensure that the edges are square and cut at right angles. Crop each photo by positioning the cropping blocks so that the areas of the photo that do not improve the composition are eliminated and the best portion of the photograph is preserved. With the photograph or the human or animal, concentrate on cropping it so that the focus is on the head or face. When you have found a crop that works, tape the L-shaped pieces together and mark off and trim your final selections.

Critique Discussion Points

How successfully does each crop work?

How is cropping an improvement to the original?

What unnecessary components in the original have been eliminated through cropping?

How has the focal point in each photo changed or been improved?

Are the cropped images compositionally well balanced?

Vocabulary

crop/cropping, cropping blocks, focal point, hierarchy, balance

References and Resources

Man Ray, Richard Avedon, Ansel Adams, Henry Wolf, Annie Leibovitz, Otto Storch, Fred Woodward, DJ Stout

In Review

1. When is it more appropriate to use an illustration as opposed to a photograph?
2. How is a graphically reduced image different from a continuous-tone image?
3. What are the differences between a mark, logotype, logo, and trademark?
4. What is a graphics standards manual? How is it used?
5. Why are symbols an important part of designing wayfinding systems?
6. What are the differences between a pie chart, bar chart, and graph? How is each one used?

4 COLOR *and* DESIGN

objectives

Explore the dimensions of color related to issues of visual communication.

Explain how color is perceived and processed by the eye and brain.

Identify key color systems and describe their relevance to graphic art.

Define color terminology using visual examples.

Present significant color theories that are useful in contemporary design.

Investigate color psychology, symbolism, and cultural influences as they affect your understanding and use of them.

Reveal strategies for choosing color schemes.

Discuss the impact of color in composition.

introduction

The role of color in visual communication is complex. It is undoubtedly the most researched; most visually powerful; and since the advent of computers, the most technical of all of the elements of design. It enhances the viewer's response on a variety of levels; it heightens the viewer's perception and intensifies emotional and psychological reaction. To become proficient with color, you must spend time studying it and working with it.

This chapter examines the fundamental dimensions of color related to science, theory, language, and practice. Crucial components of color, an exploration of color relationships, and ways of applying this knowledge to the practice of design will be presented.

COLOR SYSTEMS

Numerous color systems have been developed that attempt to order color so it can be comprehended more easily. Some of the systems are relatively simple, while others are technical. Some systems, such as the color wheel, are theory-based, demonstrating the order and relationships between purely saturated color hues. Other systems, such as Albert H. Munsell's color solid, was designed based on human perception as a standard for organizing color for industry and education.[1] His model was the first widely accepted color order system and along with others, influenced the 1931 Commission Internationale de l'Eclairage (International Commission of Illumination) in the development of a global color standard for science and industry.

The result was the CIE chromaticity model, which is used to measure hue, value, and chroma. The model also serves as the basis for computer color. Other color systems function as tools for specifying color as ink formulas for the printing industry. This chapter will discuss those systems and others, but first you need to understand how color is perceived at the source.

COLOR PERCEPTION

Color perception is a complex physiological function. Artists do not have to be proficient in their knowledge of human physiology, but they should have a basic understanding of eye and brain functions in the perception of light and form. The retina, the light-sensitive surface lining on the back of the eye, can be compared to film in a movie camera. Within the tissue of the retina are receptors referred to as rods and cones. Rods detect lightness and darkness, or tones; and cones detect color sensations, or hues (see Visual 4–1).

Rays of light illuminate objects in the world of vision and reflect them back to the eye. The eye functions like a lens, which perceives the light information that is then carried to the brain via the optic nerve. Hundreds of thousands of light messages are sent through the optic nerve at the same time. The brain processes the messages to provide you with an apparently seamless view of the world. It is remarkable that the color you perceive on objects is not tangible.

That is, what you see is not actually color, but vibrating wavelengths that are emitted from the surface of every object. For example, a red ball is reflecting red wavelengths and absorbing all other wavelengths. In fact, the wavelengths being absorbed can be thought of as the perfect light complement to the color wavelength being reflected.

Wavelengths are a form of energy that makes up the visible spectrum. They are part of the electromagnetic field, which also produces microwaves, radio waves, infrared radiation, and X-rays. Each color hue has its own wavelength. Wavelengths also determine a color's intensity, which is dependent on the amount of available light (see Visual 4–2). You can observe the intensity of a color diminish in an object by watching it during a sunset or by dimming artificial light.

---

[1]See A. H. Munsell, *A Color Notation*, 12th ed. (New Windsor, NY: Munsell Color Co., 1975).

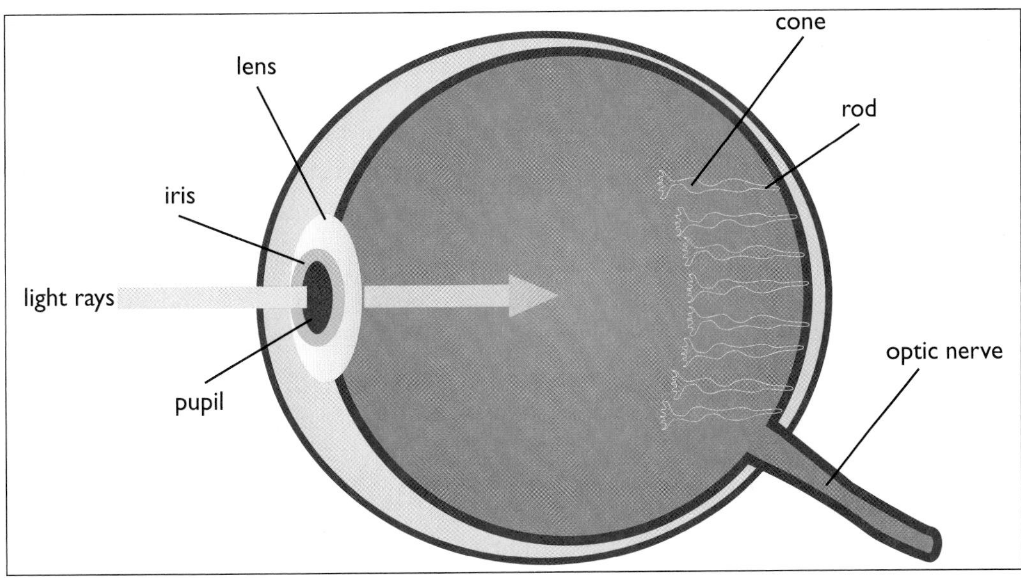

visual |4-1|

The eye sends visual information to the brain for processing via the optic nerve. Some of the features in this diagram are larger than actual scale to illustrate their appearance.

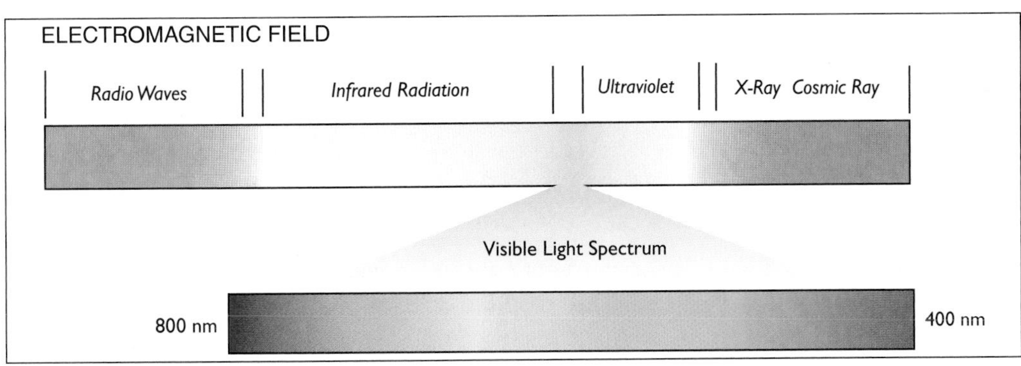

visual |4-2|

The visible light spectrum is a narrow band in the electromagnetic field.

ADDITIVE SYSTEM

Having discussed how the human eye perceives light, it is appropriate now to introduce the additive color system, which is dependent on light (see Visual 4–3). The additive system makes all colors visible. It is the color system of white light. The light necessary to see color can come from the sun; from a natural source; or from artificial sources such as incandescent, florescent, and halogen light. Artists and designers must pay attention to the source of light in which they work. The different light sources can significantly change the effect of color in a design image.

visual 4-3

The spectral blended color scheme used for this CD package is transparent, which heightens the effect of color light. The banded color simulates the visual effect of light projected through a prism. It also mimics the design look experienced when visiting the Web site for the Pleats Please clothing line. *(Jewel case design by Sayuri Studio)*

Isaac Newton may have been the first person to study light. He performed an experiment in 1666 using a prism and a ray of light to discover, in essence, the additive color system.

He discovered that white light is composed of a blend of red, green, and blue primary hues.

Mixing any two of those colors will yield a secondary hue. Blue and green yield cyan, the complement of red. Blue and red yield magenta, the complement of green. Red and green yield yellow, the complement of blue. Therefore, the secondary hues in the additive system are cyan, magenta, and yellow (see Visual 4–4).

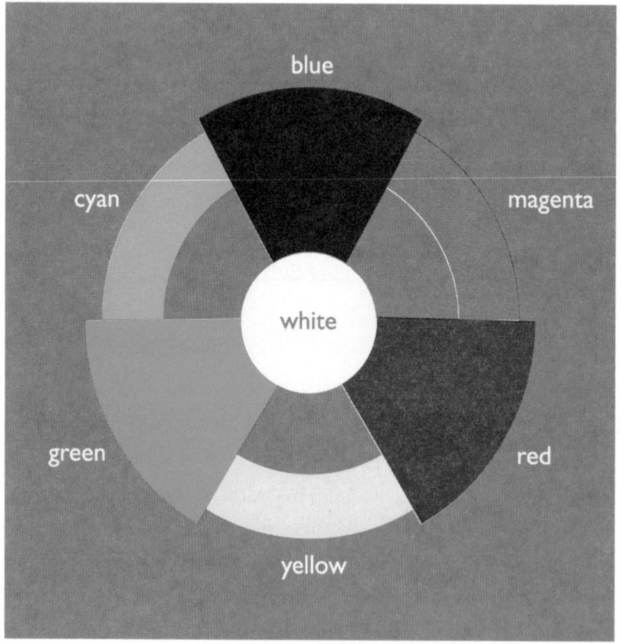

visual 4-4

Mixing the three primary colors in the additive system yields white (white light). The colors seen here are not as vibrant or luminous as when viewed on a computer monitor.

Some of the principles of the additive system (for example, green and red mixing to make yellow) run counter to people's intuitive sense of how color works. That is because they first learned about color in grade school, mixing paint and crayons, which is color pigment. Remember that the medium for the additive system is light. It is the system that forms the basis for color photography, film and video, computer imaging, and television.

The principle behind all of those media is the projection of a fine blend of red, green, and blue light. Varying the amount of each primary hue projected yields a varying intensity, which re-creates the full spectrum of color in your eye. You can see that effect by looking closely at the edge of a TV screen (see Visual 4–5).

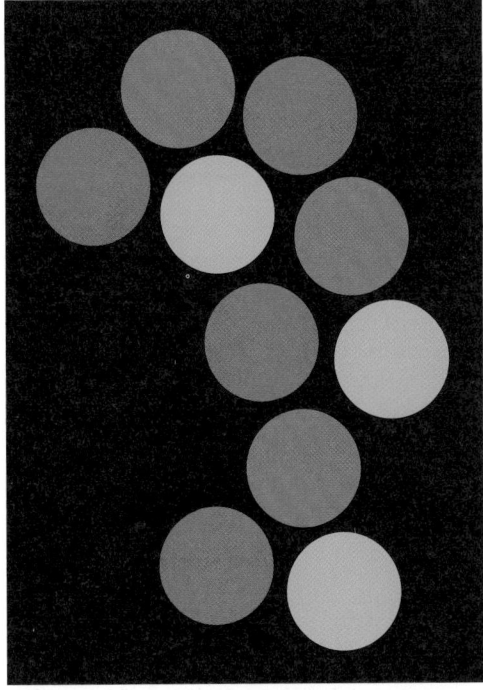

visual 4-5

Television screens and computer monitors display three separate patterns of red, green, and blue dots called pixels. The pixels form a lattice of individual colors emitting points of light that creates a full color picture.

SUBTRACTIVE SYSTEM

The subtractive color system is based on mixing color pigments. As colors are mixed, they render a subtracting effect, which essentially filters the light striking the new color's surface. When two colors are mixed, a new color is created because the mixing has changed its wavelength.

The additive and subtractive systems are interdependent. The secondary hues of the additive system are the primary hues of the subtractive system. Cyan (blue), magenta (red), and yellow are the subtractive primaries. In color printing, cyan, magenta, and yellow are referred to as process primary colors. As they are recombined on a printing press, with the addition of black to enhance value, they re-create the color known in the visible, natural world. A trip to a printing press facility early in your study of design is a valuable experience that will help you understand these processes and their application to design. In the world of mixing paint and other forms of pigment, the blue and red that are considered primary hues differ from the hues cyan and magenta. Cyan is lighter and leans more toward a blue-green than the primary blue you learned about in school. Magenta is lighter and more pink than the rich reds achieved in most pigments. Yellow is slightly lighter and brighter.

Keep in mind that there are many hue shifts within each hue and between sets of hues (see Visual 4–6).

Traditional color wheels have been used for centuries to explain and illustrate subtractive color relationships. Johann Wolfgang von Goethe is responsible for developing the first color wheel using blue, red, and yellow as primary hues and purple, green, and orange as secondary hues (see Visual 4–7). Models such as Goethe's are valuable for understanding color relationships.

But the theory on which the models are based does not always translate well into the practice of mixing color. In Goethe's model, for example, when blue, red, and yellow are mixed together, the

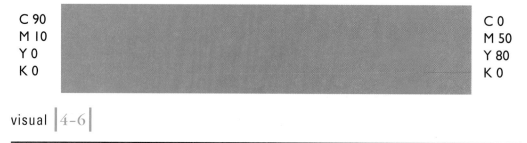

visual 4-6

This blend from blue to orange illustrates the many colors that exist between the two hues. Because these hues cross the color wheel, the colors seen in the middle area approach neutral gray.

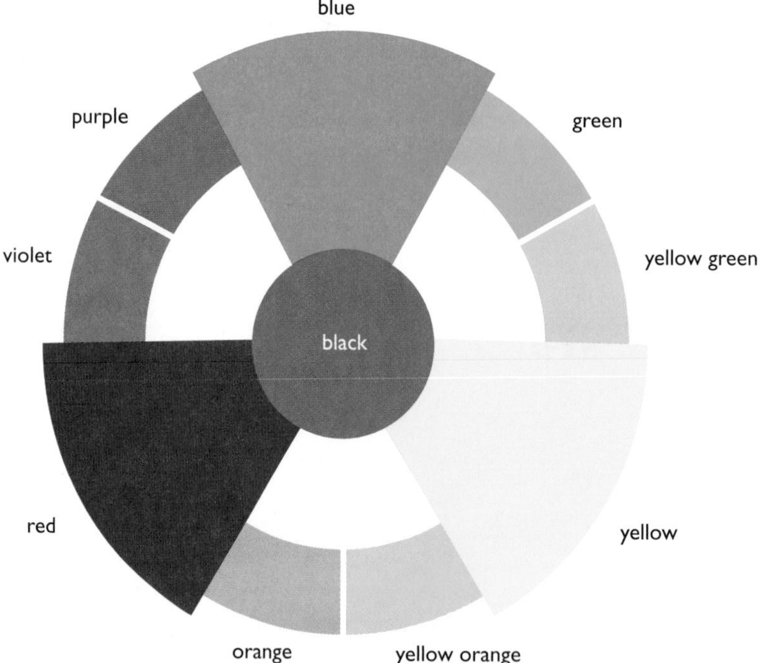

visual 4-7

This color wheel identifies primary, secondary, and tertiary hues. The black is actually an equal mix of 50 percent cyan, magenta, and yellow.

result is supposed to yield black. But you know from experience that mixing the primaries makes a grayish-brown color.

The secondary hues of mixing pigments are purple, green, and orange. The purple, green, and orange you get depend on the parent hues used to mix them (see Visual 4–8).

Hues found between primary and secondary are called tertiary. Red-purple, yellow-orange, and blue-green are examples. In addition to tertiary colors, intermediate hues can be made by mixing secondary and tertiary hues to achieve, theoretically, all of the colors in a spectrum.

Any two primary hues and the colors between them are called analogous hues. All primary, secondary, tertiary, and intermediate hues are fully saturated pure color—they are pure in the sense that they contain no white, black, or gray.

Other models have been developed that use a variation of color groupings as primary and secondary hues. Most of the models do a poor job of representing the full color range between any set of hues. They present a limited window of the many hues that exist between two colors.

That is evident in Visual 4–8, which represents only nine of the limitless number of hues that exist between the primaries. Continuous blends, achieved electronically, better illustrate the range between any two colors (see Visual 4–9).

visual | 4-8 |

Purple on the left and violet on the right are mixed from the same two parent colors—blue and red. Purple has slightly more blue, and violet has slightly more red.

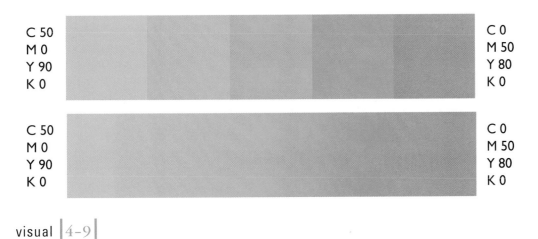

visual | 4-9 |

The top color study presents five intermittent steps from green to orange as compared with a continuous blend of the hues below.

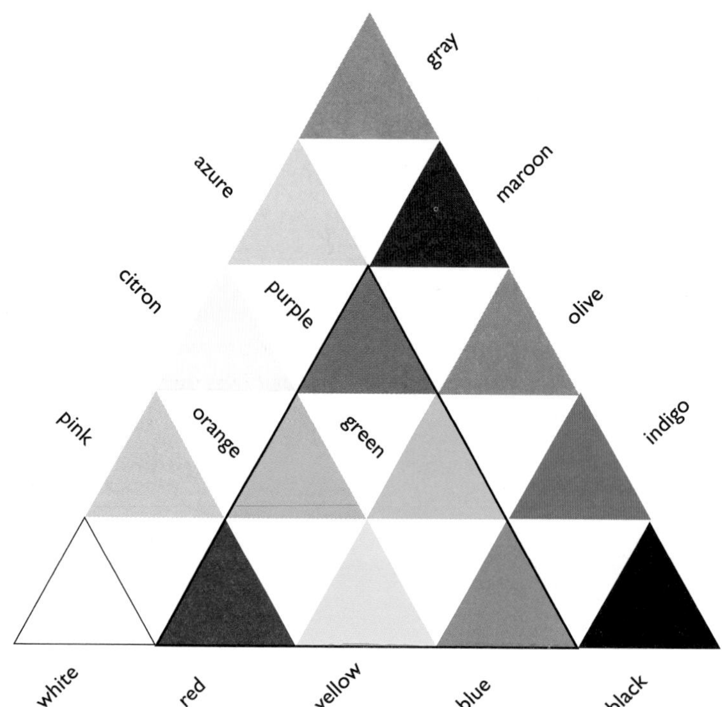

visual 4–10

The result of this model yields color mixes with expanded color names that are more useful than the simple generic names you probably learned in grade school. Any two colors on the bottom row can be followed diagonally to the color swatch they make. The inner triangle contains the basic primary and secondary hues.

Other aspects of the color wheel limit your comprehension of color relationships.

You learn, for example, that the complements are blue and orange, purple and yellow, and red and green; and so they are. But many other hue relationships can be complementary.

Turquoise, similar to cyan, and red-orange have a complementary relationship, as does yellow-orange and blue-purple and infinite opposite pairs found on a color wheel.

Color systems such as the color pyramid in Visual 4–10 have added black and white as primary colors.

Remember that simple color names such as blue and green are arbitrary when attempting to specify colors. What one person has in mind when thinking of blue is likely different from another person's perception of blue. That is why color is specified in design by precise systems or by the comparison of color swatches or pigment samples.

SPECIFICATION SYSTEMS

Choosing the right color or color scheme is a process of narrowing a general idea of color to more precise color specifications. Designers use a variety of color specification systems from early ideation to final production. A designer may begin with an intuitive idea for a color scheme (for example, yellow ochre and blue) as a general concept. Early in the development of the design, markers or cut paper swatches may be used to visualize color for the design. But when it is time to prepare the design for electronic or print production, more accurate color specifications are necessary. Graphic design software offers a variety of color systems that are integrated with the printing industry and digital multimedia design. The electronic color systems can be cross-referenced to swatch books of printed color to ensure color accuracy in print design. Now you will examine the color specification systems individually, beginning with those used in the printing industry.

Printing is based on two types of color systems, CMYK and match systems. CMYK is cyan (blue), magenta, yellow, and black. (The *K*, which stands for *key*, is used for black, which also distinguishes it from blue.) CMYK is more often referred to as process color or four-color process. Digital or conventional reflective art is prepared by breaking down or separating it into each of the four colors. The separation process filters the cyan, magenta, yellow, and black one at a time. Then each separation is converted to a dot pattern that is recorded onto metal plates. The four plates are then fastened to drums located at four separate stations on a four-color printing press. Sheets of paper are run through the press, receiving an impression of ink from the plate at each station. The four colors are printed on top of each other, recombined to reproduce the color in the original design. Four-color process is used when the original art is continuous or blended tones.

Match systems are used when the color is solid and isolated within shapes or backgrounds (see Visual 4–11). As the name suggests, desired color areas in the original design are matched to an ink formula. Those formulas are selected from a book that presents a printed swatch accompanied by a number. The number is provided to a printer, and the corresponding ink formula is used to print only those areas specified. The color numbering system that is the worldwide industry standard is

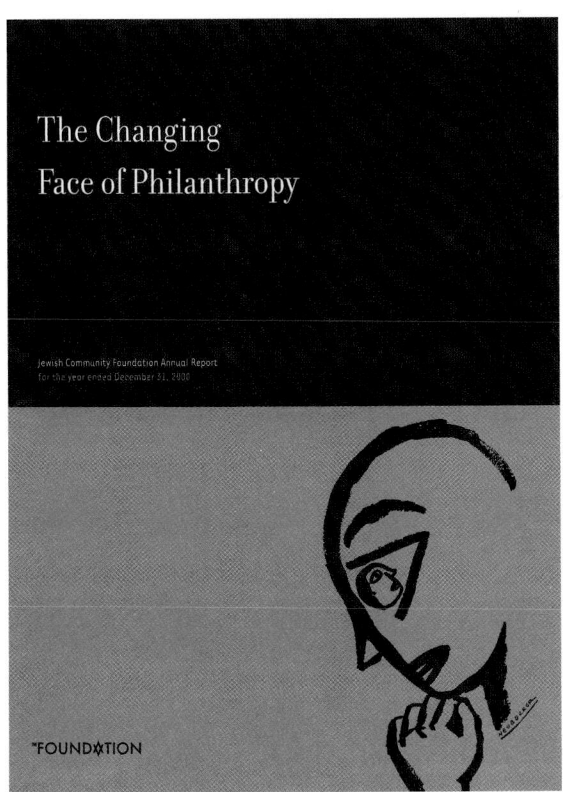

visual |4–11|

The Changing
Face of Philanthropy
Jewish Community Foundation Annual Report
for the year ended December 31, 2000
FOUNDATION

Two match colors, orange and black, constitute the printed color in this annual report design. The white type is the color of the paper. When one color is printed in the area of another, it is referred to as reversed out or knocked out. The black creates a sense of confinement to the lower half of the composition. *(Annual report design by KBDA)*

the PANTONE MATCHING SYSTEM (PMS) (see Visual 4–12). Other systems include TRUMATCH, TOYO, and Focaltone. Those and other similar systems work the same way PANTONE does (see Visual 4–13). All of the color systems are generally available for specifying color in electronic media. You may be familiar with some of the systems if you have used graphic software.

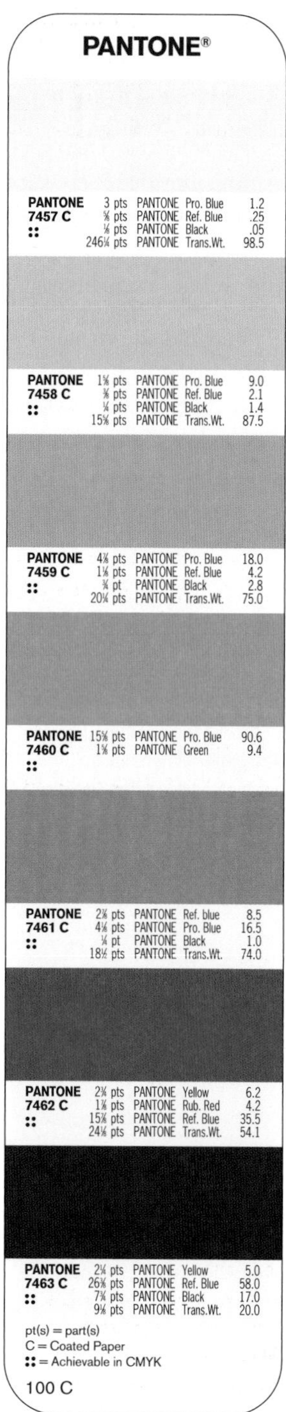

visual | 4–12 |

Match color, also called a special color, can be specified for area color fill in typography, graphic elements, and borders. Each swatch provides the color number (the *u* indicates uncoated paper) and the ink formula prepared by a printer.

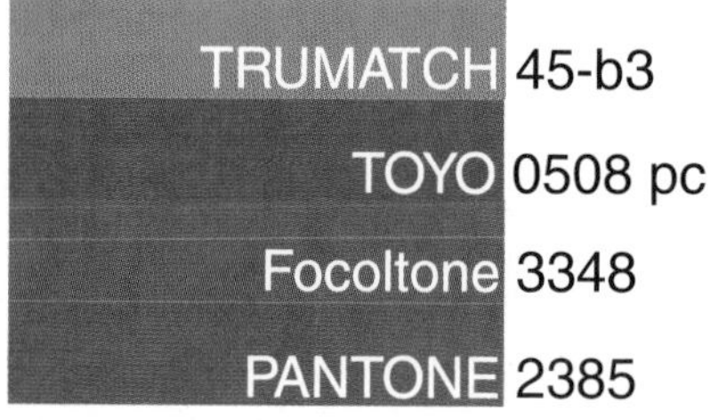

visual | 4–13 |

These four violet-purple hues were specified from swatch libraries in Adobe Illustrator.

Design and imagery that are created and produced digitally can be prepared in any of the systems mentioned previously. Most design software provides the CMYK system by default.

Colors often appear different on a computer monitor compared to when they are printed. That is because they differ in the way they are viewed. Colors can be specified and cross-referenced to a printed swatch to ensure color integrity when converted from digital to printed form.

It is important to note that match colors are more vibrant than CMYK process color because there are limits to what the CMYK mixes can achieve. It is particularly evident in blues and purples; some deep reds; and, of course, florescent colors. But for the most part, CMYK does a good job of re-creating a full color range. To clarify, CMYK and match systems are used in printing. Both systems are available in digital software and in printed swatch books for specifying color.

Color used for multimedia design or Web design requires the red, green, and blue (RGB) system.

RGB is the primary hue system of light. Any media venue that relies on projected light, such as photography, DVD, video games, computer and television monitors, and film, depends on RGB. The RGB system is the default palette for most photo- and multimedia-based graphic software. Each hue—red, green, and blue—can be adjusted in 1-point increments of brightness from 0 to 255. Because there is no translation of color from digital light to printed ink, what is seen on the screen is generally what you get. The variance occurs between the designer's monitor and the user's monitor or projection screens.

Designing for the Web has a specific color limitation. Web graphics are often designed on Mac systems and consumed on PC systems. For the color to be consistent from one platform to another, the hexadecimal system was developed. There are 216 common colors derived from the system that constitute the Web palette. Most Web software provides the colors from the hexadecimal system. RGB colors can be used and converted to this system (see Visual 4–14). RGB colors are brighter than CMYK colors—projected light is luminous; pigments are reflective.

You can see the difference by converting color from RGB to CMYK in electronic design. Most software provides an option to convert color in a document from one color system to another and from color to gray scale.

THE LANGUAGE OF COLOR

The language of color has evolved from research in theory, technology, and the practice of design. Sometimes the terms speak about specific aspects of color; and sometimes color speaks its own language—with symbolic, cultural, and psychological meaning. This section will explore and define color terminology in words and images by offering color analyses of professional design.

WEB 255/204/0

WEB 255/255/0

WEB 102/204/153

WEB 102/51/204

WEB 204/51/102

visual |4–14|

The hexadecimal color system is intended specifically for Web design. The range of color choices seems limited but actually provides a decent palette. By limiting the palette, the amount of digital information to be processed is manageable, which allows Web pages to open more quickly. This system is set up in increments of fifty-one units each of RGB.

COLOR TERMINOLOGY

Hue is the same as color. It is the inherent color referred to by a name or formula. You should learn as many color names as possible. You also would find it beneficial to learn which CMYK percentages are used to build basic primary and secondary hues (see Visual 4–15).

Saturation refers to the purity of a color. Pure hues that are fully saturated are at their highest level of intensity (see Visual 4–16). Intensity corresponds approximately to the value of primary and secondary hues. The lighter hues, yellow and orange, are more intense than the darker hues, blue and purple. Red and green have similar values and fall in between.

Adding black, white, or midtones contaminates a pure hue and affects the intensity level (see Visual 4–17). When black or gray is introduced, pure hues immediately lose their brilliance.

The smallest amount of black mixed with yellow dulls the impact of yellow, changing it to a somber green. Black has a similar effect with each of the primary and secondary hues—it changes their color name: red to maroon, green to olive drab, blue to indigo, orange to sienna, and purple to puce. Gray is not as profound but has a similar effect, making the hues murky. White has a lively effect on blue and purple as it brings them out of the dark value range.

Chroma is similar to saturation. Munsell describes chroma as the amount of colorant present in a pigment.[2]

The more colorant, the more saturated the hue. There is a subtle distinction between saturation and chroma.

The former is about dulling a pure hue by adding gray tones, and the latter is about the presence of hue in a pigment. The CMYK tool selector in graphics software illustrates the concept of chroma. The lower the percentage, the less color presence; the higher the percentage, the higher the color presence. It is not really a matter of adding white at all.

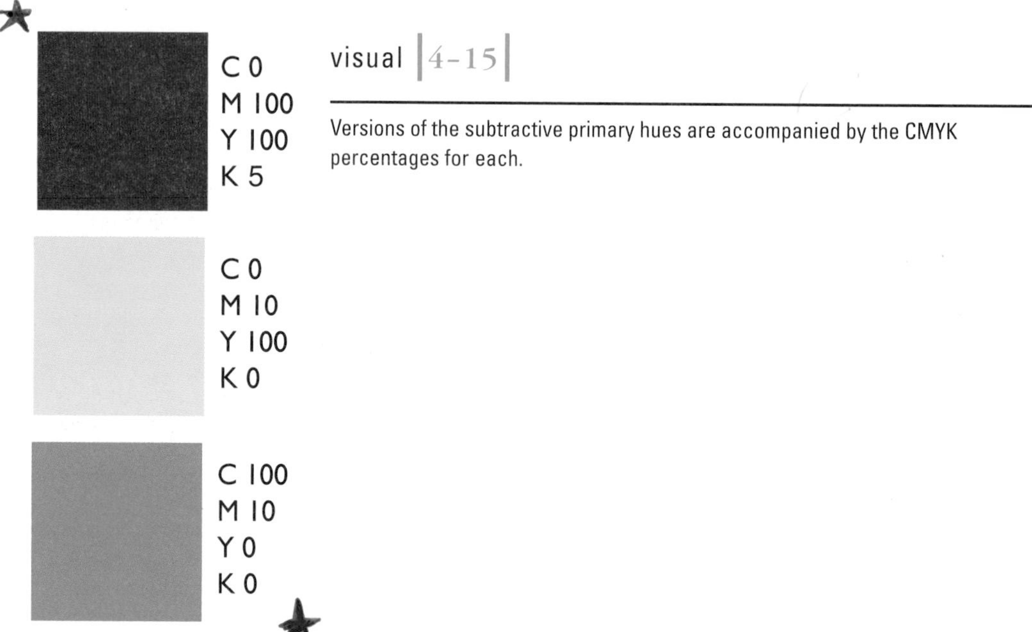

visual | 4–15 |

Versions of the subtractive primary hues are accompanied by the CMYK percentages for each.

[2]Ibid.

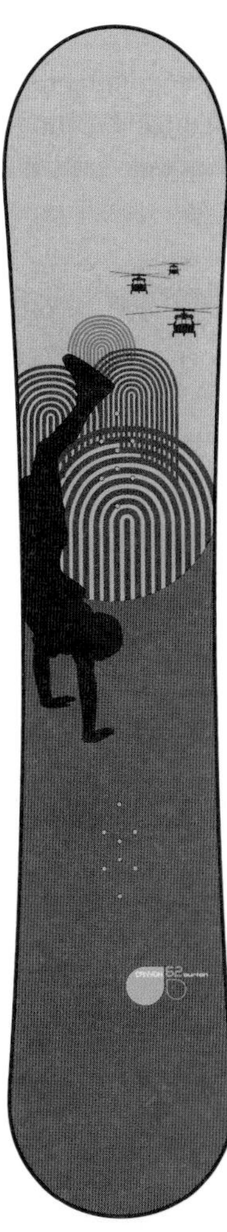

visual 4-16

In these snowboard graphics, orange is the brightest of the colors. The figure in the board on the left is silhouetted by the red and blue background areas that are more saturated; that is, they contain more of their inherent hue but are not as bright. The somber green in the right board has lost a significant amount of saturation, because of the presence of black in the color. *(Graphics by Jager Di Paola Kemp)*

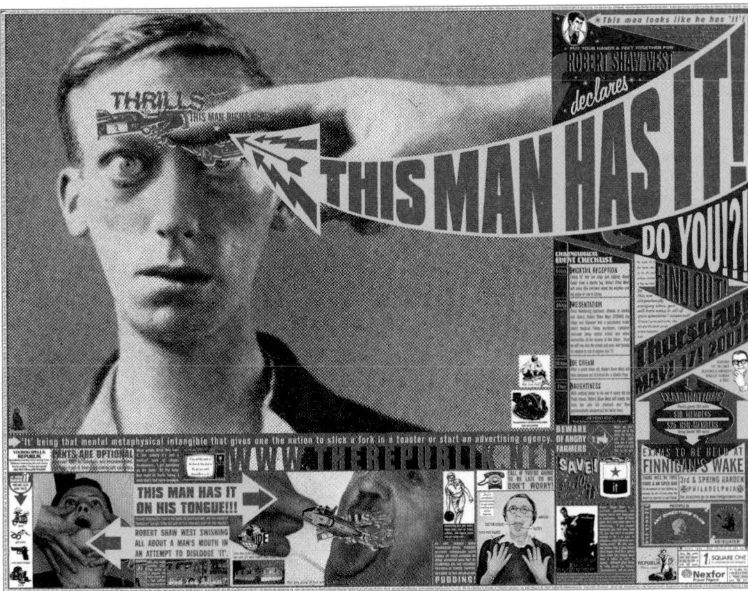

visual 4-17

The photographic imagery in this design is practically colorless umber tones. They lend an eclectic, retro look to the design and exist in stark contrast to the highly saturated red-orange colors in the type and border graphics. *(Self promotion design by Brian Murry)*

Value is lightness or darkness. Value can exist without color in grays, black, and white; but it also is present in colors. Each hue has a value that can be compared with gray tones (see Visual 4–18a). Knowing the value of the basic hues can help in choosing a color scheme. The complements, for example, offer interesting value relationships. Red and green are very similar in value, so they contrast only in their hue. Purple and yellow have the highest value contrast of any set of complements (see Visual 4–18b).

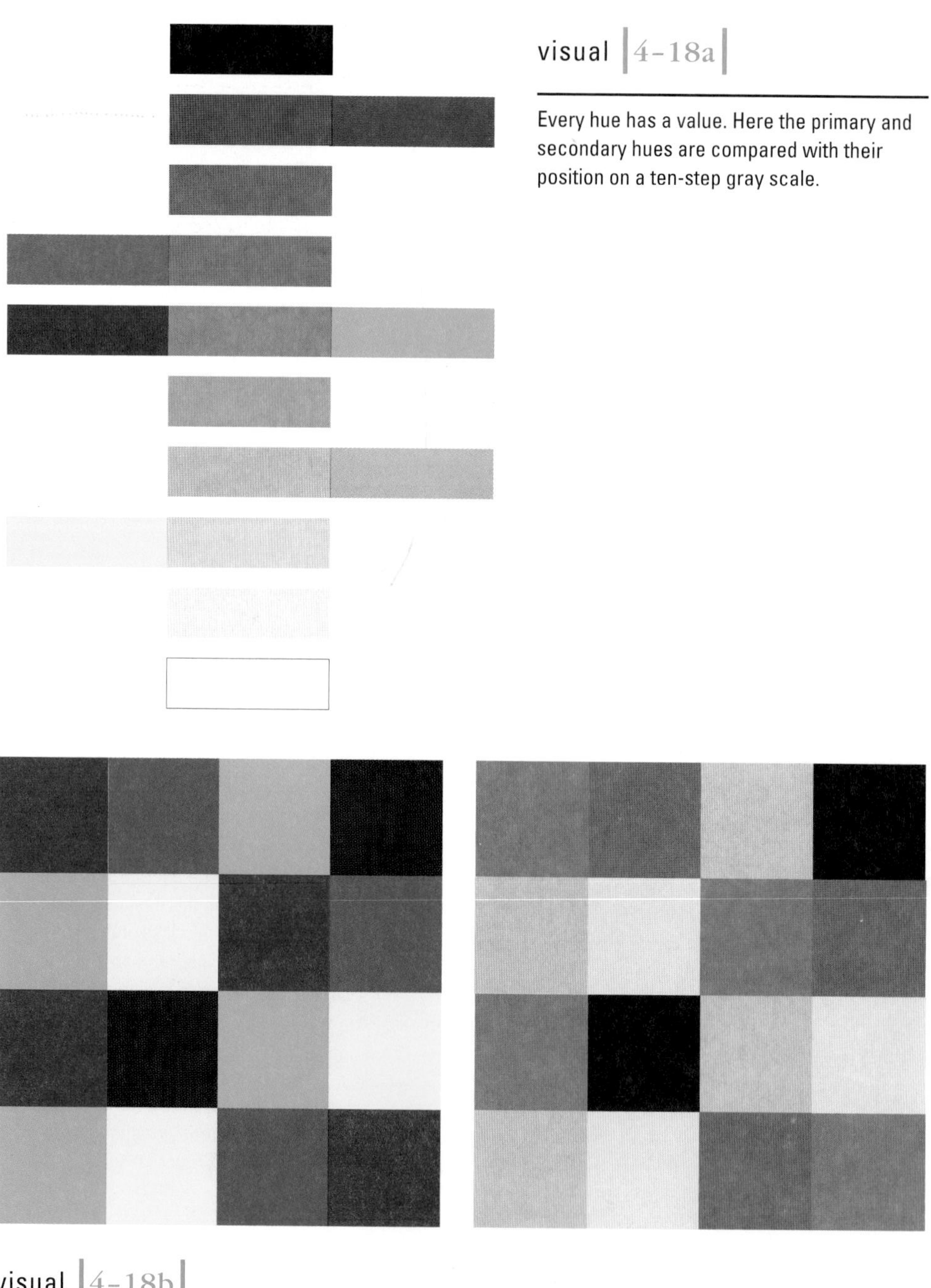

visual 4–18a

Every hue has a value. Here the primary and secondary hues are compared with their position on a ten-step gray scale.

visual 4–18b

A checkerboard arrangement of four colors is translated to corresponding gray values.

Tint is adding white to a pure hue. As most hues are tinted or lightened with white, they also are made brighter. White yields new color names when mixed with red, purple, yellow, and blue. The results are pink, lavender, citron, and azure, respectively (see Visual 4–19). Orange and green are made brighter as more white is added to each, but they hold their color integrity. A high ratio of white added to the hues yields a category of colors referred to as pastels (see Visual 4–20).

visual | 4–19 |

The arrangement of cups glazed in tinted colors dominates this photo design. These tints are deeper in color than pastels, which produces an appetizing and festive color scheme. *(Exhibition catalog by Chronicle Books)*

C/0 M/10 Y/5 K/0

C/0 M/10 Y/15 K/0

C/0 M/0 Y/25 K/0

C/15 M/0 Y/25 K/0

C/20 M/0 Y/0 K/0

C/12 M/12 Y/0 K/0

visual | 4–20 |

This arrangement of primary and secondary hues is tinted to pastels. CMYK percentages indicate the negligible quantities of actual color in each.

Shade is the mix of black with a color. The term *shade* is often misused to describe hue. A shade of blue is a mix of blue and black, not a variation in its hue. Adding black to the hues yields dramatic color changes. In small amounts, black has an insidious effect on yellow and orange. But in higher proportions, black produces handsome, deep earth tones in these hues. Blue, green, and purple seem to be most compatible with black, holding their color identity as they are mixed (see Visual 4–21).

Tones are grays, also referred to as midtones. Achromatic gray is mixed from black and white and is the same as a tone. Tones run the range from light to dark values in the gray scale. Grays deaden the brilliance of pure hues. Darker grays have a similar effect on hues as black, and lighter grays have a similar effect on hues as white. Tones mixed with yellow produce rich, colorful earth browns that resemble ochre and umber. When tones are added to hues that match them in value, you can observe an absolute shift in saturation without a shift in value (see Visual 4–22).

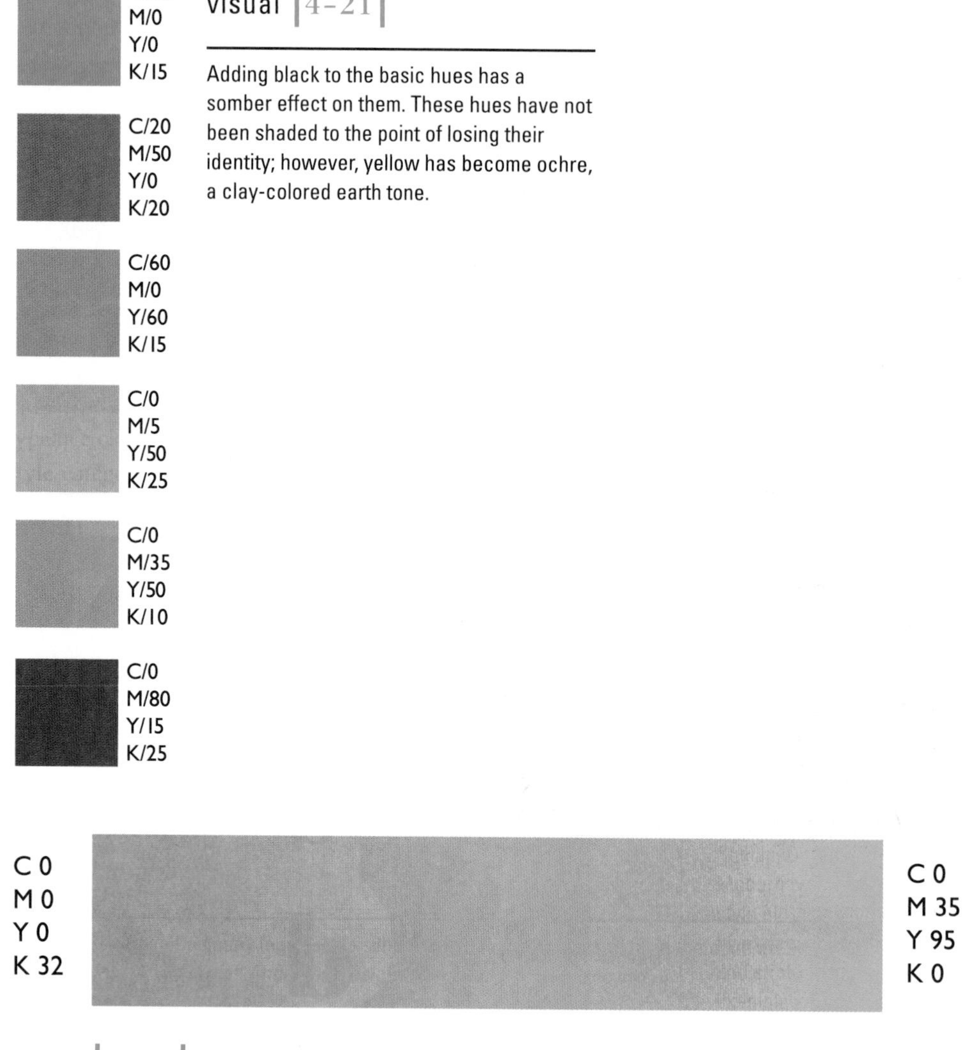

visual 4–21

Adding black to the basic hues has a somber effect on them. These hues have not been shaded to the point of losing their identity; however, yellow has become ochre, a clay-colored earth tone.

visual 4–22

The orange and gray match in value, demonstrating the effect of a midtone as it blends to a pure hue.

Monochromatic is a single color mixed with tints, shades, or tones. In printing, a monochromatic color scheme can be attained with a process called duotone, which is a gray scale and one hue. Monochromatic color schemes can effectively simulate the presence of other hues by virtue of the effect that tints, shades, and tones have on individual colors (see Visual 4–23).

THEORY AND INTERACTION

Anyone serious about a career in the visual arts needs to invest some time learning about color theories and understanding their impact on practical application. Of all of the color concepts, two theories profoundly and commonly affect the color decisions that designers make everyday. Knowing those two theories and their applications will help you order and manage color decisions artistically and intellectually.

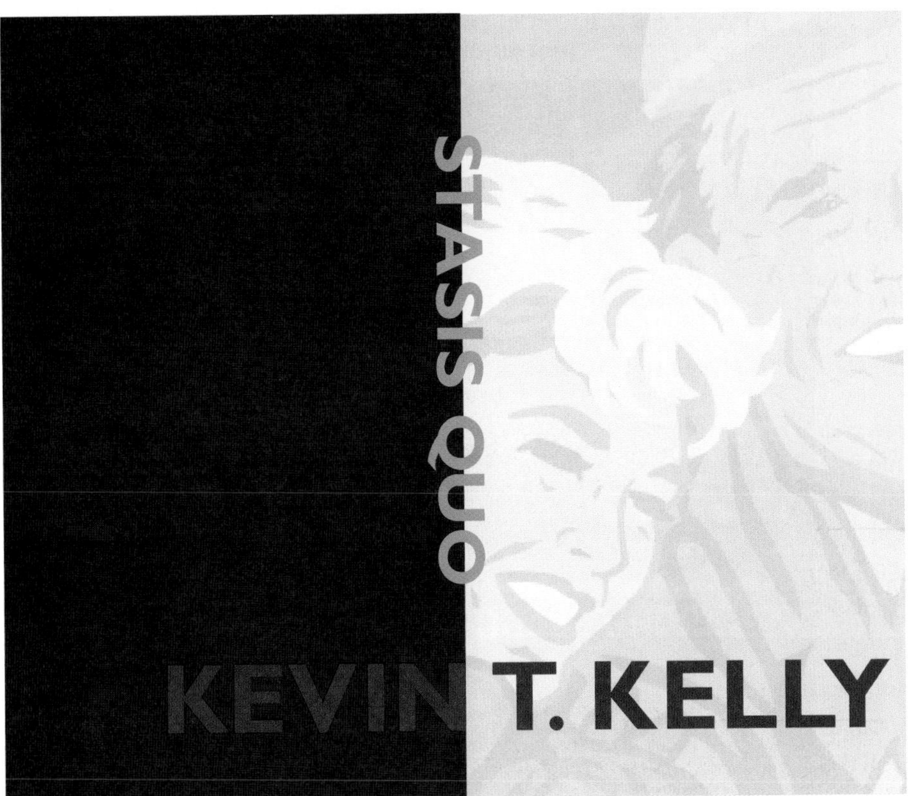

visual | 4–23 |

The graphic image used on the right half of this cover is a detail from a larger work by the artist whose work is featured in the catalog. The monochromatic image was cropped from the original full-color image and digitally converted from full color using a duotone filter. *(Exhibition catalog cover by Mark Thomas)*

The first theory is that color can be examined with regard to a set of contrasts. In particular are the seven contrasts explored and defined by Johannes Itten.[3] The second theory advances the idea that the appearance of a color depends on the influence or interaction it has with surrounding or adjacent colors. That theory is thoroughly explored by Josef Albers.[4] This chapter will examine both theories and their application to design.

Much of what has already been presented about color in this chapter lays the groundwork for a discussion of Itten's seven contrasts: value, hue, saturation, complement, temperature, size, and simultaneous contrast.

Contrast of value is the most basic color relationship. Designers often work in black and white by necessity or aesthetic choice. Black-and-white imagery offers a high degree of contrast surpassed for legibility contrast only by black and yellow, the color choice for many publications and signs (see Visual 4–24).

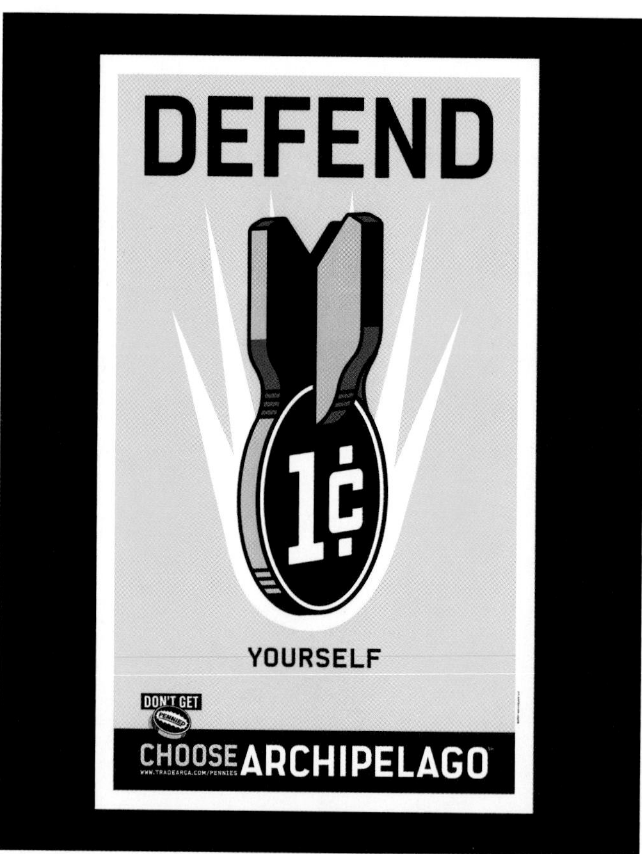

visual 4–24

The simplified and streamlined use of type and illustration has a high degree of legibility with a black-and-yellow color scheme. *(Poster design by Duffy Design)*

---

[3]See J. Itten, *The Elements of Color* (New York: John Wiley & Sons, 1970).

[4]See J. Albers, *Interaction of Color* (New Haven, CT: Yale University Press, 1963).

As has been discussed, each of the hues has a value. Some combinations of pure hues have little value contrast. For example, orange, green, and red are very similar, whereas purple, yellow, and green have a broader value range.

Contrast of hue is what distinguishes one color from another (see Visual 4–25). Often logos, advertisements, and brands need to function in black and white and in color. When a color image relies exclusively on contrast of hue, it is ineffective when translated to black and white.

Contrast of saturation is a juxtaposition of hues with varying purity. Adjusting the value of pure hues can be done by adding only white, black, or gray. To make purple lighter, you need to add white or light gray. In doing so, you lighten the color and weaken its saturation. Saturated colors tend to appear closer compared with weak colors, which recede. Using a color scheme of saturated to weaker hues creates depth through the effect of atmospheric perspective (see Visual 4–26).

A complementary contrast is based on any two hues directly opposed on the color wheel. In some ways, true complements exist only in theory, especially with regard to pigments.

visual | 4–25 |

The immediate response to this illustrated design is the bold use of color. The bold energy is achieved by using a variety of saturated, contrasting hues. The playful quality of the illustration is supported by the variety of colors. *(Phone card design by Metzler & Associates)*

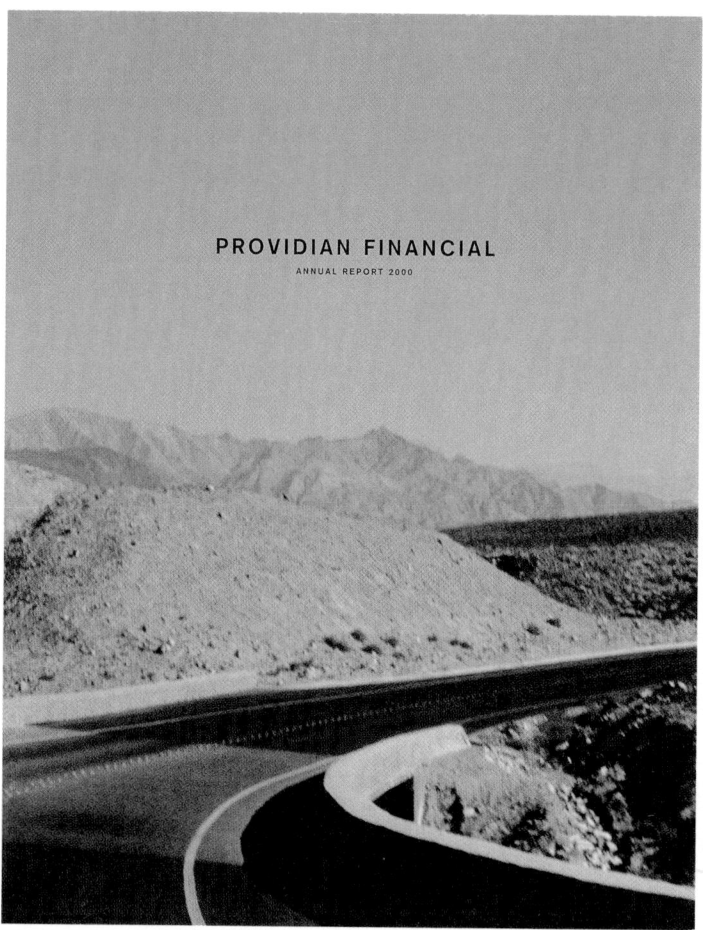

visual 4–26

Landscape photographs are good examples of aerial perspective. Colors weaken as they recede into space, losing their contrast to surrounding shapes. *(Annual report cover design by Cahan & Associates)*

The requirements for a true, perfect complement is that when mixed, they produce an absolute neutral (see Visual 4–27).

A complement is composed of a precise mix of two primaries in opposition to the remaining primary; for example, green (yellow and blue) and red. Complementary contrast is the simplest relationship for the basis of a color scheme. The relationship is curious because complements are vivid opposites that, when placed adjacent to one another, bring out the full potential of each (see Visual 4–28).

Contrast of temperature is the relative warm-cold relationship between hues. Color temperature is psychologically linked to conditions in nature—the hot yellow-orange of the sun, the cool green grass, the cold blue sky, or the warm reds and oranges of autumn leaves. It is generally accepted that red, orange, and yellow are warm colors and blue, green, and purple are cool colors.

Warm colors advance and cool colors recede, again taking their cues from nature. Within any hue range of analogous colors, a relative shift between warm and cool can be observed (see Visual 4–29). It is worth noting that most color pairs contain aspects of more than one contrast effect.

visual |4-27|

A complementary blend of blue-purple and yellow illustrates the difficulty in achieving a true complementary relationship in pigments. The area in the center of the blend (chromatic gray) is influenced by the parent colors, making it difficult to identify an absolute neutral.

visual |4-28|

Complements such as this orange-red/blue-purple color scheme produce a high-contrast energy that is fitting for the subject. *(Magazine spread design by Barbara Reyes and Peter Yates; illustration by Phil Mucci)*

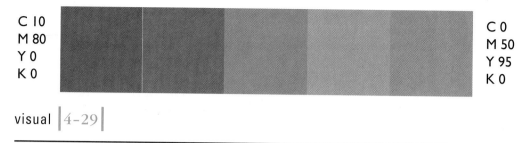

visual 4–29

All of the colors in this study are considered warm. But when the parent colors are compared, a relative shift in temperature can be seen. The magenta-red is relatively cooler than the orange.

Blue and orange are complements. They differ in value and present a warm-cool contrast. If you want to limit the coexistence of contrasts, adjust colors with regard to their complementary nature, value, or temperature (see Visual 4–30).

Contrast of extension is the comparison of quantities of color. It is a judgment of how much of one color compared to another color is needed to achieve harmony or balance. In the contrast in Visual 4–31, the design mantra coined by Mies van der Rohe, "less is more," can be vividly observed.

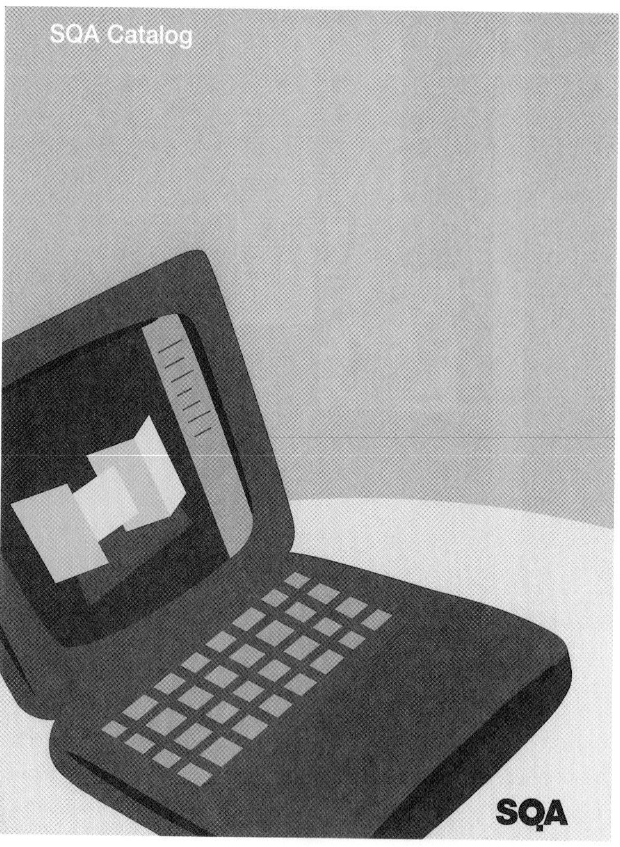

visual 4–30

The blue-orange color scheme is both complementary and contrasting in temperature. *(Catalog design by Herman Miller Inc.)*

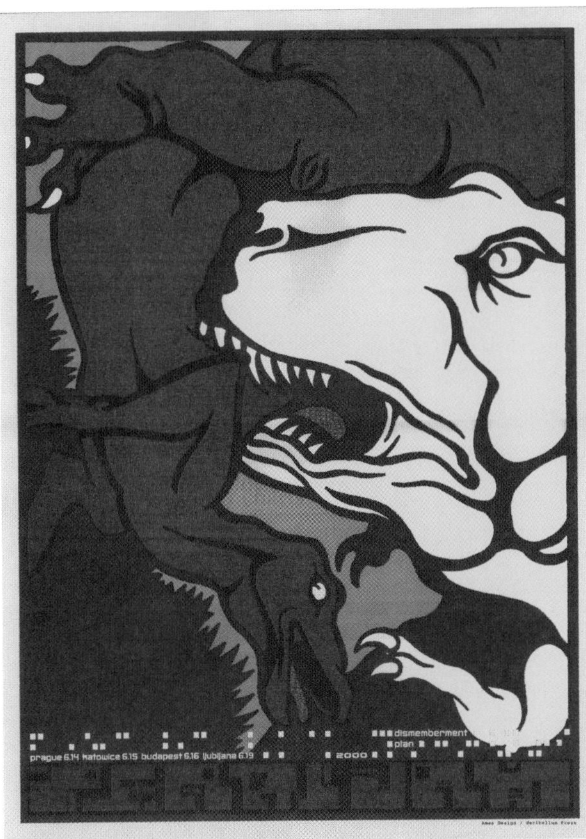

visual 4–31

The smaller percentage of the green area, contrasted by the reds and oranges, reinforces the scale of the dinosaur in the foreground, helping the dinosaur to dominate the composition. *(Poster design by Ames Design)*

Often the impact and intensity of smaller color elements are more profound than larger elements.

Certain color combinations cause color vibrations because of a combination of their size and value. The visual effect causes certain colors to expand beyond their edges (see Visual 4–32).

Other color relationships cause hues to remain contained within their edges; for example, a black square in a yellow color field.

Simultaneous contrast is perhaps the most subtle and subjective of the seven contrasts—no doubt because the phenomenon is dependent literally on the "eye of the beholder." The eye is ever searching for color harmony through color complements. When a complement is not present, the eye physically attempts to provide one. That occurs as an optical illusion, but it affects the way individuals process color. There are numerous figures that effectively illustrate this phenomenon.

It can be experienced by staring at a color that "burns" itself onto the retina of the eye.

Looking away at a neutral or white space produces the sensations of the opposing complement (see Visual 4–33). Simultaneous contrast also occurs in color relationships in which the interaction of colors affects how people perceive them (see Visual 4–34).

visual |4-32|

In this figure, the black and red stripes are physically equal in size, as are the white and green stripes. Yet the black appears wider than the red, and the white appears wider than the green. This optical effect is due to the nature of the color relationships. The red/green study shows a relationship in which the edges dissolve because the colors are complements that have a similar value. Black strives optically to stay contained within its edges, and white tends to expand optically outside its edges.

visual |4-33|

Stare at the center of the illustration for thirty seconds. Move your eye over to the dot to the right and blink quickly. You should see the black and white reversed and flashes of cyan in the red areas. *(Card announcement design by Kathleen Burch and Michael Bortolos)*

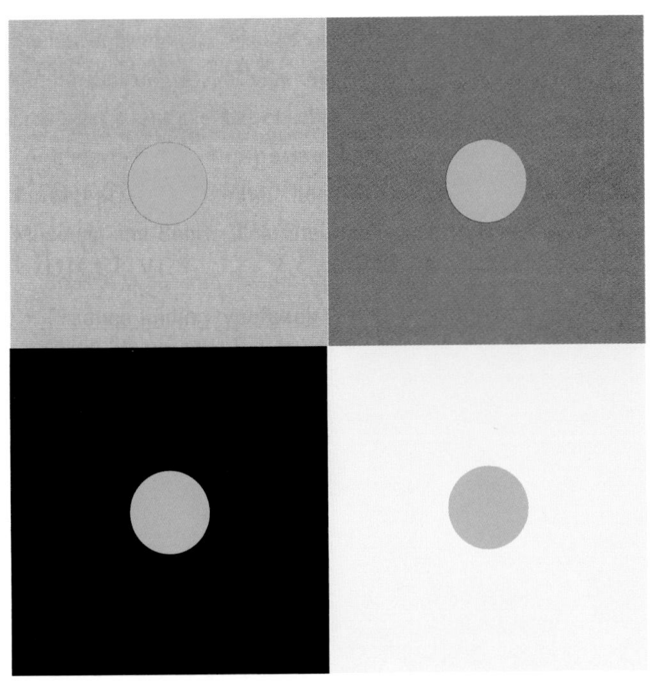

visual 4-34

Notice the significant change in the green circle as it is influenced by the four different-colored squares.

No color can exist in nature or visual art in a vacuum. As just discussed, gazing at a single color field or a deep blue sky finds the eye compulsively searching for complementary resolution.

Effective color decisions in design are critically dependent on managing color interaction.

No one has advanced the understanding of color influences and optical deception more than Albers.[5] His work is an illustrated application of the seven contrasts as they interact, producing remarkable effects.

Albers conducted most of his investigations using painted color and screen prints. Geometric figures and shapes are arranged in studies that function as basic design compositions. They lend themselves naturally to electronic media. The studies can be easily replicated and worked using digital color.

The premise for the studies is that color creates a context and that controlling the color environment affects the perception of the color. To make green look greener, place it in a red color field. To make a color appear darker, place it in a lighter context.

The essence of the color interactions demonstrates how one color can change its complexion to appear as two, how two colors can be independently influenced to appear as the same, or how color identity can be affected by surrounding colors (see Visual 4–35).

The ability to achieve the effect depends on the color choices and the size or amount of color undergoing change. At some point, as the size area of a color increases, it exerts its identity over the influence of its surroundings (see Visual 4–36).

[5]Ibid.

visual 4-35

This study is in the manner of Josef Albers, illustrating the effect of color interaction, making two different colors appear as the same color due to the influence of the background color fields.

Applying the knowledge found in color contrasts and color interaction can enhance figure-ground relationships, make type more legible, create harmony and balance, and enhance visual depth in design compositions (see Visual 4–37).

COLOR PSYCHOLOGY

Psychology plays an essential role in deciphering the meaning of color in visual communication.

Color psychology involves the affective nature of color—how color makes a person feel. This is a powerful dimension of color in all of the visual arts. Color psychology encompasses symbolic and cultural associations that also affect how individuals feel about certain colors (see Visual 4–38). Color has been associated with the sounds of musical instruments, the energy centers of the body, basic shapes, musical notes, and basic emotional responses. Color is more emotional and subjective than intellectual and objective. In fact, the standard color wheel was developed more from views of human perception and psychological response to color than any scientific theory.

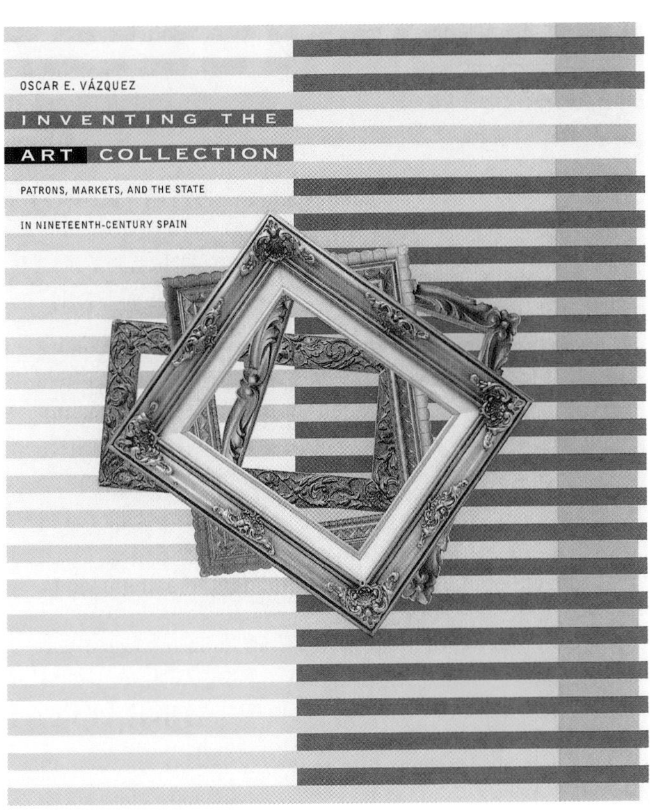

visual 4-36

The complexion of the yellow in this design is profoundly different as white and red independently influence it. *(Book jacket design by Jennifer Norton, Jerry King Musser)*

visual 4-37

The visual hierarchy and communication in this poster are enhanced by the color scheme. It contains some classic color devices, such as warm colors advancing and cool colors receding. It uses a complementary palette and strives for high legibility in the type, using effective color contrast. *(Poster design by Sayles Graphic Design)*

The trick is to learn how to use color psychology as a determinant in making effective color decisions. Each of the basic colors embodies a distinctive set of associations that can be translated into words. Knowing those associations will inform your color choices. Now you will examine some of the basic hues with regard to their universal meanings.

Purple is royal, sophisticated, and cultivated; and because of its deep value, it has an enigmatic quality (see Visual 4–39). It is associated with valor, as in the Purple Heart. It is a hue that is associated with distinctive aromas derived from fruits such as plums, grapes, and berries. Purple can have ominous qualities especially when mixed with gray or black.

Blue is expansive, serene, and reliable, as in "true blue." It is used extensively in business as a color for banks and brokerage firms. In the financial marketplace, blue conveys a sense of reliability and trust to consumers. The sky and water are the color's most familiar associations. Psychologically speaking, when a person is blue, she is sad, lonely, or depressed (see Visual 4–40). In most surveys, blue is the top pick for favorite color.

Green is growth, nature, and life-giving. Forests, fields, and farms are dominated by green. On the other hand, it also is the color of money, as in *greenback*. Green has been studied as the easiest of all colors to live with, especially as a shade or a tint. When it leans toward blue, it becomes aqua, the color of the sea in tropical environments (see Visual 4–41).

Yellow is sunlight, citrus, and energy. It is often associated with gold and, subsequently, wealth. It suggests intelligence and reason. As was mentioned earlier, yellow and black are the highest color contrast combination. Yellow can be acidic in its pure form but appealing with the addition of a small amount of red. It is a fragile color. Small amounts of any other hue, black or gray, have a significant effect on yellow (see Visual 4–42).

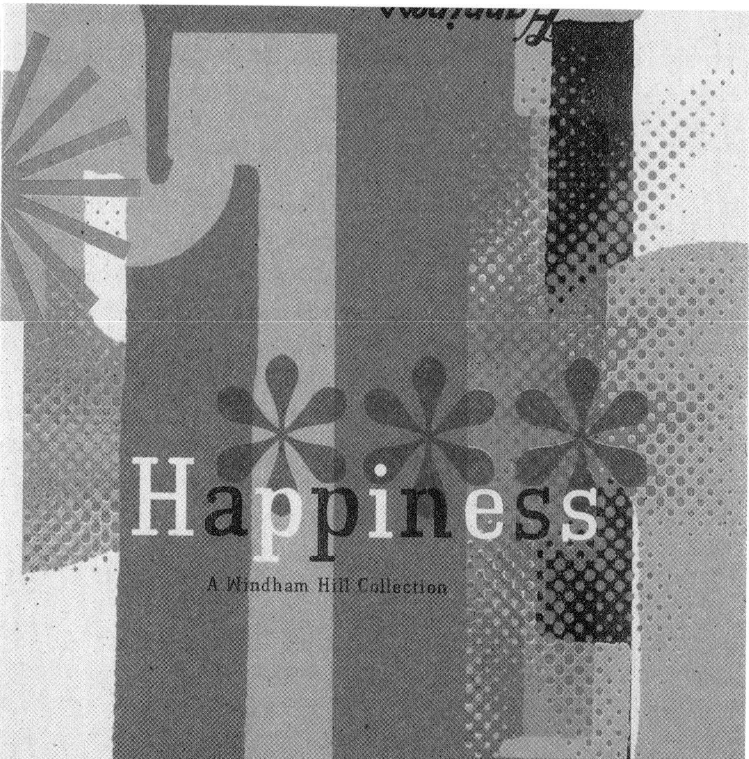

visual 4–38

The vibrant, whimsical color scheme in this CD design communicates the same message with the color as it does in word. *(CD designs by Stoltze Design)*

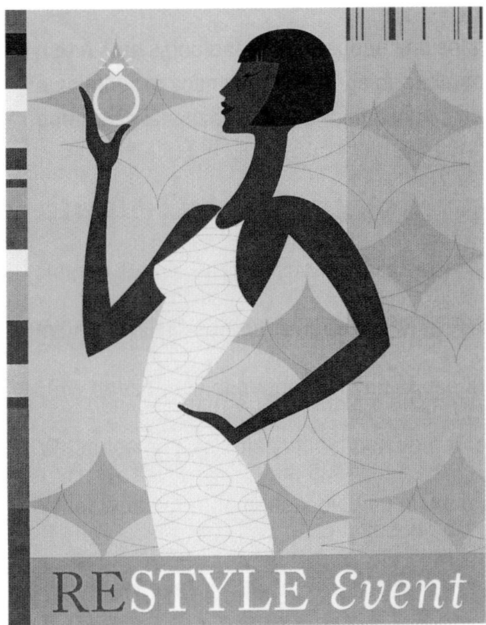

visual |4-39|

(Poster design by Design Ranch)

visual |4-40|

(Poster design by Mires Design)

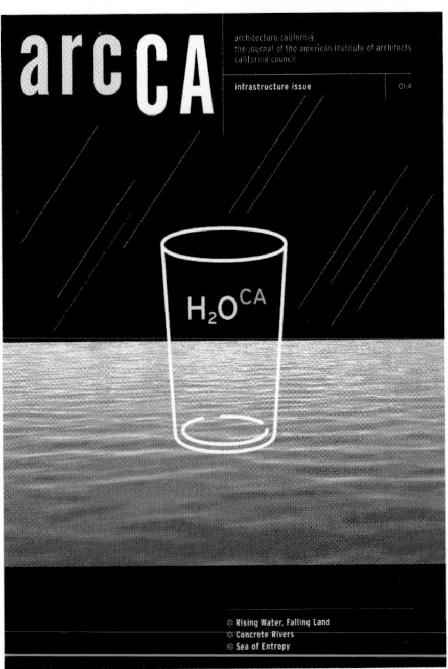

visual |4-41|

(Publication design by Aufuldish & Warinner)

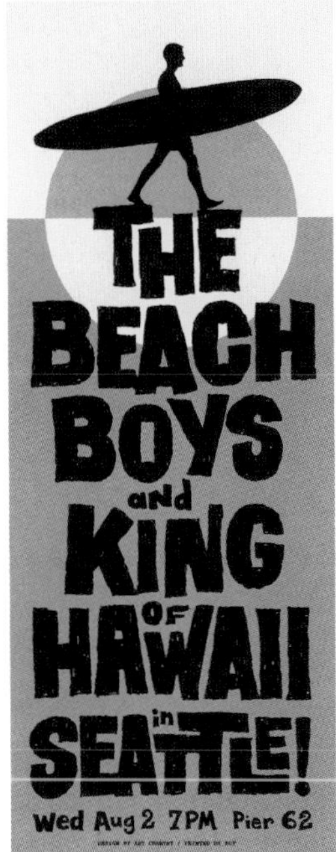

visual |4-42|

(Poster design by Art Chantry)

THE DESIGNER AT WORK

"I thrive on seeing other artists' work, but in the end I have to go off by myself and tune out entirely what my peers are up to, in order for my own voice to emerge."

— Jean Tuttle

jean tuttle

After receiving her BFA from Parsons School of Design in 1978, Jean Tuttle based her studio in Manhattan for the next twelve years. She currently lives and works in Denver, Colorado. Tuttle first became known for her hard-edged, high-energy scratchboard style. She was among the first to switch to the computer in the late 1980s; and at present, she creates all of her work using Adobe Illustrator software. While her illustration style has evolved along with digital technology, her approach to problem solving and her strong sense of design have remained constant.

Her illustration interests encompass a broad range of clients and applications. She has created illustrations for magazines, advertising, and children's publishing and has designed icons and logos for corporate communications, products, packaging, and events. Her work communicates with a graphic immediacy and a familiarity that reassures the viewer and a use of color that challenges the viewer with schemes and palettes that transcend expectation.

Over the years, Tuttle's work has won numerous awards, including recognition from American Illustration, How, Print, and The Society of Publication Designers, and a silver medal from the Society of Illustrators. Her work has been featured in *IDEA* magazine (Japan), *Step-by-Step Electronic Design*, *The Illustrator Wow! Book*, *Illustrator Illuminated*, and other publications.

Tuttle's client list includes AT&T; American Express; *Business Week*; Hasbro; Lucent Technologies; Moosehead Breweries; Reebok; *Time*; *The New York Times*; L'Oreal; *Newsweek*; *Rolling Stone*; Smith Barney; Sprint; *The Washington Post*; *The Wall Street Journal*; and the United States Census Bureau, for whom she designed the icons appearing on the Year 2000 census form.

The works presented here include an illustration titled *Susan with Bird Mask*, a personal piece that is a portrait of a close friend and classmate. The illustration received a Certificate of Merit from the Society of Illustrators 47th Annual Exhibition. Tuttle changed the colors in the photo reference to colors that reflect her friend's personality. *First Night in Hartford* was created for a *Hartford Courant* feature story. This New Year's Eve event is a family-friendly celebration filled with music, dance, and fireworks. The self-portrait, *Baby Jean*, was produced for "The Beautiful Baby Exhibit" organized by Murray Tinkelman at the Society of Illustrators in 2006. About the color choices for this piece, Tuttle comments, "Even as a kid I wasn't particularly girlish, so I purposely avoided using pinks and pastels, and pulled in cooler, stronger, more neutral tones." The work was a Certificate of Merit winning illustration at the Society of Illustrators 49th Annual Exhibition.

Orange is active, appetizing, and hot. It is made from two warm colors that result in a transitional color associated with sunsets and the seasonal changes of autumn. It has a diverse association with smells that come mostly from sweet, tangy, and hot foods and spices. Many exotic foods are orange, such as mangoes, melons, papayas, seafood, peppers, and yams (see Visual 4–43).

Red is festive, exuberant, and romantic; and it is associated with danger, blood, and imagination.

Although red covers a range of seemingly contrasting associations (festive and danger), all of its suggestive qualities can be described with the word *passion*. Red is used extensively in packaging and advertising because it brings unrestrained attention to itself (see Visual 4–44).

visual 4-43

(Product/package design by Turner Duckworth)

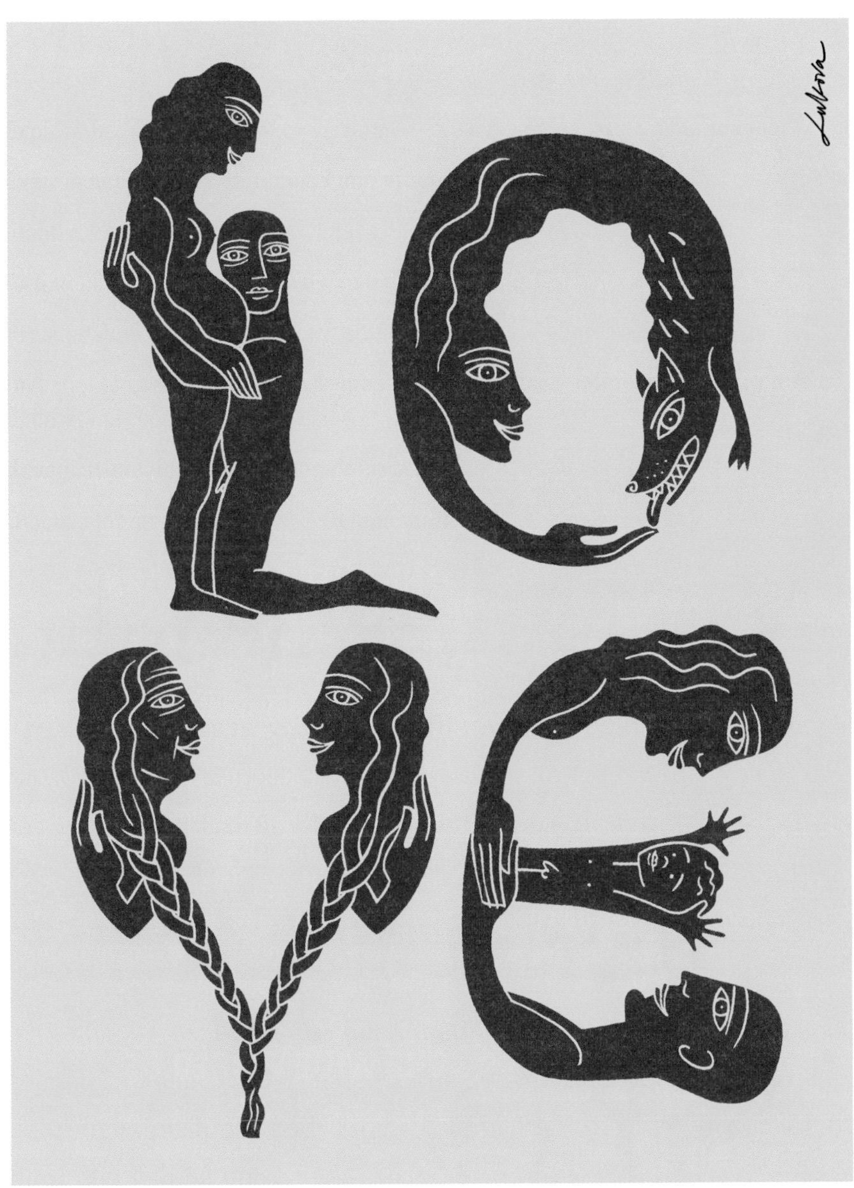

visual 4-44

(Poster design by Luba Lukova Studio)

COLOR MY WORLD

RICHARD PALATINI

Richard Palatini is senior vice president and associate creative director at Gianettino Meredith Advertising.

Palatini also is an instructor of Visual Communication at Kean University in New Jersey.

People are affected and influenced by color in many obvious and not-so-obvious ways. We use color to describe feelings: "I'm in a blue mood, "She's green with envy," and "He's got me seeing red." It's used to identify everything from military organizations (navy blue), to businesses (IBM, "Big Blue"), to life stages (baby blue). Beyond words and images, color communicates instantly and powerfully. A world without color would be a world without emotion.

1 THE "LIFE" OF COLORS

People develop feelings about color that change and evolve as they reach different life stages and they also relate to color in different ways during each stage. For example, red and blue are colors to which young children are most responsive. Adolescents are drawn to colors that are most outrageous, intense, and used in unusual ways (think green catsup!). The same red that children are drawn to is the color that adults perceive as danger.

2 THE WIDE WORLD OF COLORS

When considering use of a color, we also need to understand how well it "travels." And, more specifically, how does a specific culture perceive a color or color combination? Historically, white has been associated with mourning by the Chinese, yet, in America, white is the color of wedding gowns. Because each culture has its own color symbolism, perceptive designers

I know will often research countries and regions of the world to more fully understand what specific colors represent to them.

Be aware that in today's mobile global society, people will bring their color "baggage" with them on their travels. Still, individuals can also seek to assimilate into their new societal environment by emulating the new colors they find there. It's most important to consider all these factors when making color decisions that have "international travel" on their itinerary.

3 COLOR WITH FEELING

Think of the emotional response you want to elicit from your audience. Is it serene, sensual, exciting, powerful? Whatever it is, there are colors and color combinations for each and every one. Using light to midtones of greens, lavenders or blues and in combination will communicate that peaceful, serene feeling.

Dense purples, deep reds, and intense pinks are sensually provocative. Combining them with black will only increase the sensation. And, while black is THE power color, combining it with another hue can be even more powerful, such as black with a regal purple or royal blue. Many colors can bring feelings of excitement, but these should be warm and vivid. If your audience is young, consider vibrant warms and cools from every color family especially in combination.

4 CRIMES OF COLOR

Sometimes, breaking the laws of color can be the right thing to do. In creating a distinct identity it's better to be different than to use the right symbolic color. Car rental companies are a perfect example of this. Hertz's color is yellow, Avis is red, and National is green. Each has created its own distinct, yet appropriate color personality. Remember, it's OK to be different but it must be with a clear purpose in mind.

Color can be the most direct and memorable way of making your communication, whatever it may be, effective and successful. Consider your audience, their emotions, and culture and life stage. Understand how colors communicate your message best, and when necessary, break the rules.

Color in Design

Because color appeals so strongly to emotions, people tend to choose colors based on preference.

In design, colors must be selected for their ability to enhance communication and composition (see Visual 4–45). Relying on an understanding of how color is perceived, color systems, color terms, theory, and psychology provides a basis for exploring options for application. Researching color from an informed stance results in a sound rationale for your color choices.

Palettes and Color Schemes

To establish a palette or color scheme, you must establish the theme and content of the design.

Color may be limited by budget or aesthetic concerns depending on whether you use process color or match color.

Color must support the communication message. Your goal is to determine what needs to be said and support it with an appropriate palette. Content determines color. Often designers must use supplied photographs or illustrations. Colors found within those subjects can enhance and unify other design elements such as type and other graphic elements.

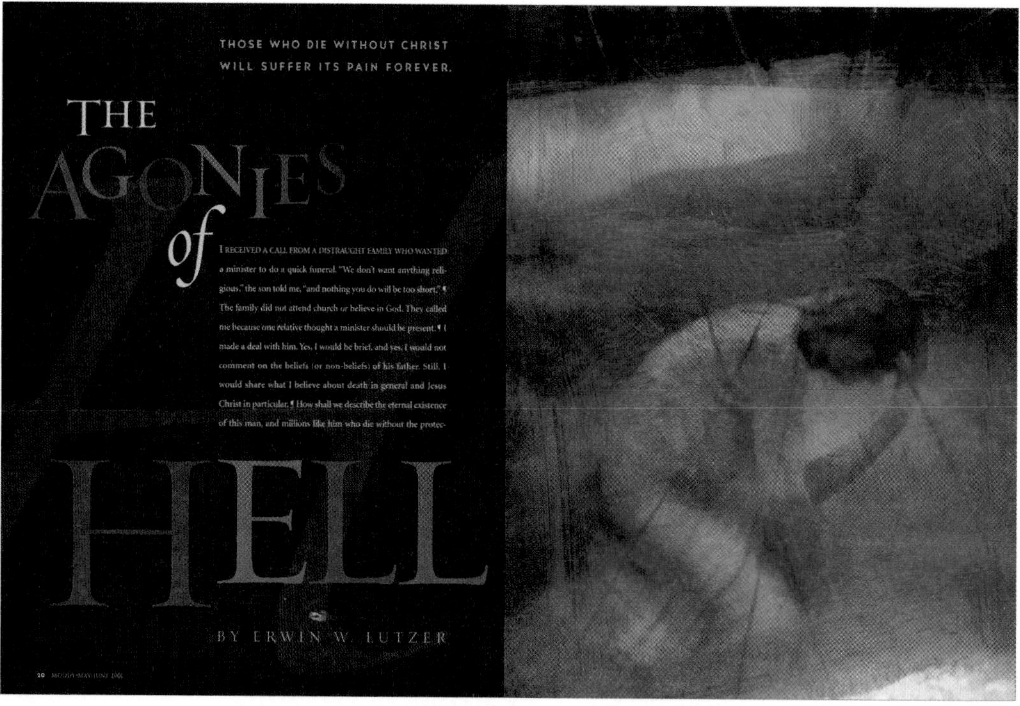

THOSE WHO DIE WITHOUT CHRIST WILL SUFFER ITS PAIN FOREVER.

THE AGONIES of HELL

I RECEIVED A CALL FROM A DISTRAUGHT FAMILY WHO WANTED a minister to do a quick funeral. "We don't want anything religious," the son told me, "and nothing you do will be too short." ¶ The family did not attend church or believe in God. They called me because one relative thought a minister should be present. ¶ I made a deal with him. Yes, I would be brief, and yes, I would not comment on the beliefs (or non-beliefs) of his father. Still, I would share what I believe about death in general and Jesus Christ in particular. ¶ How shall we describe the eternal existence of this man, and millions like him who die without the protec-

BY ERWIN W. LUTZER

visual 4–45

Bright, warm colors are enhanced on a black background. The color of the type reflects the color of the image. Both are communicating the same message. *(Magazine spread design by Tyler Darden)*

If you are building a color scheme from scratch, work with a color triad. Triads should be built from two related colors, such as yellow and orange, and one contrasting color, such as blue (see Visual 4–46). As you explore your palette, adjust the contrast of the original colors using Itten's seven color contrasts as a guide.

Accents can be added to the triad depending on the nature of the design, but avoid having too many colors competing for identity in the design. Establish a hierarchy for color with regard to quantity and quality of its use (see Visual 4–47).

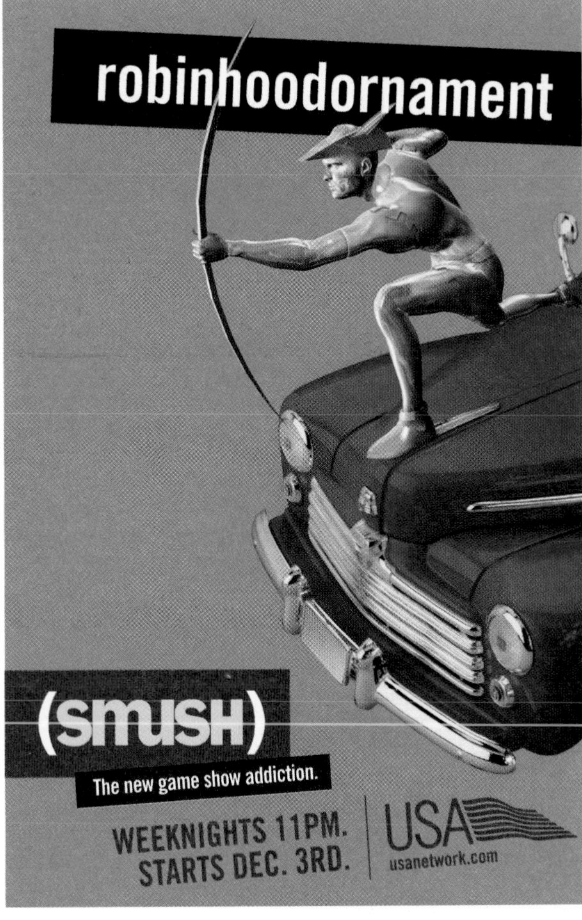

visual | 4–46 |

The color triad of yellow, orange, and blue heightens the clean use of imagery and type. *(Poster design by Bird Design)*

visual 4–47

This simple color scheme exemplifies the effective use of a color hierarchy. The color of typographic elements echoes the color of bands in the background. A thoughtful juxtaposition of colors found in the top and bottom creates strong unity and communication. *(Poster design art direction by Stewart Pack)*

Color and Composition

Most design can function in black and white. Black and white can be the right aesthetic choice in some cases. The majority of design images, however, are produced in full color.

Color intensifies and embellishes shape, line, texture, and type in a composition; and color can enhance depth and help direct eye movement through a composition (see Visual 4–48).

Color is used to classify, identify, and code, helping to distinguish one thing from another (see Visual 4–49). Color also creates variety, supports balance, and establishes pattern, unifying all of the design elements, as shown in Visual 4–50.

A variety of ways to explore color use are available in the process of creating a design or graphic solution. Keep a supply of printed color swatches in your toolbox. Color-aid paper is a good source. It has a high-quality pigment surface that is actually screen-printed ink. Those sets of color paper

In Review

1. Colored light is the basis for what color system?
2. How are the additive and subtractive color systems interdependent?
3. What two terms describe the hues found between the primary and secondary colors?
4. What is the name of the industry standard for specifying match color?
5. What is the distinction between chroma and saturation?
6. What two color theories have profoundly affected designers' understanding and use of color in design?
7. Discuss the effects associated with contrast of extension and simultaneous contrast.
8. Define color triad and discuss how it is used in design to devise a color scheme.
9. Choose a color, describe its qualities, and present an analysis of its potential use in a design.

5 MANAGING *Effective* DESIGN

objectives

Discuss the role of organization and format as basic design issues

Present various grid systems for organizing compositions

Explain the functions of eye movement and strategies for controlling it

Identify and discuss key visual relationships that every designer must know

Present illusory phenomena that affect visual perception

Examine structures in nature and the constructed environment as sources for graphic designers

introduction

By definition, design is organization. Designers determine which elements to use and how to use them effectively to create visual interest and communicate an intended message. Managing visual organization is taking an active, informed role in the design process. This chapter will examine ways to manage the organization of design through the use of fundamental, universal strategies and techniques. You are now familiar with the principles and elements of design. You will learn what professionals know about governing key visual and conceptual relationships that support effective design. This chapter also will introduce integral ways of using visual principles and relationships to establish visual organization and artistic control. Finally, it will examine the origins of design in nature to help you understand the structure of design, aesthetic references, and sources for inspiration.

VISUAL ORGANIZATION

Organization is central to good design. You must consider many factors to achieve visual organization; but primarily, you need to know how to manage the surface elements that are seen and the "hidden" structures that are transparent in the composition. Lines, shapes, and color are seen. Format, orientation, grids, eye movement, and theme are transparent or subliminal structures that achieve harmony in the viewer's eye. It also is important to know something about how the viewer experiences visual information.

The eye and brain work together to organize and make sense of the visual world as people see it. At the turn of the twentieth century, a group of German psychologists including Max Wetheimer, Kurt Koffka, and Wolfgang Kohler (whose work as a research psychologist is discussed in Chapter 6), studied the phenomenon of how humans perceive and organize the visual world. What the psychologists determined is that people tend to cluster shapes, colors, textures, and other visual elements in an attempt to process a "whole image."

In his 1890 publication *On Gestalt Qualities*, Christian von Ehrenfels was the first to use the term *gestalt*, which translates from German to mean "form" or "the way things come together." The group of psychologists coined a related phrase, "the whole is greater than the sum of the parts." It means that, when viewed together, the interaction of design elements is more dynamic than each of the elements are individually (see Visual 5–1).

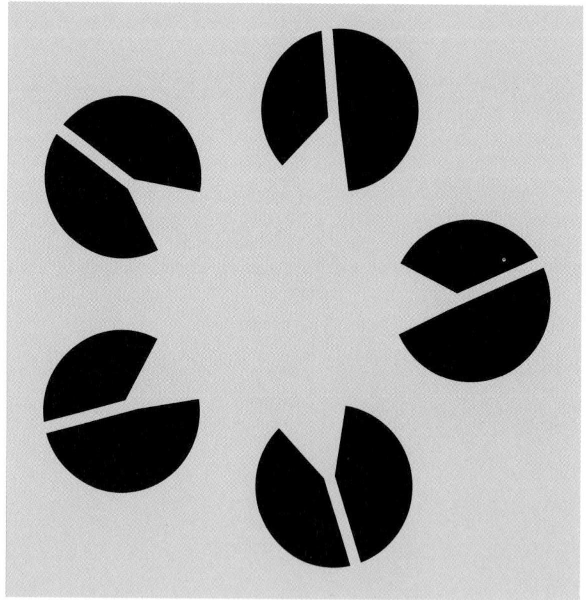

visual 5–1

The parts in this pictogram include five black circles and a star with lines projecting from its five points. The overlapping of the circles and star produces a new set of shapes and relationships. The positive and negative shapes have come together to create a whole image that transcends the presence of the individual parts. This graphic technique is often used to design logotypes and pictograms. Perceptual psychologists refer to this optical effect as subjective contour.

When looking at nature, people accept what they see as harmonious and "whole." Perhaps this is why nature has been such a popular subject for artists through the centuries. But when artists attempt to re-create nature in a painting or drawing, attaining visual harmony and wholeness is the result of arranging and rearranging the elements until a "good gestalt" is achieved. Here, good organization in design results from an informed decision-making process that involves creative thinking, combined with an understanding of how visual organization works. A good place to begin is to learn visual organization from the outside in.

Organization as a Whole

Overall organization involves four primary considerations:

- Format and orientation
- Underlying structure (grid systems)
- Eye movement
- Theme and motif

From ideation to execution, each design decision must be supported by a rationale or reason. Often choices are made intuitively because they "feel right." Although it is important to trust your instincts, it is equally important to test them. Testing your decisions is a matter of questioning the relevance of each decision with regard to the design objective. This is not always a linear, sequential process. Designers often work with components and elements that do not offer immediate resolution. But, by continually questioning and working the problem, designers find that the pieces ultimately fall into place.

Format and Orientation

In the design world, the term **format** is used two ways. It is the surface area that contains the design composition. The shape, size, and general makeup of the format is determined by the venue or kind of design—that is, packaging, publications, Web sites, posters, calendars, banners, etc. Venues are aligned and determined with the design objective in mind, which means that formats are often outside the control of a designer. Unconventional formats, however, offer creative design challenges (see Visual 5–2).

In printing production, format refers to the arrangement of the design components as they will be printed, cut, scored, and assembled. It is important to consider the relationship between the design format and production format from the beginning of the design process. Decisions that are made in a design are affected in the production stage. If they are not in tune with each other, the design will need to be reworked. A good practice is to consult production services early to avoid problems later. Even if you are not taking your design to full production, you should think ahead about format sizes and construct prototypes and comprehensives (comps) of your designs. Laser printers, large-format plotter printers, boards used for mounting, and other preparations for presentation of work are affected by formatting decisions that need to be considered early in the design process.

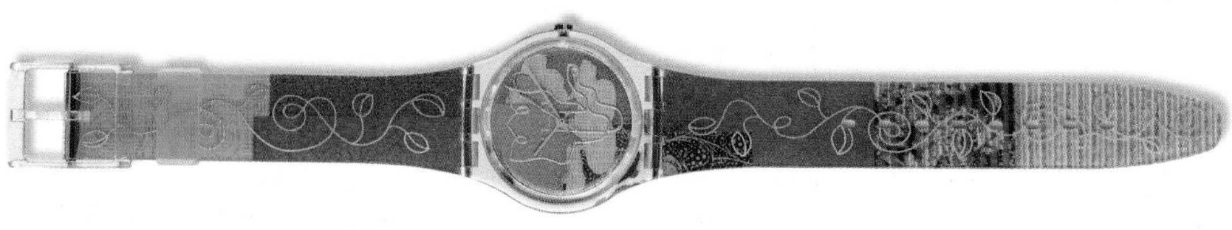

visual | 5-2 |

Venue formats are often outside the control of the designer and can have a huge impact on a design. In this example, the designer was challenged to conceive and apply a design with an Indian motif to the limited and dynamic surface space of a watch face and band. *(Design by Doppelgänger Inc.)*

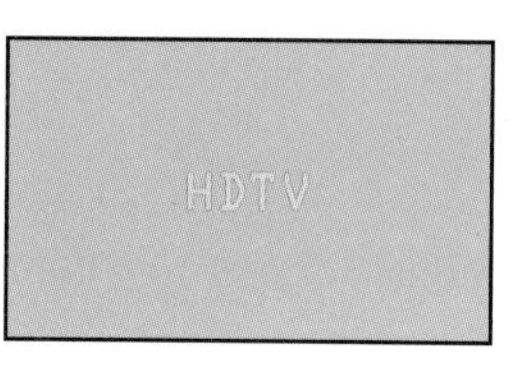

visual | 5-3 |

The wider panoramic format of the movie screen has a comfortable viewing proportion. Films that are presented on a conventional television lose action that occurs on the sides. The proportions of letterbox and Cinemascope are 2.35:1, although optically they appear different in this illustration because of the signature band adjustment at the top and bottom. HDTV has a less panoramic proportion of 16:9.

Orientation is the point of view determined by the designer, and it is the way the viewer is meant to relate visually to a design or an image. However, orientation begins with thinking about how the viewer relates to the world. Humans generally perceive the world standing or sitting perpendicular to the ground. This is a fundamental, stable viewpoint by which every nonperpendicular relationship is measured. The brain is so conditioned to this perpendicular relationship that even when people tilt their head to view any environment or image, their brain perceives it as perpendicular to the ground.

A person's field of vision is an oval shape with the width roughly double the height. The film industry screen formats of Cinemascope and letterbox are designed to mimic the same proportions (see Visual 5–3). Although people's field of vision is oval in nature, they tend to view the world in a rectangular frame. That tendency is culturally reinforced by the overwhelming use of the rectangle in architecture, art, design, and technology (see Visual 5–4).

ARCHITECTURE WEEK

visual |5-4|

Architectural forms tend to be perceived as vertical rectangles. This perception serves as the basis for the logo design for *ArchitectureWeek*, where the rectangularity of the letter forms and their elongation, reminiscent of a skyline, reinforce the periodical's focus on architecture. *(Design by Atelier Works)*

The proportions and configuration of a format set up a psychological association that affects the way an image will be read. A horizontal format is associated with the horizon, nature, and serenity. Vertical represents contemporary, architectural qualities; and a square implies a neutral, stable feel (see Visual 1-5a, Visual 1-5b, and Visual 1-5c in Chapter 1).

Grid Systems

Grids have been used for centuries as a means of scaling smaller images to larger works or to break down the observed world into smaller, more manageable sections. For those same reasons, graphic artists today use the grid; but because design is more about arranging, grids also are used to help achieve good organization. Grids can be built from square (arithmetic), rectangular (geometric), triangular, and even varying-sized units. The square arithmetic grid is composed of equal-sized square units arranged in a series: 1, 2, 3, 4, etc. The geometric grid is composed of units that are built using multiples. Units might be 1 × 2 or 1 × 1.5. Grids also can be built from arithmetic progressions such as, 1, 3, 5, and 7. What makes that a progression is that the value between each number in the progression is constant. In these examples, the numeric values can be translated into a visual form used to build a grid (see Visual 5–5a,Visual 5–5b,Visual 5–5c, and Visual 5–5d).

Grids are useful for defining key alignments and intersecting points within a composition.

They also provide a means of organizing and determining where to place graphic elements, imagery, and text; and they function as the underlying structure that is transparent to the eye (see Visual 5–6). A grid offers the designer a means for making efficient decisions. Using a grid is particularly useful when there are many elements and layers to organize.

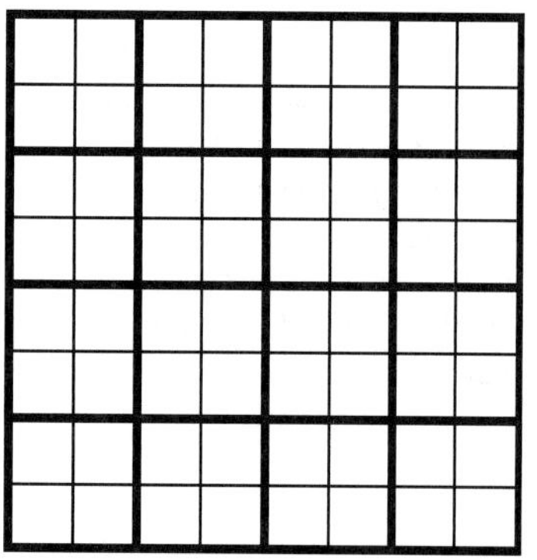

visual |5–5a|

In this arithmetic grid, the sixteen larger units have been subdivided into sets of four for a total of sixty-four smaller units. Subdividing grids identifies dominant and subordinate intersecting points to use for the placement of elements.

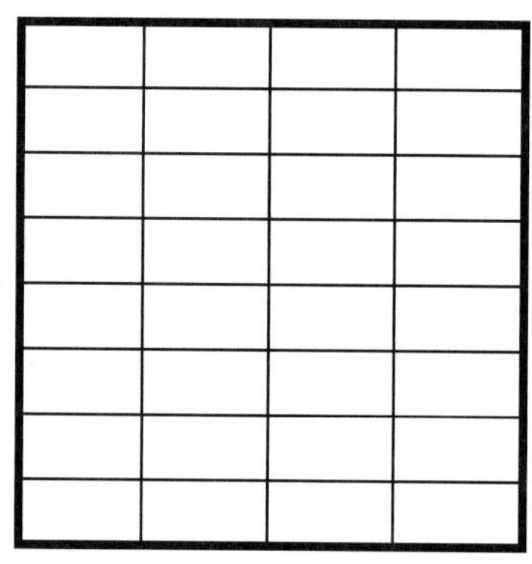

visual |5–5b|

Geometric units are rectangular and in this case have a 1×2 proportion. This grid provides a different set of relationships from the arithmetic grid, suggesting an aesthetic distinction that would likely yield a different design. The alignment of intersecting points creates an angle that is more gradual than that of the arithmetic grid.

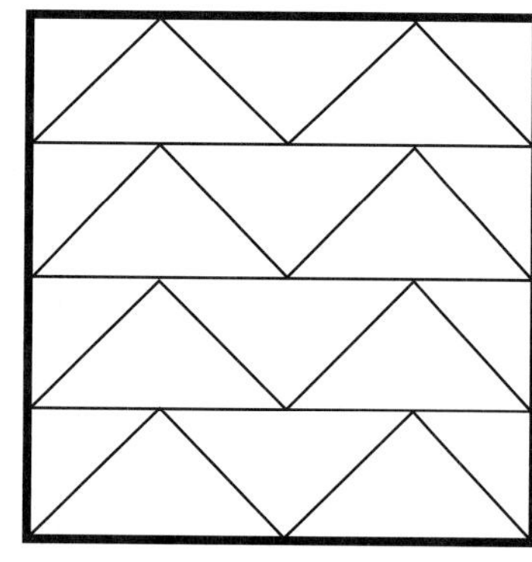

visual |5–5c|

A grid built of triangles offers a departure from rectangular grids. Here the grid suggests a strong sense of overlap and depth with a bias toward diagonal alignments. The diagonals also create a repetitive movement that could profoundly influence the design on its surface.

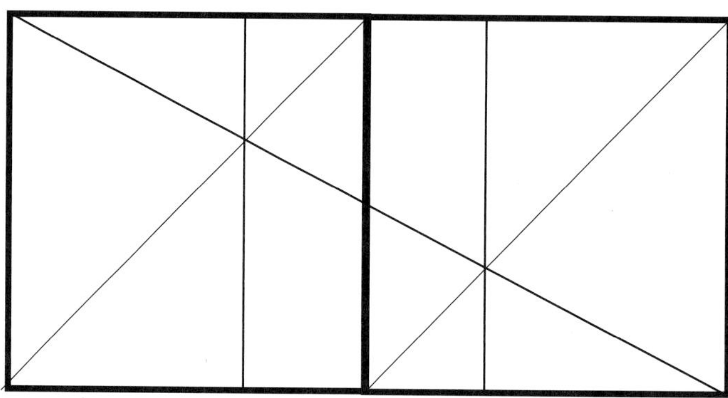

visual |5–5d|

This grid is useful for page layout. It was built from a series of intersecting lines.
Begin with two rectangles or squares, which in this example serve as pages for a publication. Draw a line diagonally through either set of opposing corners. Now draw a line through the corners of the individual rectangles. Draw a vertical line through each of the intersecting points created by the intersecting diagonals.
The resulting vertical rectangles can be used as areas for the placement of text and images in publications.

Grid systems also can be combined to establish a hierarchy to manage both the outer proportions and internal placement of design elements. For example, a golden rectangle can be used in conjunction with a set of simple arithmetic and geometric grids that subdivide the squares and rectangles. The resulting grid hierarchy begins to suggest internal relationships and a direction for eye movement (see Visual 5–7).

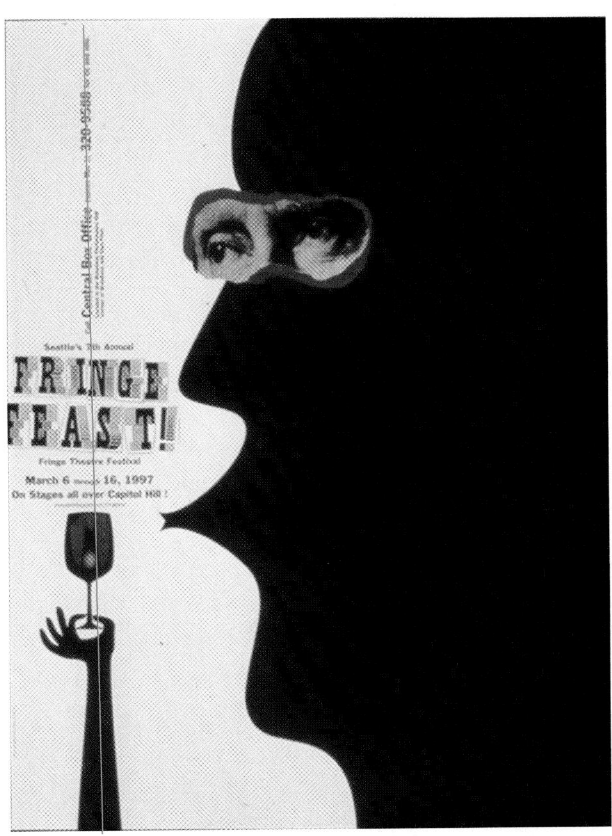

visual |5-6|

A grid provides a system or format for organizing the elements in a composition. It can be a simple division, like the invisible line that serves as a means of aligning visuals in this poster design. *(Poster design by Modern Dog)*

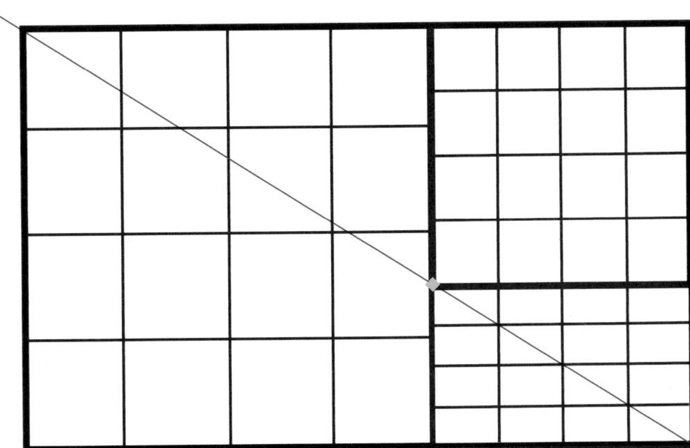

visual |5-7|

Combining systems can suggest scale changes, movement, and emphasis, as in this grid, which begins with a golden rectangle and is further subdivided. The subdivided grids are two arithmetic systems and one geometric system. As the units decrease in size, a sense of spiraling movement is created, established around a pivoting focal point identified by the green diamond.

Eye Movement

The human eye is a wonderfully complex instrument. The eye works in conjunction with the brain to perceive the world. Physiologically, the eye provides people with neural impulses that are recorded on the brain's visual cortex. The best analogy is that the eye and brain work like a movie camera. The lens works like the eye; and the film is like the retina on the visual cortex of the brain, recording the world as it is perceived. One distinct difference between the eye and a camera lens is that the eye is continually moving or quivering, allowing the images that people perceive to be recorded on the retina.

This quivering or rapid scanning of the eye is a built-in survival feature of human physiology that helps people distinguish shape, pattern, and color. Therefore, it is difficult to maintain a fixed stare on any point within a picture. The tendency is for people to want to move their eyes around, scanning various features in an image. When people fix their eyes on a point on a picture, they perceive the rest of the image in their peripheral vision. The longer they stare, the more faded the images in the periphery become. Therefore, the bias is for the viewer's eye to want to scan; and so it does. Controlling eye movement in a composition, then, is a matter of directing the natural scanning tendency of the viewer's eye.

But what kinds of arrangements, alignments, and shapes attract and move the eye? The eye tends to gravitate to areas of most complexity first. In pictures of people, the eye is always attracted to the face and particularly the eyes. The combination of the graphic complexity in a face and the fact that the face embodies the essence of human expression leads the eye to examine the face for clues about meaning (see Visual 5–8).

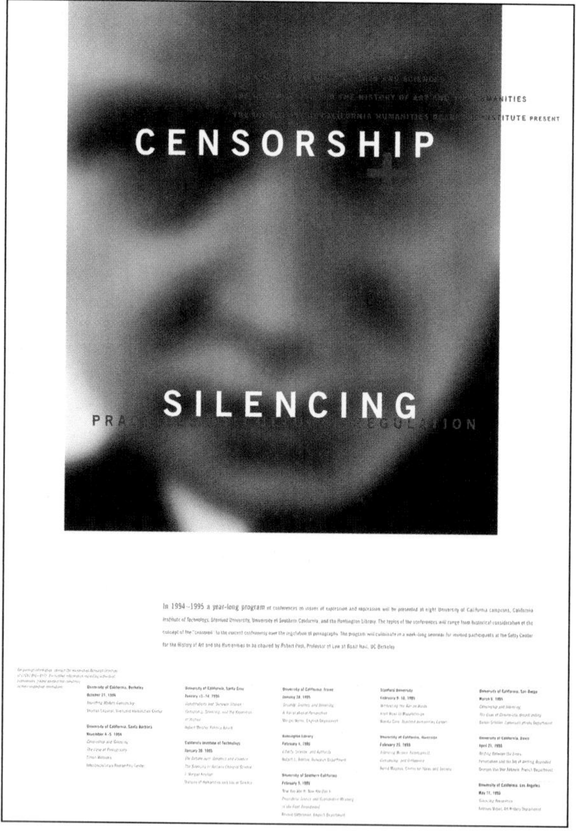

visual 5–8

In this poster promoting a series of lectures on censorship, the viewer's eye is immediately drawn to the face, particularly the subject's eyes and mouth, where the poster's primary message is delivered. *(Design by Adams Morioka)*

Light and dark contrasts create distinct shapes and line edges that attract the eye. Vertical and horizontal lines or edges are stable, functioning as constant axes. Angled lines, edges, and alignments that operate counter to the vertical and horizontal, guide eye movement (see Visual 5–9). Isolated elements set in neutral areas away from more complex patterns or grouped elements also attract attention.

An effective strategy is to establish a visual hierarchy to direct eye movement. A rhythmic loop can be created that takes the eye on a journey over the surface and into the depths of the composition with built-in resting places, or white space. Textures and graphic details can offer the eye a reason to sustain interest, examining the picture again (see Visual 5–10).

Theme and Motif

Theme in design is a subject or topic being represented. It also can be thought of as the quality or character of a represented idea. As such, a visual theme determines the elements to use and the appropriate ways to use them. Theme serves as a conceptual scheme for making organizational decisions. Theme may be presented as the premise of a story, a symbolic association, or the use of a visual metaphor.

Motif is a concept related to theme. The appearance of the overall image in a design is referred to as motif. Motif is the inherent pattern or arrangement of the overall image. Descriptions of motif are often culturally referential; for example, an Arabesque motif, a seasonal motif, and an urban motif. There are three general kinds of overall images: nonobjective, abstract, and realistic.

Nonobjective, or nonrepresentational, images have no resemblance to anything recognizable.

These images are built from geometric and natural elements that make no attempt to depict the real world. Nonobjective images function mainly on a formal level, concerned with general relationships of basic elements. Conveying a theme with nonobjective imagery is conveying a quality or feeling that is interpreted rather than described (see Visual 5–11). Abstract images resemble the physical world but are a simplification or distortion of the things in it.

visual |5–9|

In this composition, eye movement tends to follow the light blue line and the edges of the orange and yellow against the dark blue. The angles are countered by the regular placement of the yellow diamonds. The yellow diamonds and the dark blue area bring attention to the conspicuous circle and the isolated orange diamond.
The grouped row of orange diamonds along the bottom edge of the composition call briefly for the viewer's attention.

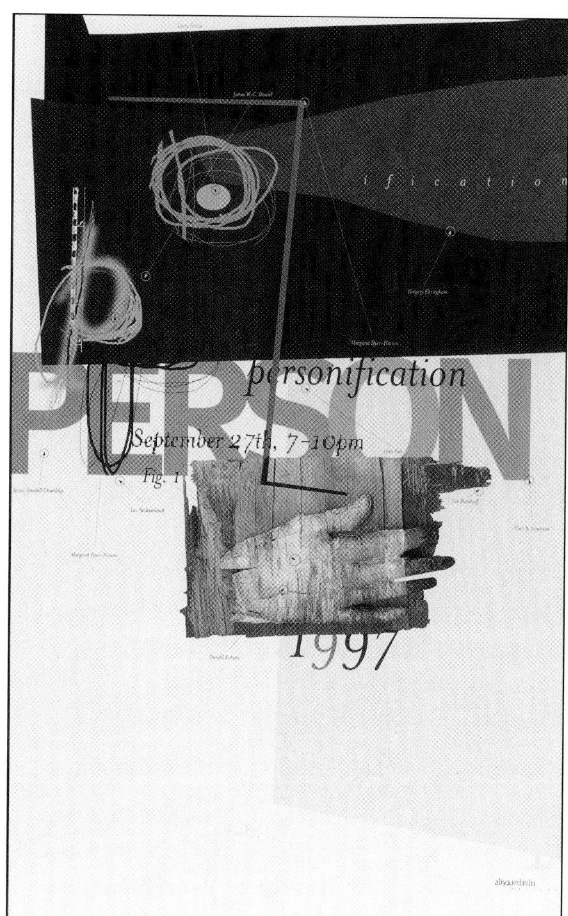

visual 5–10

This poster promoting the opening of a gallery exhibition features samples from work by each artist represented in the exhibition. This imagery and the typographic content about the opening and exhibition are strategically scaled and positioned to create a well-balanced composition, supported by neutral areas of black-and-white space that leads the viewer's eye from one design element to the next. *(Design by The Partnership)*

In theory, all images are abstract because they are re-creations of the physical world. But within the realm of the visual arts, images are classified by their degree of coherence to the world you see and live in (see Visual 5–12).

Realistic or representational imagery replicates the real world in a descriptive manner. Represented objects have defined and namable referents to the real world, although they may contain symbolic meaning (see Visual 5–13).

Theme and motif are used in design to create a graphic look that promotes the overall idea. Often the theme is given as part of the design problem, but it can sometimes be the job of a designer to determine a theme. In either case, a theme must be researched and developed so the imagery used to represent it is appropriate, accurate, and ultimately understood by the audience.

A theme is usually generated with a word concept that can be translated into graphic form. Some common thematic categories include animals, industry, music, seasons, places, sports, weather, holidays, culture, and historic periods. Narrowing a broad theme to a specific concept can provide more pointed communication. For example, winter might be narrowed to snow (and more specifically translated to snowflake) as a motif or symbol used to represent the broader original theme.

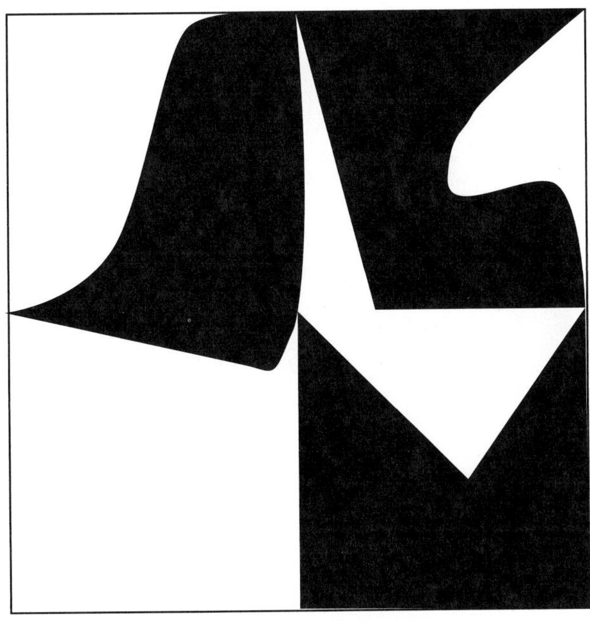

visual |5-11|

Nonobjective imagery relies on shape relationships and a formal visual vocabulary to communicate. This composition is about the tension created between points and edges and the precarious balance of the shapes. The shapes also seem stuck in their position with no room to move. The prevailing feeling conveyed here in the relationship between the shapes is a sense of confinement and incompatibility.

visual |5-12|

Every identity program created at Malcolm Grear Designers is the result of extensive research, conceptualization, and refinement leading to a specific and relevant design solution. The new identity for Vanderbilt, integrating the oak leaf and acorn within the *V* letterform, has symbolic (seed of knowledge, strength, and steadfastness) and historic references. Additionally, the form's incorporation of these elements reflects Vanderbilt's status as an active arboretum. The New Bedford Whaling Museum identity enhances and leverages the museum's reputation as the largest museum in America devoted to the history of "whaling in the age of sail." *(Identity symbols by Malcolm Grear Designers)*

Design Criticism Model

The purpose of the Design Criticism Model is to expand your vocabulary and critical-thinking skills. It is adapted from a model developed by Edmund Feldman, *Varieties of Visual Experience*, and is directed toward a discussion of design imagery. You can use this model in critiques or in writing about your work or the work of others. Most of this discussion involves an examination of compositional organization and visual relationships.

Four Levels of Visual Inquiry

Level I	**Description:** Facts, no personal feelings
A. *Identify the venue—the form of the design.*	illustration, poster, package, book, photograph, Web page, advertisement, etc.
Identify the media (studio tools).	painted, offset printed, collage, electronic, hand- or machine-fabricated, etc.
B. *State the size, dimension, and point of view (dictated by venue and media).*	
C. *Determine the kind of image.*	**Nonobjective**—has no referents to namable objects in the real world. These images are generally geometric or organic lines and shapes used to create a look or pattern. **Abstract**—refers to commonly understood, namable objects from the real world; however, the image is distorted or significantly simplified with regard to color and form. **Realistic** or representational—refers to commonly understood, namable objects reflecting detailed attributes of the real world or surreal world.
D. *Identify content or subject.*	In realistic and abstract work, this is people, buildings, animals, automobiles, etc.; and for nonobjective, this describes line configuration, shapes, forms, and use of typographic forms.
E. *Describe the overall arrangement.*	color, patterns, textures, motif, etc. This specifies properties of the arrangement, such as vertical, horizontal, diagonal, ragged, or smooth.
F. *Research background information.*	dates, name(s), period style, "school", movement, design, or historical references

Level II	**Analysis:** Examine compositional form and its function.
A. *Discuss the use of principles of visual organization.*	Visual hierarchy to serve overall organization—unity, theme, proportion, variety, balance, movement, orientation, dominance, scale, and variations of these
B. *Discuss the use of elements of visual organization.*	line, shape, form (graphic and typographic), size, space, color, and texture
C. *Discuss the appropriate use of media.*	Includes studio/artist materials and the form that the communication assumes—venue (e.g., book, television, digital monitor, billboard, and print)

Level III	**Interpreting the Message:** Find meaning in the image. Determining the communication mode of the image provides insight as to how the image functions and how the image serves the message. Semiotics helps to decode and interpret the meaning of "signs" in media, communication, and culture. Semiotics is a field that studies how meanings are made. Consider the following modes of communication extracted from semiotics.
A. *Is the image communicating a specific viewpoint or message?*	The image is a ***sign symbol***, which conveys a "one-to-one" correspondence to its referent (e.g., a stop sign and traffic light).
B. *Does the image stand for or represent something else?*	The image is a ***symbol*** (e.g., a cross and national flag). Logotypes are considered symbols.
C. *Does the image physically or perceptually resemble or imitate that to which it refers?*	The image is an ***icon***, which possess similar qualities to the referent (e.g., a portrait, diagram, and scale model).
D. *Does the image signify a connection to some physical or causal event?*	The image is an ***index***, which shows evidence of something observed or inferred (e.g., smoke, a clock, and a footprint).
E. *Can the image be observed from a variety of viewpoints?*	The image is a ***metaphor***, which is open to interpretation and can be "read" on many levels (e.g., a Georgia O'Keefe flower painting, a Brad Holland illustration, and a Brancussi "egg form" sculpture).
Level IV	*Evaluation:* Making a judgment on the effectiveness of the communication/message An expressed opinion based on a rationale
A. *Your judgment or opinion is more meaningful when it is based on a critical inquiry that includes description, analysis, and interpretation of the image and its message. Levels I–III initiate thought, dialogue, and necessary research of the subject, providing a rationale for your evaluation.*	
B. *You do not have to reach a conclusion in the evaluation. The evaluation can lead to further questions that require additional investigation.*	

THE DESIGNER AT WORK

"The education of an artist and designer does not stop with a diploma—art is a profession for a lifetime and it is your devotion—so believe in what you do. Be proud to call yourself a designer."

— Luba Lukova

luba lukova

A graduate of the Academy of Fine Art in Sofia, Bulgaria, Luba Lukova never dreamed that she would be a practicing designer in New York City. The then-Communist government assigned the outspoken Lukova to a position in Blagoevgrad, a tiny town in southwestern Bulgaria, far from the capital and city life. However, as a designer in Blagoevgrad, Lukova found ways to present her dissident views, producing theater posters with subtle messages that hinted at the censorship and restrictions the Communist government had imposed on her native country. In 1989, the Berlin Wall came down, marking the end of the Communist regime; and shortly after, Lukova was granted an international passport to travel to the United States. In 1991, she traveled to Fort Collins, Colorado, for an international poster exhibition that included many of her posters. On the way home, at a stopover in New York City, Lukova saw an issue of *The New York Times.* On an impulse, she contacted the paper and landed an illustration assignment. The work became steady, and Lukova decided to stay and set up permanent residence in New York City. She now works as a freelance illustrator and designer, producing illustration and design for local publishers and organizations as well as national and international clients. She continues to produce illustrations on a regular basis for *The New York Times* Op-Ed section.

As a young artist, Lukova was greatly influenced by the Russian playwright and writer Anton Chekhov. Knowing this, it is not surprising that many of her poster commissions have been for theater productions. Deriving her inspiration from the production, Lukova believes that in addition to promoting a play, posters prolong the life of the production long after the play has ended. Lukova's poster images combine simplicity with energy. Her palette is typically composed of aggressive primary colors. Her posters communicate the spirit of a play with a bold intensity that immediately captures a viewer's attention.

Although she is probably best known for her theater posters and illustrations for *The New York Times*, in recent years, Lukova has turned her attention to gallery installations, architectural works, and books. Her works are included in the permanent collection of The Museum of Modern Art (MOMA) in New York City; the Toyama Prefectural Museum of Modern Art; the Museum fur Kunst und Geverbe in Hamburg; The Library of Congress in Washington, D.C.; and Bibliothèque nationale de France. Her solo exhibitions have been held at UNESCO, Paris, France; DDD Gallery, Osaka, Japan; La MaMa, New York; and Avla NLB Gallery, Ljubljana, Slovenia.

In a postcard promoting her own exhibition, Lukova uses a visual metaphor to communicate the show's theme and support its title.

Lukova continues to express her political beliefs in her artistic endeavors. This gallery installation is from a recent show of her work.

This poster, created for a 1999 production of the *Taming of the Shrew*, shows how Lukova's illustrations and hand-drawn type work together to communicate a raw intensity that commands attention.

visual 5-13

This illustration for *The New York Times* Book Review is an example of realism or representational imagery, which often involves exaggeration to project an editorial point of view, as in this caricature of Neil Young. *(Illustration by C. F. Payne; art direction by Steven Heller)*

Visual Relationships

Controlling the relationships of visual elements is the art of aesthetic judgment. Controlling graphic continuity, determining the character and quality of the elements, and deciding questions such as, "how much is enough?" and "what kind should be used?" are the type of issues that make art of design. The arrangement of elements also taps artistic sensibilities.

Making decisions about where elements should be placed and how they should interact requires a measure of intuition and logic. The essential objective is to create visual interest. Investigative, preliminary studies allow for the exploration, development, refinement of visual relationships, and compositional arrangements that will engage the eye and mind of the viewer.

Figure and Ground

The relationship between figure and ground is perhaps the most fundamental in design composition. Shape and contrast affect the figure-ground interaction most profoundly. Keep in mind that the ground, or space around a figure, has shape as well. Visual shapes can exist independently, overlap one another, or have a transparent quality depending on the figure-ground arrangement.

There are three basic arrangements:

- Simple figure-ground arrangement is the coherent, independent presence of a shape juxtaposed in a space that serves as the ground. The space can be compressed or shallow, or it can create the illusion of depth. In simple figure-ground arrangement, the figure is positive and generally active and the ground is negative and generally passive (see Visual 5–14).
- Figure-ground reversal is a graphic effect in which figure can function as ground and ground as figure. Shapes form in the space between figures and create a visual inversion. The reversal can be a dynamic way to activate neutral space in a composition (see Visual 5–12 and Visual 5–15).
- Ambiguous figure-ground arrangement finds the viewer uncertain about the relationship between form and space. The trick to controlling figure-ground ambiguity effectively is to create an arrangement that is disorienting yet comprehensible (see Visual 5–16).

visual | 5–14 |

The playful use of typography and illustration for this self-promotion relies on a simple figure-ground relationship. All of the elements are placed against a neutral background to allow the distinctiveness of each element to read clearly with the others. *(Self-promotion design by Scorsone/Drueding)*

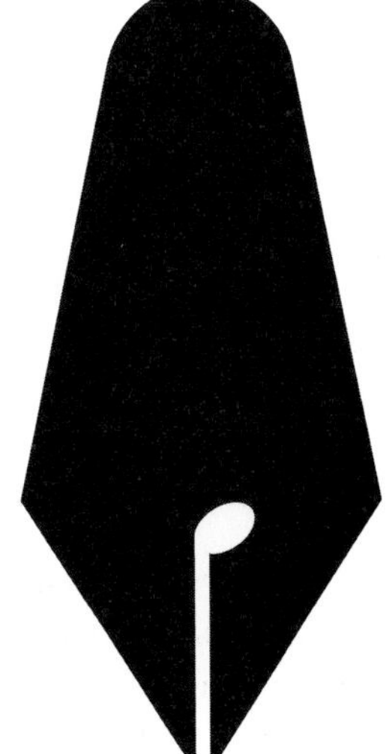

visual | 5–15 |

This clever and elegant logotype was designed for a composer. The figure of a musical note is reversed onto a pen nib. The image reversal yields a visual solution that offers economy by combining two images into one. (*Logo design by Dogstar*)

visual 5-16

Figure-ground ambiguity is what designer McRay Magleby had in mind when he created the graphics for this Earth Day poster. The positive image of the mother, the profile of the head, and the resulting kiss are intertwined, engaging the viewer in a visual mystery of form and concept. *(Poster design by McRay Magleby)*

Closure

Closure literally refers to the condition of being closed. A form that is entirely closed can be thought of as fully described or complete (see Visual 5–17a and Visual 5–17b). However, a form can be interrupted or incomplete and still be understood. There is a limit to how incomplete a form can be represented yet still be comprehended.

Visual 5–18a, Visual 5–18b, Visual 5–18c, and Visual 5–18d present a sequence of illustrations of the St. Louis Arch. The question is, "How much can be removed from the arch, yet still have it read as complete?" In Visual 5–18a, Visual 5–18b, and even Visual 5–18c, there is enough information for the eye to complete the form. In Visual 5–18d, however, it is difficult to complete the form in the way the viewer recognizes it. In that case, closure is about presenting form in a way that permits viewers to complete it in their mind's eye. This visual relationship is widely used to create visual interest for the viewer.

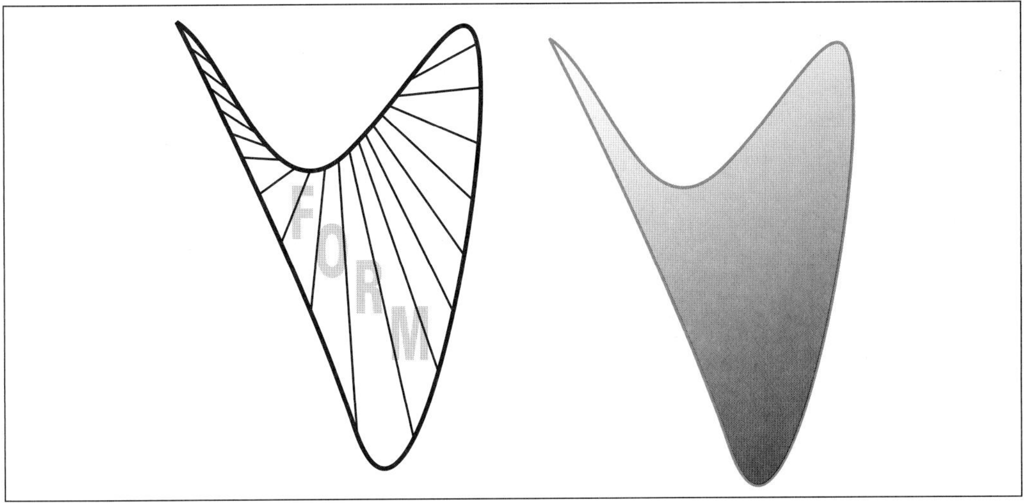

visual |5-17a and b|

Forms can be described as open or closed. In Visual 5-17a, the open form is seen as transparent, functioning like a wire framework that you can see through. Closed forms are opaque and built from solid planes like the one in visual 5-17b. Both forms are examples of complete or described closure.

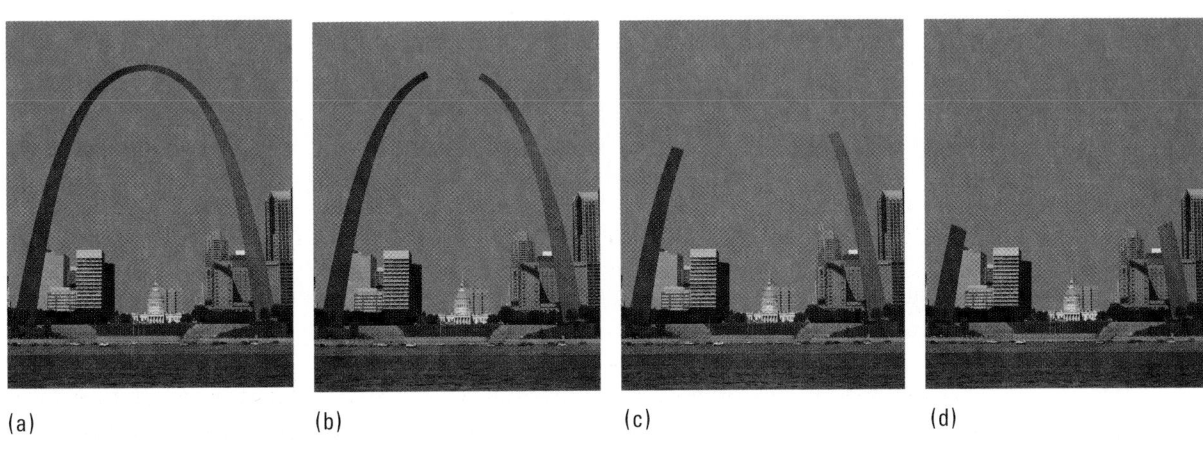

(a) (b) (c) (d)

visual |5-18|

This series of images of the St. Louis Arch provides an example of incomplete closure.

Closure also depends on relative position, that is, the distance from one object or shape to another. When related shapes are too far apart, they have no relationship; but when they are positioned closer to each other, the relationship can become meaningful. They can exist as complements or create a visual tension. A classic example of this type of closure from art history is in Michelangelo's painting *The Creation of Adam.* In this famous scene, God reaches his pointed finger outward toward the finger on Adam's hand. The fingers almost touch, which promotes a sense of birth or creation. If the fingers were farther apart or touching, the quality of the relationship would be much different (see Visual 5–19).

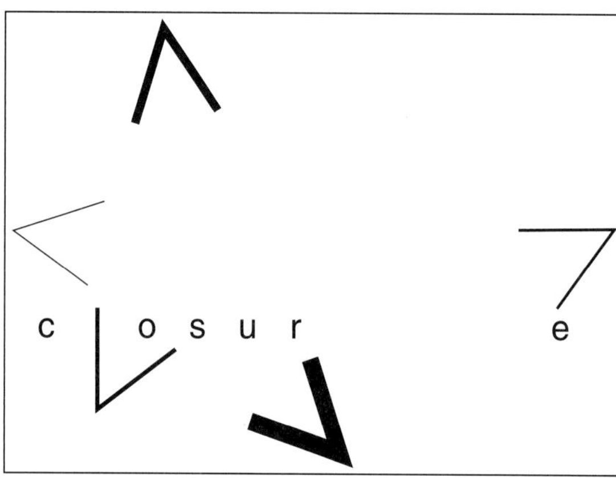

visual 5-19

The *e* and adjacent angle can be associated with the other letterforms and angles by similarity. But because of the distant proximity, they do not appear as though they belong to the rest of the word. Their proximity needs to be adjusted closer to complete the word *closure* and the accompanying star shape. Presenting the five component angles of the star apart from one another allows viewers to participate more actively by completing the star shape in their mind's eye.

Contrast

When you think of contrast, you think of a relationship between light and dark. That is, of course, one kind of contrast; but there are many others. A related term used often in the visual arts for contrast is *juxtaposition*, which refers to a relational, comparative placement of two or more elements.

The possibilities are endless: negative versus positive, jagged versus straight, geometric versus organic, serene versus chaotic, rough versus smooth, random versus orderly, saturated versus pastel, static versus kinetic, monumental versus diminutive, etc. These contrasting relationships can be visually articulated using combinations of the elements of design. Contrast serves the higher principle—variety. Achieving unity through variety is the art of arranging unlike elements and making them work together. Contrast of size, order, weight, direction, configuration, value, color, texture, and form creates visual interest by presenting an opposing context that allows one to complement the other. Curved looks more curved when placed in proximity to straight. Blue looks more blue when it is surrounded by its complement, orange. Regular looks more regular when an irregular element is present (see Visual 5–20a, Visual 5–20b, and Visual 5–20c).

Anomaly

Visual anomaly is the presence of an element or a visual relationship that is unlike others that dominate a composition. It functions as a particular type of contrast—a contrast of nonconformity.

Anomaly can create a lively, animated quality. It can be subtle or prominent. It often brings playful attention to the point where it occurs. When it is skillfully aligned with a communication message, the use of anomaly can make an otherwise ordinary design unique (see Visual 5–21).

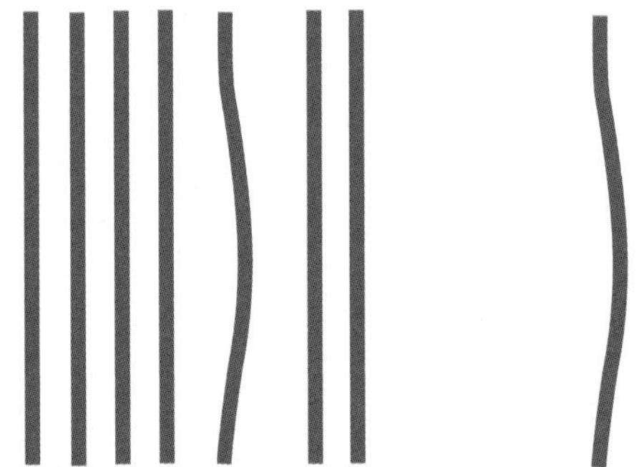

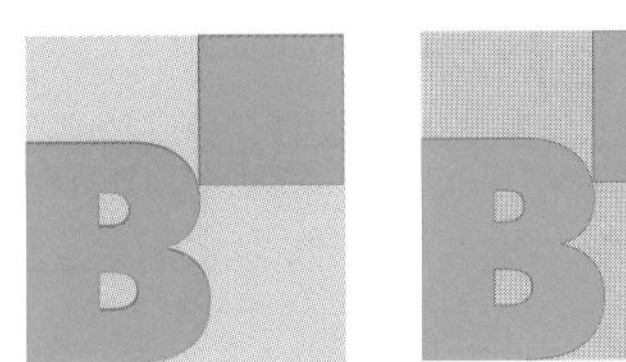

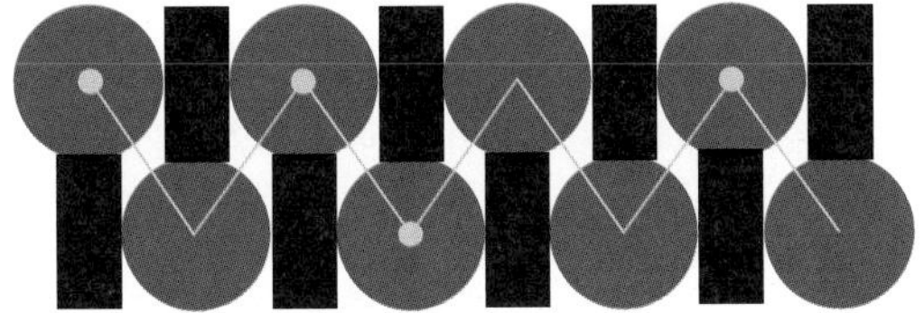

visual | 5–20a to c |

(a) In the context of a series of straight vertical lines, the curved line creates a tension that makes it appear more curved. (b) When placed on a complementary color field, the contrast of the blue *B* and square are heightened as compared with the neutral gray ground. (c) In a more subtle contrast, the regular rhythm of the circle and rectangle shape is countered by the intermittent rhythm of the small circle and zigzag line.

visual | 5–21 |

This logotype uses a four-unit grid arrangement with one different element. The diagonal unit is an example of visual anomaly. It serves as the focal point and focus of the communication for an orthodontist whose business is straightening teeth. The designer makes a subtle but critical decision to soften the corners of the square units to represent the qualities of a tooth. *(Logotype design by Charlene Catt-Lyon, Catt-Lyon Design)*

Emphasis and Focal Point

Look at any visual image; and as your eye scans it, you may notice that your eye tends to return to one point—the focal point. As you attempt to find meaning in the image, the focal point usually contains the key to understanding the intent. It is where the artist wants to lead your eye. Often the element that dominates the visual hierarchy of a composition is located at the focal point. Emphasis refers to an area of interest, such as a place where lines converge, a light figure in an area of darkness, an area of complexity, or a detail in an otherwise uncomplicated field.

You just learned that visual anomaly creates a visual point of interest as well. Emphasis serves hierarchy. An area of emphasis is dominant and often is supported in the hierarchy of a composition by contrasting areas. Once the area of emphasis is located, the viewer tends to read all other elements in relationship to it (see Visual 5–22a,Visual 5–22b, and Visual 5–22c).

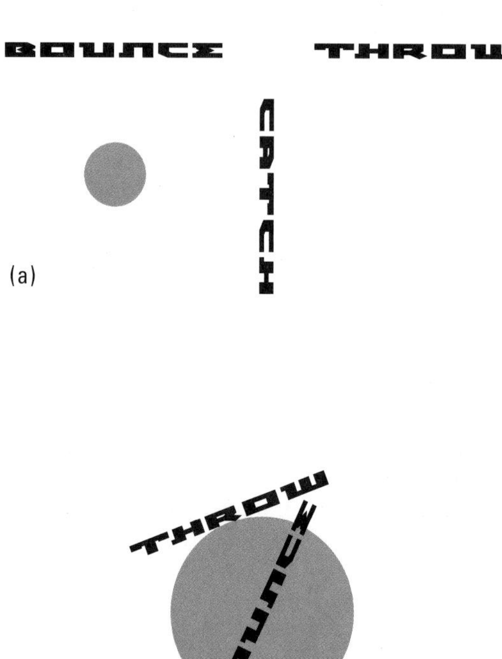

(a)

(b)

visual | 5–22a to c |

The arrangements in these three visuals contain the same basic elements. The dominant element in each one is the orange ball. The support elements are words that communicate an action practiced with a ball. The word elements interact with the ball, which functions as the focal point in each arrangement. In Visual 5-22a, isolation brings attention or emphasis to the ball. It fits precisely in the center of the *T*, supporting a subliminal relationship to the word elements. In Visual 5-22b, the size of the ball compared with the words is what calls the viewer's attention. The scale of the ball seems to be expanding as the ball presses against the words *throw* and *catch.* The diagonal orientation suggests a circular motion that reinforces the ball as a focal point. Visual 5-22c presents an arrangement of the word elements as lines converging toward the ball. Convergence is a function of perspective that leads the eye to a point in space that, by definition, creates a focal point.

(c)

It is worth noting that all designs do not rely on emphasis and focal point. Decorative arts such as textile design rely on a regular pattern of equally distributed elements.

Space and Illusion

This chapter already discussed effects of color and shape interaction that can be illusory in nature. Simultaneous contrast, vibrating color, effect of color backgrounds, afterimage, subjective contour, and certain figure-ground relationships create illusory phenomena that fools the eye. Optical illusions play a role in the design of imagery. High-contrast imagery often developed for logotypes, symbol design, and pictographs can require optical adjusting for the viewer's eye to perceive them properly. In the discussion of *Gestalt*, you learned that the eye seeks order, trying to make sense of patterns, groupings, and visual relationships. Visual relationships are based on context, but they are affected by perception. Illusory phenomena have been studied to learn more about how the human eye and brain work to perceive the world. The research yields valuable insights for visual artists. Illusions based on depth cues relate to an artist's use of linear and overlapping perspective (see Visual 5–23, Visual 5–24, Visual 5–25, and Visual 5–26).

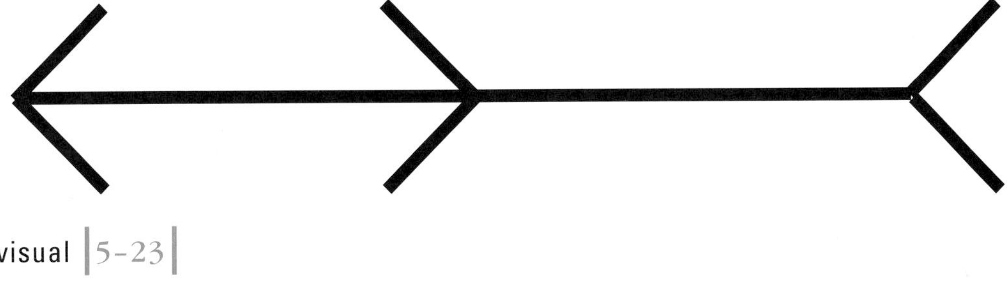

visual |5-23|

In the Mueller-Lyer illusion, line segments between the angles "in" and the angles "out" are mathematically equal, although they appear different in length. The explanation for this is based on a person's intuitive understanding of perspective (depth and distance cues). The angles "in" are associated with closer, and the angles "out" are associated with farther away.

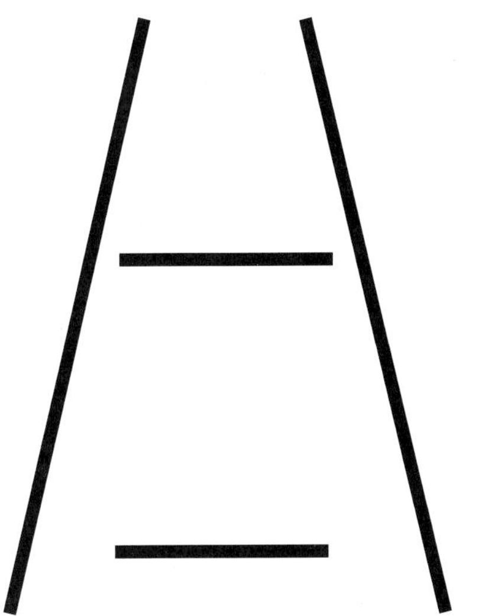

visual |5-24|

This illusion developed by Mario Ponzo is based on a similar explanation. Both horizontal lines are equal length. The line segment that crosses the two converging lines exists in a context that you associate with farther away.

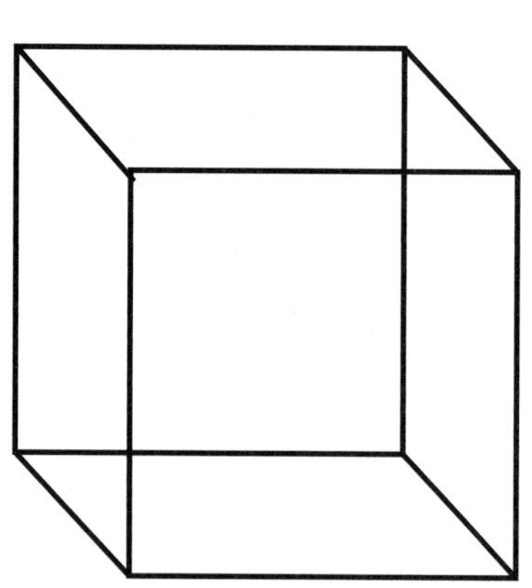

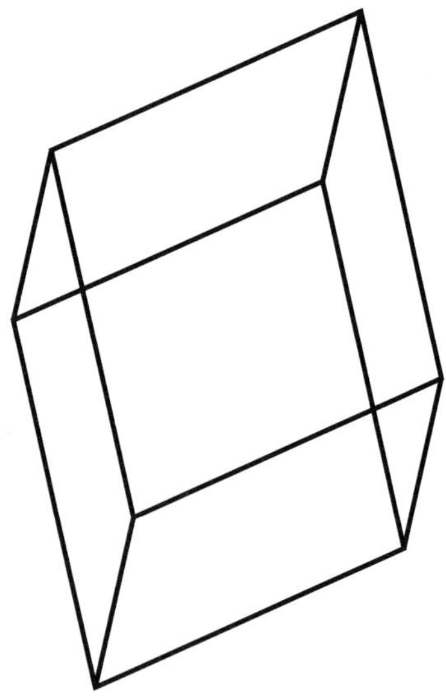

visual 5-25

The Necker cube (left) and rhomboid (right) are examples of depth-ambiguous figures. These figures, presented as "open forms" without a background, flip from front to back. In either case, the "fronts" are perceived as smaller.

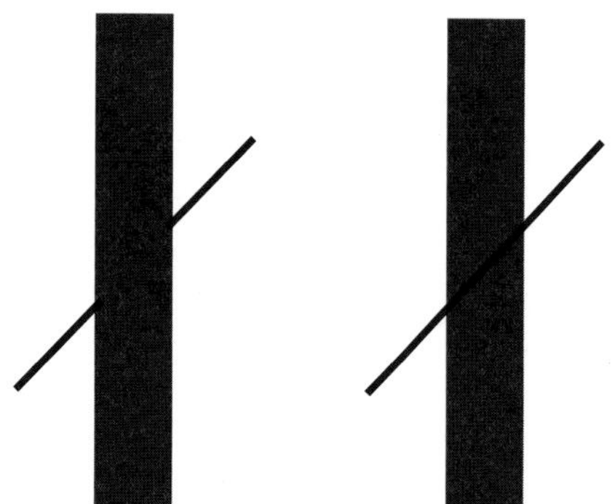

visual 5-26

Johann Poggendorf described an illusion based on overlapping. On the left, the diagonal line is interrupted by the rectangle—it appears disjointed. The counterpart on the right offers a different result.

Other optical illusions depend on context cues or relative size perception (see Visual 5–27 and Visual 5–28). Graphic artists routinely make adjustments to imagery based on relative size. Making refinements to imagery that is susceptible to such effects first requires that you recognize them. While these examples are "clinical" in nature, the theory behind them applies to certain kinds of visual imagery. You will undoubtedly encounter these illusory effects. You will have to determine whether they are desired and adapt the design accordingly.

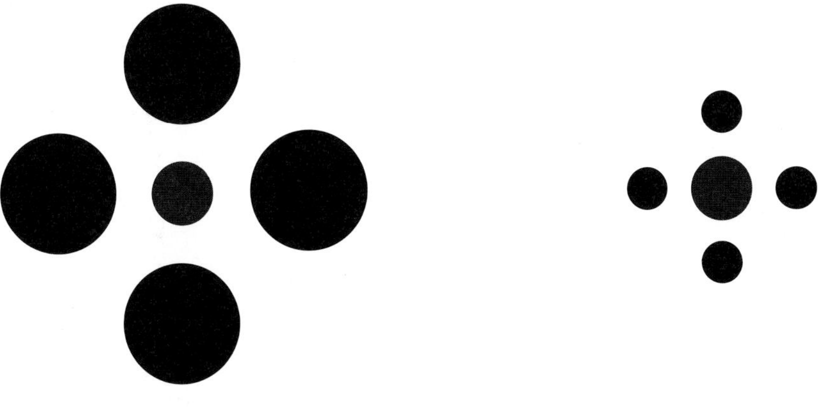

visual |5-27|

The two center circles appear different in size—the Hermann Ebbinghaus illusion.

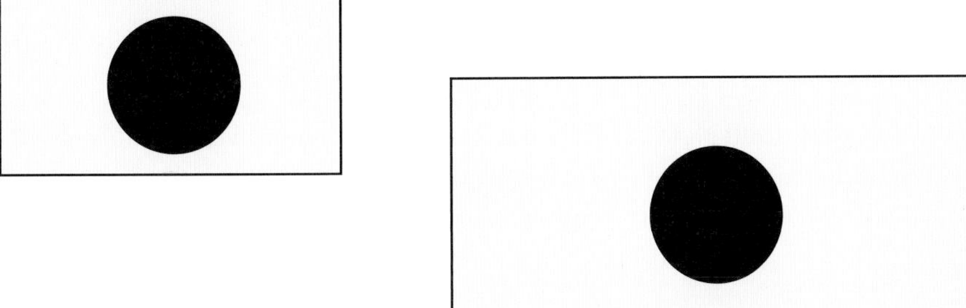

visual |5-28|

The circle and rectangle is a variation of the Ebbinghaus illusion. They rely on a scale comparison. It has been cited as an explanation for why the moon appears larger when it is closer to the horizon.

Origins and Inspirations

You could think of the visual world as comprised of three realms: microscopic, macroscopic, and the world in between that is experienced with the naked eye. What is curious and fascinating about the microscopic world of molecules and atoms and the macroscopic world of the cosmos is that they resemble each other. *Powers of Ten*, a film by Ray and Charles Eames, is a brilliant illustration of the scale of the universe. It zooms out from a man's hand to 10^{24}, which is to the end of the visible universe, and back in to 10^{-16}, revealing the molecular structures inside the man's hand. An important lesson here is that careful observation of natural and constructed worlds can reveal a rich source for inspiration and for design structures.

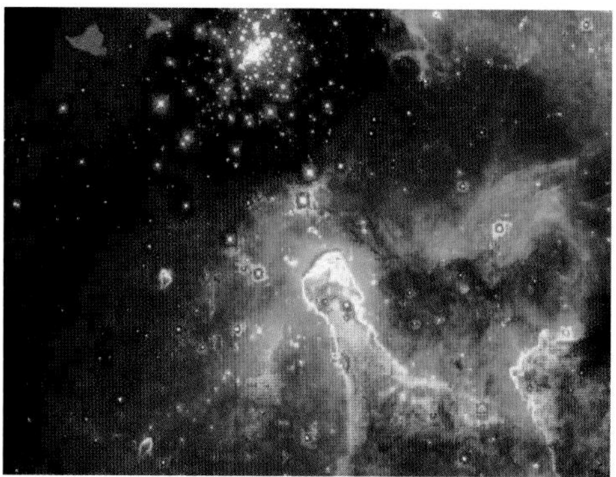

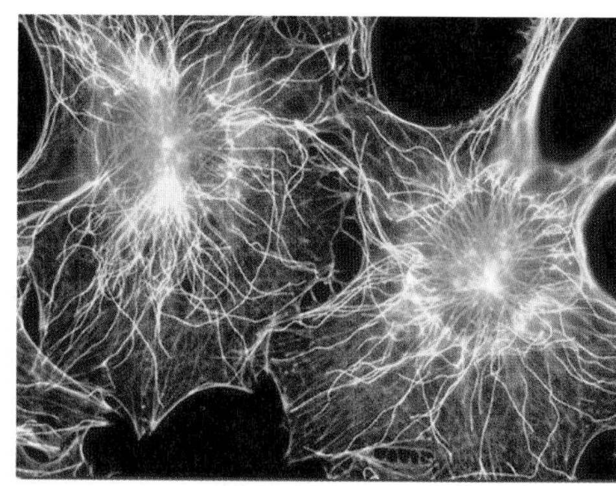

visual | 5–29 |

The left NASA photo image is a view of a galaxy with enhanced color in comparison to a photomicrograph of structural protein of mouse cells. While the forms are not exactly alike, their nucleic structures resemble each other. There are countless examples of repeated and reciprocal structures and systems in nature. *(Photomicrograph (right) by Dr. Torsten Whittman, University of California, San Francisco)*

Design and Nature

Visual artists examine the world with a critical eye, often seeing what others overlook. It is important to develop an observational curiosity of the visual world, examine it, and study it. Where do the shapes, structures, and systems you use to design come from? (see Visual 5–30 and Visual 5–31)

visual | 5–30 |

M. C. Escher created imaginative spaces using illusions and precise figure-ground relationships. His inspiration and subject matter was derived from a careful examination of shapes in nature. His observations of animal forms and animal behavior yielded creative views of animals in repeated patterns with many visual surprises. *(Smaller and Smaller, 1956. Wood engraving and woodcut in black and brown, printed from four blocks by M. C. Escher.)*

visual 5-31

The bird and fish shapes are carefully designed to interlock as they pass one another. They share not only a figure-ground relationship but also an ecological dependency. *(Sky and Water I, 1938. Woodcut by M. C. Escher.)*

You can see them in the natural world as a vocabulary of forms that are initiated by growth, built by animals, or developed from changing conditions. Shapes in nature tend to occur out of function for survival and economy of use. Some of the basic shapes in nature include the sphere, polygon, spiral, helix (or coil), and branch (see Visual 5–32a, Visual 5–32b, and Visual 5–32c). From the outside, an eggshell has amazing resistance to cracking; yet from the inside, an egg is fragile enough for a weak chick to crack its way out. The hexagonal-shaped honeycomb is an efficient structure used by bees to store honey. The growth of tree branches and many forms of shells and mollusks is based on a spiral. Certain plants rely on a helix shape to coil around other structures for growth. Animals such as the squid and most stemmed plant growth are examples of branching. Those basic shapes have served as content and structure for artists through the millennia. In nature as in design, they are the building blocks for more complex structures. The design of many architectural forms, such as domes, metal grids, and modular forms, owe their aesthetic beauty and structural integrity to forms in nature. Nature often uses and reuses the same basic shapes in variation. In design, basic shapes also are used in different ways or in variation (see Visual 5–33).

Taking a close, slow look at forms in nature can offer a rich source of inspiration and a lesson in basic design. Take your sketchbook to the zoo, a botanical garden, a forest, or your own backyard. Study the growth patterns of plants and flowers. Use a magnifying glass to view details. Look at the way branches grow on trees and flowers. Make careful sketches and notes describing the things you see. You may already have a collection of shells, insects, or plant forms that you can begin to study in drawings. Collect samples of other different life-forms; you may use them as references for subjects or even design systems. Try to find examples in your nature exploration of each of the basic shapes. Many life-forms are complex structures built from more than one of the basic shapes or built from variations of the same shape. Finally, look for ways to integrate inspiration from nature into your design. Also look at how other designers rely on and use shapes, structures, and systems from nature (see Visual 1-27, Visual 4-38, Visual 5–12, and Visual 5–16).

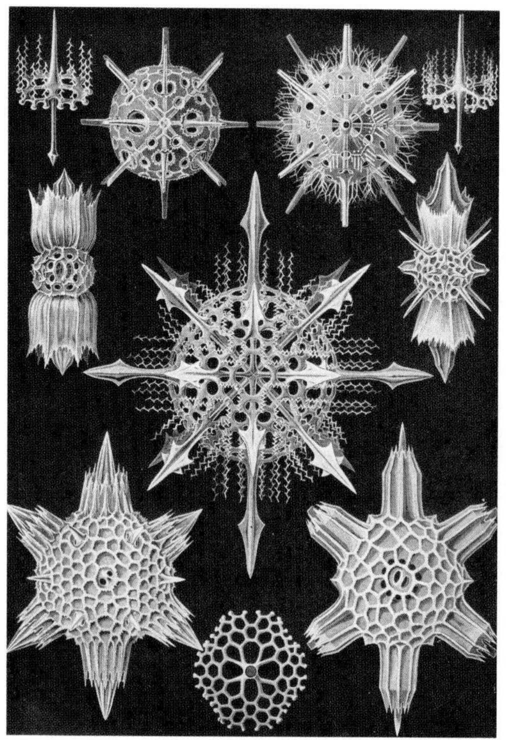

(a)

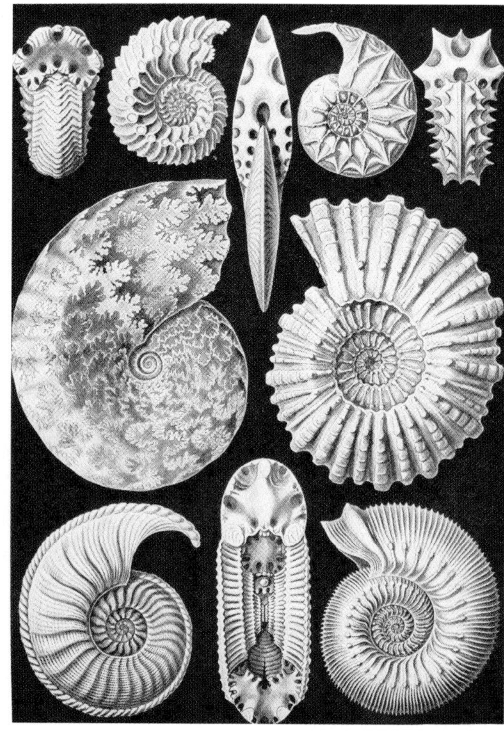

(b)

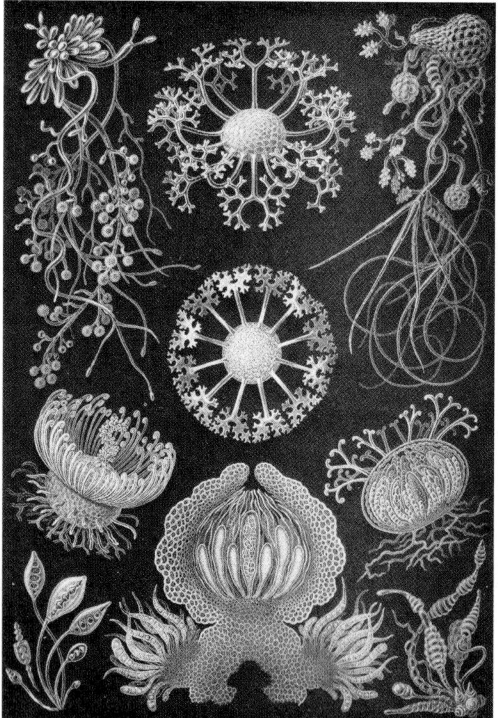

(c)

visual |5-32a to c|

Ernst Haeckel (1834–1919), biologist and philosopher, made amazing drawings of organisms he studied with the naked eye and with microscopes. Visual 5-32a is a series of drawings of marine protozoa, examples of polygons. Visual 5-32b presents variations of shell forms based on the spiral. Visual 5-32c is a page of drawings of fungi. These forms offer a combination of branching, coiling, and sphere shapes.

visual |5-33|

This playfully enchanting 3-D illustration was designed to promote and enhance the DVD review column in *The New York Times*. The review column is published quarterly and often utilizes seasonal themes. The fall theme for this illustration combines an imaginative use of a leaf form as a "headdress" for the falling characters in contrast to the circular shape of the DVDs, which is incorporated into the image as a bicycle wheel. *(Illustration by Chris Sickles, Red Nose Studios)*

SUMMARY

Organizing visual elements and information into a cohesive, engaging graphic image is the work of graphic designers. Attention must be given to the manner in which the design is organized. The key is to give careful consideration to the relationship of the elements as they come together to create a whole image. Formal control, visual illusion, and aesthetic choices affect visual relationships. Designers must work to achieve a resonance among all of the elements as they come together, like the individual sounds in a symphony. The aspects of overall organization, format, orientation, grid systems, eye movement, and theme function together like a transparent stage for the performance. The elements are combined to create visual relationships such as figure and ground, closure, contrast, anomaly, emphasis, and focal point, which give form to the idea. The designer is the conductor, ensuring that the communication message and the visual form it takes work in concert to serve the same composition.

projects

Project Title Contrast Studies

Objectives

Explore a variety of forms of contrast in compositions

Achieve visual unity by managing variety in two contrasting compositions

Work with a design process that includes preliminary study of elements, composition, and application of materials

Work with a process that involves the refinement of hand skills to draw and paint a design image

Develop a visual vocabulary of lines and shapes from verbal content

Work to achieve economy in the relationship and arrangement of elements

Communicate a concept using nonobjective imagery

Description

Design two contrasting compositions based on one of the following sets of complements: negative/positive, jagged/straight, geometric/organic, serene/chaotic, rough/smooth, random/orderly, saturated/pastel, static/kinetic, or monumental/diminutive. Use primarily basic geometric and nonobjective shapes and lines. Strive for economy in the compositions.

Choose three sets of complements to study in preliminary marker sketches. The format for the sketches is 4 inches by 4 inches.

Choose one of the sets of sketches to develop into a final compositional study. The final study is two 8-inch by 8-inch images presented together to illustrate the two contrasts. (Refer to the discussion of contrasts in this chapter.)

Limitations and Materials

Use a bristol board (two-ply or four-ply) for the final images. Work with black-and-white designer gouache to paint the final boards with flat and round paintbrushes. Mount the final studies on gray board with a 3-inch border. Present them together. This assignment also can be done as a cut-paper assignment with black-and-white cover stock.

Critique Discussion Points

How does each composition achieve unity?

Describe the overall character or quality of each composition.

Which visual relationship primarily drives the design?

How is economy achieved in each composition?

Vocabulary

contrast, unity, economy, nonobjective, negative space, positive shape, kinetic

Evaluation Criteria

Composition

Craft

Communication of Contrasting Word Concepts

Effective Use of Economy

Project Title Proportion Study with Line, Point, and Edge

Objectives

Work with external and internal proportions

Use a grid to place design elements in a composition

Explore a refining process of generating elements

Work with repetition, scale changes, proximity, quantity, motif, and closure to produce a design composition

Communicate a theme in an abstract composition using basic elements

Description

Create a composition using the golden rectangle and grid system as an underlying structure to visually convey a force of nature theme using line, point, and edge. Begin with a golden rectangle that is 11 inches on the shortest side. Subdivide the three main areas into smaller grid units using arithmetic, geometric, or triangular grids (see Visual 5–5a, Visual 5–5b, Visual 5–5c, Visual 5–5d, and Visual 5–7). Ink this proportional grid system on cover stock with a fine marker and use it as a template for a design. Work to create implied alignments with elements placed in the grid system. Choose a force of nature (for example, wind, rain, snow, or flood) as a theme. Placing layers of tracing paper over the grid system and using lines, points (dots), and edges (shapes), begin generating design elements that illustrate the chosen theme. Use at least ten layers of tracings to produce the content elements for the final composition. You can cut sections from earlier tracings and incorporate them into the final layer(s). Edit and refine the drawn elements and produce a final precisely drawn tracing of your composition. Carefully transfer the design to illustration board and paint it with black gouache. Do a color translation as an extension of the assignment.

Limitations and Materials

tracing paper, black markers, compass, straightedge, pencil, 16-inch by 20-inch illustration board, designer gouache, fine round and flat brushes, graphite paper (for transfer)

Critique Discussion Points

Discuss your process from the first tracing to the final board.

How did the grid system dictate the placement of elements?

Identify two visual relationships. How are they serving the overall design?

Identify a good design decision and one design decision you would like to change.

Vocabulary

repetition, scale changes, proximity, quantity, motif, closure, grid, golden rectangle, proportion, abstract

Evaluation Criteria

Composition

Craft

Communication of the Force of Nature Concept

Adherence to the Criteria

Project Title Letterform Study

Objectives

Make compositional decisions using letterforms as design elements

Study type as shape

Work with a variety of high-contrast visual relationships

Manage a variety of figure-ground relationships in the same composition

Description

Produce a composition composed of nine smaller letterform compositions.

Using a variety of single letterforms, begin by generating 25 to 30 black-and-white studies that are 3 inches by 3 inches. Variety is the key—variety of typefaces, scale changes, figure-ground relationships, anomaly, closure, emphasis, orientation, and proximity in the small compositions. Cut the small studies carefully into 3-inch squares. Create a new, larger composition using nine of the small studies arranged in a nine-unit grid, three studies across by three studies down. Work to create overall continuity (unity) and rhythm from one unit to the next.

Hint: To create visual interest, partially obscure the identity of the letterforms through cropping, rotating, or reversing within the small compositions.

Limitations and Materials

Generate type from a computer or a photocopy from printed sources. For the final composition, use clean, good-quality laser prints or photocopies. Use a studio knife and metal straightedge to cut small studies. Glue the nine studies in a square grid arrangement on cover stock and mount to a piece of gray board with a 3-inch border.

Critique Discussion Points

Describe the use of variety in the design.

How is variety controlled in the overall composition?

Identify a type of figure-ground relationship at work in the design.

Describe in one word a quality that the design conveys. Point to the visual relationships that support this.

Vocabulary

variety, scale changes, figure-ground relationships, anomaly, closure, emphasis, orientation, proximity

Evaluation Criteria

Composition

Craft

Ability to Achieve Variety

Adherence to the Criteria

In Review

1. What does the Gestalt phrase *The whole is greater than the sum of the parts* mean?
2. Discuss two ways that format is used in graphic design.
3. What are the unique implications of horizontal, vertical, and square formats?
4. What are the advantages of using a grid in design compositions?
5. Discuss the various visual relationships that control eye movement.
6. What are the three general classifications of motif?
7. How does figure-ground reversal differ from figure-ground ambiguity?
8. Identify two visual illusions and discuss how you would compensate for their effect in a design.
9. Find in a work of professional design one of the basic shapes in nature. Describe the use of the shape and offer a reason why you think the designer chose to use it.

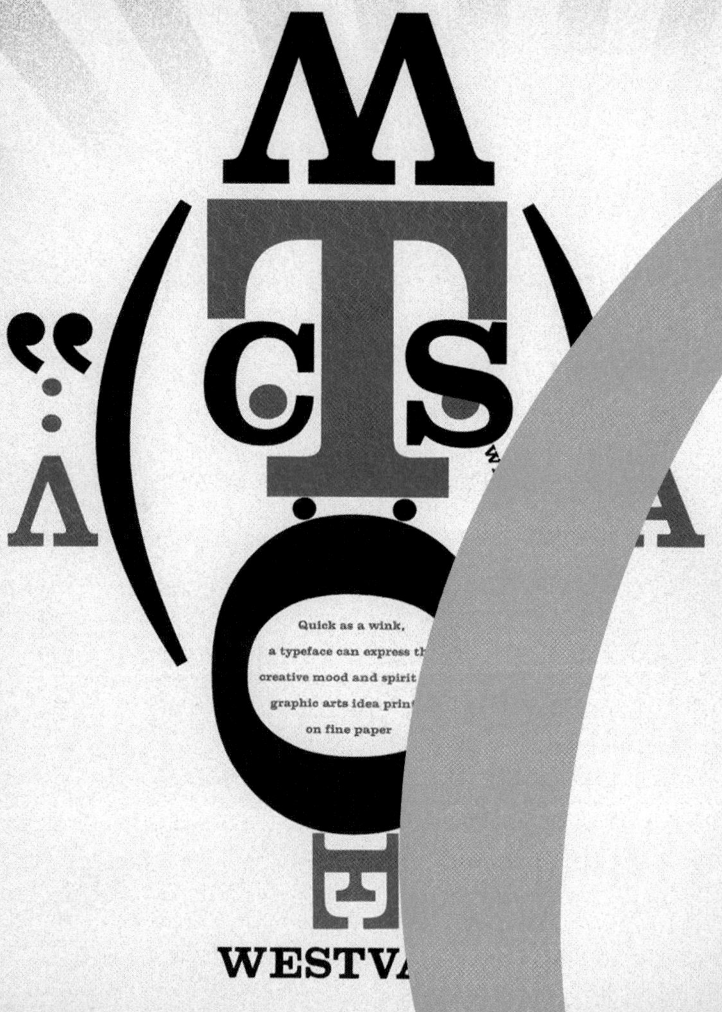
Bradbury Thompson
Quick as a wink,
a typeface can express th
creative mood and spirit
graphic arts idea print
on fine paper
WESTVA

6 RESEARCH *and* VISUAL COMMUNICATION

objectives

Explore processes and methods of research used in the field of visual communication

Apply methods of research to project-based design

Explore processes/methods for research in visual communication

Investigate four components of visual communication: motive, message, audience, and image

Present a Research Project Guide

Present a design criticism model for understanding design imagery

Explain the value of teamwork in problem solving

Explore the relationship between design and communication

Complete research projects

Explore a variety of research tools for the communication arts

introduction

The word *research* is derived from the French term *recerchier,* which means "to thoroughly investigate." Other meanings for research include intellectual inquiry or examination, experiments aimed at the discovery and interpretation of facts, and the collecting of information on a specific subject. Art educator and author Dr. Laura Chapman defines research as "to search again." In that elegant and simple definition, Dr. Chapman captures the essence of research—an activity that, by its nature, is an ongoing process.

In the creation and production of visual art, research is often conducted. Sometimes research is deliberate and methodical; and in other instances, it is intuitive and unsystematic. Intuition is a valuable form of human knowledge that relies on personal experience. The problem is that there is a limit to the depth and breadth of personal experience that each person possesses. When a problem requires a person to know something outside personal experience or knowledge, more methodical research is needed for conducting informed inquiry. But it is important to distinguish information gathering from useful inquiry and examination. An example of the former is printing pages of text and photographs about flowers from the Internet. Simply possessing the information is only the first step in conducting meaningful and useful research.

The information becomes useful only when it has been examined in the context of solving a specific problem. The problem may be to design a program for the Santa Fe Opera. If it is determined that the use of a flower as a visual metaphor is appropriate, then a particular desert flower indigenous to the high deserts of that area of New Mexico would be appropriate.

Research for communication design can be thought of as a journey that leads you to a design solution. This chapter will examine appropriate methods of research for exploring and examining the purpose of a design, the communication message, the audience, and the image itself. The chapter also will examine a variety of physical and intellectual tools used for research in visual communication.

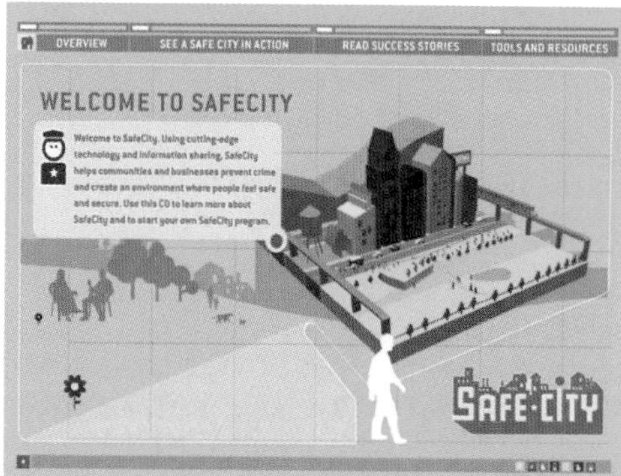

visual 6–1

The purpose of this interactive CD is to help businesses and communities use technology and effective communication to reduce crime. The look is serious yet inviting. The resonating blue motif offers a calming effect. The information graphics are contrasted with retro-designed illustrated graphics. A great deal of research is necessary to create a complex, layered design. *(Interactive CD design by Catalyst Studios)*

COMMUNICATION IN DESIGN

The incorporation of a communication objective distinguishes graphic design and illustration from other visual arts. Managing effective design is managing both the visual elements and accompanying communication objectives. A package or book cover must represent the contents within. A corporate logo must represent the image and nature of a company's business. An advertisement must deliver a pointed message about a product or service.

Communication directs design decisions. What needs to be said by the designer and understood by the audience is the essence of communication design. It is important to understand what needs to be communicated and what to use in the design to support that need. Class assignments have many of the same components as a "real" design project. You are given a set of objectives, limitations, and a time frame to complete the work. Then you are to study the objectives to gain an understanding of what you are being challenged to do. Objectives generally contain the information you need to establish your direction. Most importantly, you must determine the communication components before you begin to explore visual solutions. In beginning design assignments, these components are more basic, but they provide the conceptual framework that serves as the communication criteria.

It is important to understand that whether presented by an instructor or a client, the element of communication is a given that originates from the outside. It is the job of the student and the practicing designer to understand the nature of the need and develop a plan to incorporate it into an effective design solution. Once incorporated, the communication message often serves as the design objective (see Visual 6–2).

Communication design begins with verbal language. Advertising, marketing, publications, packaging, multimedia, and the images needed to support those communication venues rely on concepts that are first considered as written or spoken messages. Communication artists must learn the skills necessary to translate verbal language into visual communication.

In some ways, the verbal message is a conceptual element that must be considered in conjunction with the visual elements. Verbal messages drive the decision-making process that ultimately determines graphic content and the form it needs to take. Translating verbal concepts into visual form is a matter of testing ideas. Sometimes it is obvious that a verbal concept has limited potential as an image. For example, *rational thinking,* as it reads, would be a challenging concept to illustrate. Having to work with such a message may require brainstorming sessions to rethink an approach so it is workable.

The concept *ancient drummer* is inherently rich with visual potential. However, because there are many ways to interpret the concept, it is important to consider the audience, possible venues, and the communication message to guide your design decisions. That requires a clarification of the concept that can be determined by developing a series of related questions.

For example, what culture does the drummer represent? What does a drum from that culture look like? What point of view is most dramatic? Those questions define and refine the concept so it can be worked in an appropriate way.

visual |6-2|

The objective of this advocacy design is to promote voting. The final design is a curious but effective message. It relies on the words and the image together to communicate the intended message. The essence of the illustration is saying, "You have no voice." When combined with the words, the message is complete. *(Poster design by Modern Dog)*

visual |6-3|

Each of these drums is a reproduction of historic First Nations designs, from left to right, an Arapaho hand drum, a Northwest Coastal design, and an Iroquois water drum. While each drum design is of Native American origin, it is different in function and purpose. It is critical to specify your design direction with accurate visual references to clearly establish your intentions. *(Left to right: Arapaho natural rawhide drum design by Alvin Talksdifferent; Thunderbird, Whale, and Human drum design by Na Na Quish; Iroquois Water Drum design of Cayuga Nation artist)*

PACK YOUR BRAIN

ROSE GONNELLA

Rose Gonnella is an educator, an artist, a designer, and a writer. Gonnella has exhibited her art nationally and internationally in collections such as the Smithsonian National Museum of American Art. She also has written numerous books and articles on creativity, art, and architecture.

Why are some professional artists and designers or students of the arts bubbling fonts of creativity that flow with a seemingly endless stream of ideas? Energetically creative people weren't born with minds filled with visual and mental information. Ideas spring from a brain (and heart) packed with experience and knowledge. Creative people are curious and passionate about learning. Curiosity is the foundation of creativity.

Creative people fuel their brains everyday by absorbing as much mental and visual stimuli as can be tolerated before passing out at the end of an evening. Even in sleep, creative people find ideas.

Upon waking, a creative person will jot down the weird and wacky juxtapositions of imagery and dialogue that comes during a dream.

1 INSPIRATION AND IDEAS ARE A PRODUCT OF PROACTIVE MIND.

Creative people are listeners, doers, hobbyists, collectors, museum goers, travelers, scavengers, revelers, searchers, adventurers—with the exploring done through far-reaching experience or simply by reading books. Creative people are hunters and gatherers who constantly look and fill their living space with interesting scraps of paper, all sorts of printed matter, oddly shaped paper clips, doodads, gadgets, and, of course, books. Creative people take notes yet understand that what they accumulate on any given day probably has no particular immediate purpose. Creative people invest in learning and searching for its own sake. The search for inspiration and ideas is an investment.

Time is needed to sponge up information from a myriad of sources. Time is needed to experience.

And, in time, your brain fills up with all manner of stimulation. The stored information, images, and ideas are calmly waiting to be reordered, reconfigured, refreshed, and put to creative use. The stockpile lies dormant until a spark ignites it: you are asked to find a solution to a creative problem. And BANG!, stored information explodes and ideas pop.

But you can't pull out of your head what is not in your head. Creativity does not happen in a vacuum. You have to pack your brain (fortunately there is always room for more). When you ask the question, "How do I get a great idea?" the response is, "Reach into your brain and yank it out OR get up, get out, and gather what you need." Research. Excellent ideas come from what preexists in your brain from previous research, discovery, and exploration, or from what you actively put there for the instance. If you are designing a brochure to save the whales, it is time that you (a) went on a whale watch, (b) watched a documentary about whales, (c) visit a public aquarium that has whales, or (d) read and search the Web. But don't rely on the Web alone. Experience comes best with personal field experiences.

2

WHAT DO TEETH HAVE TO DO WITH TEA BAGS?

Nothing. Isolated visual and intellectual information gathered for the pure joy and pleasure of salvaging, searching, research, observation, or accidental discovery (such as, visiting a flea market, reading a book on Northwest Coast Indian masks, poking through the Japanese bookstore near Rockefeller Center in New York City, bird watching, or coming upon a mural by Thomas Hart Benton at the city hall in Jefferson City, Missouri) will not be useful until the material is compared, related, combined, synthesized, and composed.

Meaning comes from relationships. Keeping your mind wide open to comparing and combining disparate objects, ideas, and imagery creates visual poetry and fresh ideas. A design found on the ceiling of the Uffizi Gallery in Florence might make a great composition juxtaposed with an image of clouds.

In isolation, an image of clouds is seen as itself. Seen together, an image of a floral tapestry and clouds may suggest an entirely new and evocative meaning. Some people look into the night sky and see stars. Creative people look at the stars and also see horses, crabs, lions, and warriors. Now, what do teeth have to do with tea bags?

Open your mind and let the possibilities pour in.

PSYCHOLOGICAL FOUNDATIONS AND VISUAL COMMUNICATION

Understanding relationships between verbal language and visual communication gives designers and illustrators important tools for communicating with an intended audience. An audience is a group of people with a specific profile, referred to in marketing as a demographic. To understand any group and the individuals in it, you need to consider the psychological foundations that influence the members of the group. Those psychological foundations include how people *behave*, how they *think*, how they *feel*, and how they *interact* with one another. You will examine each of them as they relate to visual communication.

Behavior refers to the actions or reactions of a person, usually in response to environmental factors. Behavior can be unconscious or conscious, involuntary or intentional. A generally accepted tenet of behavioral psychologists is that it takes two weeks to begin to change a behavior. You can test this on yourself with a simple research task. Choose a kitchen appliance, a wastebasket, or another useful object that you use frequently. Move it to a different location in the room or on the countertop. In the first few days, you will notice that your behavior is to go to the original location first. As you proceed through the next few days, you will find yourself going to the new location more often. Eventually, you will change your behavior as you train your orientation to the new location. Keep track of the number of times you involuntarily choose the new location. This example underscores how behaviors can become habits and how changing your intentions, (i.e., moving the object to a new place) can change your behavioral relationship to the use of the object.

Behavioral outcomes, or *what is determined to be a desired response*, are a key aspect in design communication that intends to persuade the viewer (see Visual 6–4). Knowing how an individual or a group behaves provides critical information when attempting to market ideas or concepts to them. It is why daytime television runs medical health advertisements geared toward senior citizens, certain sporting events advertise beer and cars, and the X Games focus on messages to youth markets.

Thinking is another word for cognition. The term *cognition* is derived from the Latin for *cogito*, "to think." Cognition also refers to a person's mental processes, the processing of information and intellectual understanding or comprehension. Thinking or cognitive awareness can involve the process of learning or acquiring knowledge. Communication design can involve verbal meaning and visual imagery that requires reasoning, acting, or processing information. The ability to distinguish when a design demands a cognitive response is critical to aesthetic choices and the arrangement and presentation of the overall design (see Visual 6–5). Book design, interactive information design, and educational displays and exhibits, for example, appeal to the viewer's cognitive sense and must be designed with that in mind.

Feeling is emotional expression that produces psychological change. Expressions of emotion can include anxiety, rapture, rage, delight, animosity, or compassion. Feelings also can be thought of as sensations related to and experienced through the sense of touch, visual perception, olfactory

visual 6–4

This poster design is a satirical commentary promoting an anti-war message. It presents the viewer with behavioral alternatives. The pictographic images also make a comment on the obvious contrast between constructive and destructive behavior. *(Poster design by Scorsone/Drueding, Joe Scorsone and Alice Drueding designers)*

perception (smell), auditory perception, and even taste. Graphic designers are, of course, interested primarily in visual perception when it relates to a viewer's emotional response. Images have the power to conjure feelings of loneliness, joy, contempt, and serenity. Certain shapes and colors evoke particular emotional responses (see Visual 6–6).

Communication designers can anticipate how an audience will feel or generally feels in a given situation. People at an amusement park will generally feel differently than a group at a poetry reading. An individual shopping on eBay has a different mind-set than someone walking through an airport in a foreign city. Countless scenarios affect how people feel about different situations and how different situations make people feel. Visual artists use color, shape, line, and texture in particular arrangements to communicate a mood or sense of feeling to their audience.

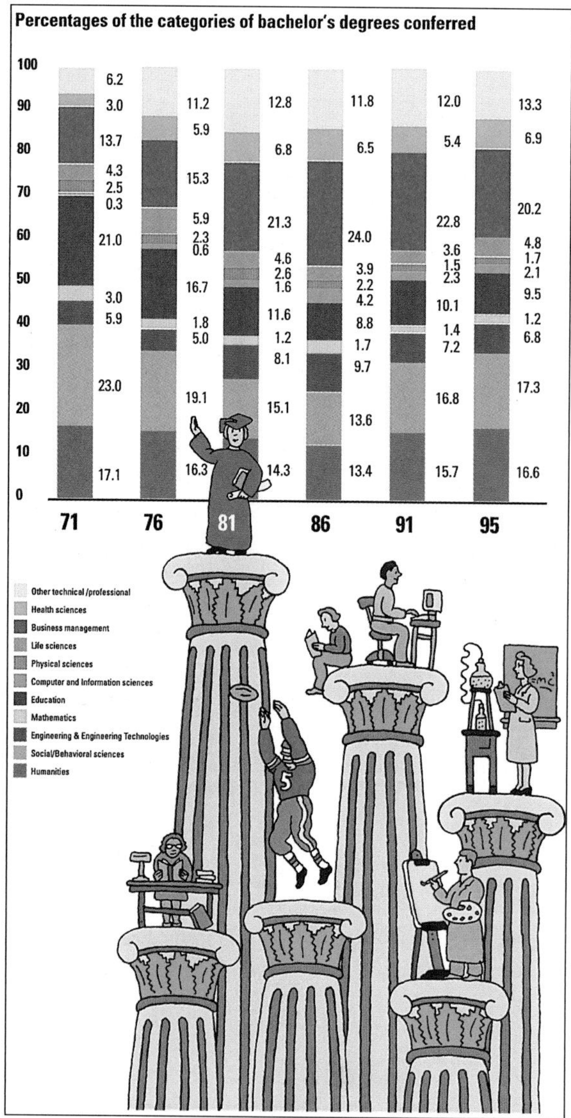

visual |6-5|

Information graphics appeal to people's cognitive senses. Charts and graphs present information that requires alytical reasoning to process. This design, presenting statistical data about college degrees, provides a visualization of the data with entertaining graphics. The graphics help the viewer appreciate the impact of the data.

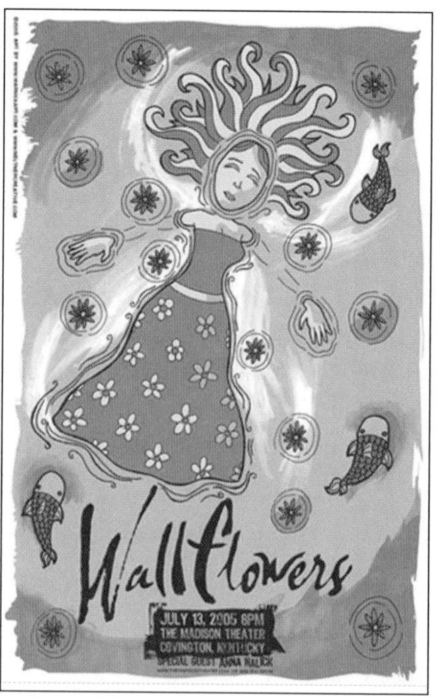

visual |6-6|

Screen-printed poster art is a medium that often excites the senses with vivid color and imagery and with physical size. This poster design promoting the Indie rock group *The Wallflowers* depicts a female figure, fish, and water flowers floating serenely in water. The playful combination of graphic elements seems to excite the viewer's sense of sound and touch. It graphically presents the feelings of floating, weightlessness, and release. The color scheme of overall soft blue tones contrasted by muted red-orange graphic elements supports the intended feel the designers had in mind. *(Poster design by Keith Neltner and Rob Warnick)*

INTERACTION

The ways and motivations for how and why people interact are very complex. Sociologists and psychologists study the phenomenon of human interaction to learn the dynamics of social structures and the relationship of the individual in these structures. People experience a plethora of socially interactive situations everyday—talking to a neighbor, shopping in a marketplace, worshiping, playing team sports, attending an entertainment event, working, or going to school. When people interact, they are engaged in a symbolic social structure that provides meaning and purpose to their life. Herbert Blumer[1] is a social psychologist who studied social interaction and is known for advancing the idea of *symbolic interaction*. **Symbolic interaction** is the process of forming meaning in support of the formation of personal identity and human socialization. Blumer identifies three core principles for symbolic interaction—meaning, language, and thought. **Meaning** is central to his thesis. How people interact with one another and with objects is based on meanings the people project on to the other individuals and objects. **Language**, verbal and visual, provides a means for people to negotiate meaning using symbols. **Thought** provides a mental construct for people to interpret and reinterpret symbols. Blumer's work has an obvious underlying connection to the formal tenets of visual communication.

To communicate with a group (an audience), you need to know something about the structure and purpose of the group and a profile of the individuals in it. For example, a teacher of an introductory design class needs to know the nature of the skill levels, interest levels, ability of the group to stay attentive, familiarity with the subject, etc., to prepare and teach the course. The designer of a sign system for a city park must consider the unique ways people interact in that environment if she is to create a successful and effective design.

PERRY LEVELS

A learning environment is a complex social structure that, by its nature, is dependent on the interaction of its members. It is also a structure in which people have extended experiences. How an individual student interacts and ultimately learns within an educational structure depends on what William Perry Jr. describes as "Levels of Intellectual Maturity"[2]. At this point, as a student of the visual arts, you should examine these levels in the context of this chapter's discussion of social interaction and with the goal of gaining personal insight. These levels, called Perry levels, are valuable to you as a student and as a future professional engaged in the ongoing process of self-education.

Perry's own research of his students at Harvard revealed valuable insight into the adult learner. His study offers a great example of how people generally develop as learners. The Perry levels provide meaningful insight into your own learning development and readiness to engage in the learning process. Which of these levels have you experienced? Note that while these levels are presented in hierarchical order, they are not strictly sequential in the way people experience them. Also, they are not specific to visual learners. A discussion later in this chapter will address aspects of visual intelligence and the visual learner.

---

[1] The Society for More Creative Speech. 1996. "Symbolic Interactionism as Defined by Herbert Blumer." http://www.thepoint.net/-usul/text/blumer.html.

[2] William G. Perry Jr., *Forms of Intellectual and Ethical Development in the College Years: A Scheme.* (New York: Holt, Rinehart and Winston, 1968).

THE DESIGNER AT WORK

Two basic ways we learn to represent and communicate the objects, actions, and feelings in our lives are with words and images. Words are an effective method of communicating complicated interrelated ideas. It is symbols however that can communicate across the language barriers created by words.

—Lance Wyman

lance wyman

Lance Wyman was born in Newark, New Jersey, in 1937 and lived the first nineteen years of his life just across the Passaic River in Kearny. His father ran a commercial fishing boat. During his grade school years, Wyman spent time with his father on the Atlantic. Kearny was an industrial area, and Wyman worked in the factories during the summers to pay college tuition. The no-nonsense functional aesthetic of the sea and the factories has been an important influence in his approach to design.

In 1960, Wyman graduated from Pratt Institute in Brooklyn, New York, with a degree in industrial design. At that time, graphic design was a European influence that was just being introduced to American universities at the graduate level. When Wyman met a student who studied logo design with Paul Rand at Yale, he knew he wanted to design logos.

He started his career in Detroit, Michigan, first with General Motors and later with the office of William Schmidt. At General Motors, he designed the packaging system for its Delco automotive parts that unified 1,200 different packages. At the Schmidt office, he did the graphics for the 1962 USA Pavilion at the trade fair in Zagreb, Yugoslavia. The theme of the exhibition was "Leisure Time." He devised an hourglass logo with a sun-and-moon image at the top and used it as a gateway to the exhibit. It was his first experience integrating logo design into a three-dimensional environment.

In 1963, Wyman joined the George Nelson office in New York and designed the graphics for the Chrysler Pavilion at the New York World's Fair, which was a series of islands with exhibits designed for kids. Devising a "pointing hand" theme logo and adapting it as the site directional signs convinced him that logos could play a more important role in an overall design program.

In 1966, Wyman went to Mexico City with Peter Murdoch to participate in a competition to design the graphics for the 1968 Mexico Olympic Games. It was the beginning of an adventure that has continued to influence his work and life. The Mexico68 logotype that he designed was instrumental in winning the competition. The resulting design program, a multidimensional integration of logos, typography, and color developed to communicate to a multilingual audience, was cited by Philip Meggs in the book *A History of Graphic Design* as ". . . one of the most successful in the evolution of visual identification . . . ." The lessons from this program have been a constant guide to Wyman's work.

The spiral of symbols serves as Wyman's home page. Enlargements isolate a building symbol for downtown Albuquerque, New Mexico, and a logotype for the Philadelphia Expo.

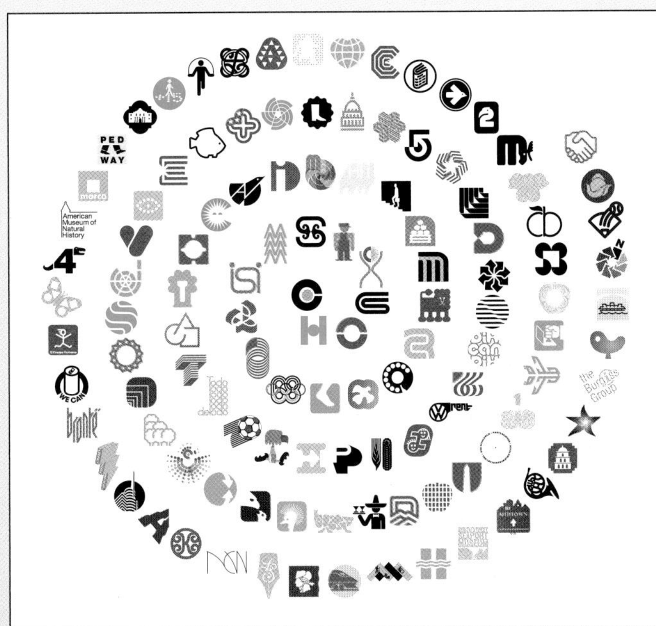

Levels of Intellectual Maturity

Dualism (concrete thinking) Some of the traits in this level include thinkers who believe things are right or wrong and good or bad. Knowledge is thought of as a set of truths. Every problem has a finite answer. Learners are reluctant to express a point of view. Authority figures have the ability to explain and give correct answers.

Multiplicity At this level, recognition of diversity of thinking exists. Uncertainty prevails because other points of view are valid. Knowledge is a matter of educated opinion. There is no single right solution to a problem. Learners listen to experts but have a right to their own opinions. Experts explain a theory or content that is viewed as their opinion.

Relativism At this level, knowledge is relative. Knowledge is not universal, but a matter of context and situation. What is true in one situation may be not be true in another. Ambiguity is part of life requiring the individual to prove reasoning for ideas. Knowledge is determined by reasoning. Based on their experiences, experts present procedures and analytic methods to help others reason and compare alternatives.

Commitment The learner develops the need to take a position. Knowledge is constructed from experience, from interaction with others, and from reflective thinking. There are many potential solutions to a problem, but they are not equally valid. Knowledge is integrated. Experts are mentors that challenge a person's assumptions to support the person's learning.

Understanding these kinds of interdisciplinary theories and concepts provides an intellectual depth for your design research. They also provide you with a substantive theoretical knowledge base to formulate a rationale for design decisions. Having solid reasons for the creative choices you make gives you a distinct advantage when you present your ideas to others. If you are convincing, you will gain creative control.

BRANCHES OF COMMUNICATION DESIGN

Communication specialists in the advertising and marketing fields understand the previously discussed psychological foundations and theories. They use them in conjunction with other profiles such as age, gender, ethnicity, geography, and income to create messages and imagery that will reach the target audience.

Designers and illustrators take the messages and craft them into visual concepts. To develop effective graphics from potential concepts, the designer must know what the communication specialist knows about the nature of the message and the audience who will receive it. A connection then needs to be made between the human psychology that drives marketing and advertising and the way communication functions in design.

The following discussion will relate the psychological foundations of human activity to the branches of communication design. It also will provide examples of each type. These branches determine the way a communication message will be delivered to an audience—that is, to persuade, inform, direct, and enhance (embellish).

Persuasive design attempts to persuade an audience to think or behave in a deliberate, sometimes different way from what they are accustomed to thinking or doing. "Support the Arts," "Be a Subscriber," and "Buy This Brand" are messages intended to persuade. Advertising, promotional, and social advocacy designs are examples of this category (see Visual 6–2).

Information design presents ideas and concepts with the intent of educating the audience.

Textbook design, Web site design, exhibit design, annual reports, charts, and diagrams all deliver information that is graphically organized and designed to assist the audience in their understanding of specific content (see Visual 6–5).

Directional design helps people find their way through architectural, virtual, or environmental spaces. Theme parks, retail centers, public spaces, Internet navigation, and transportation systems all rely on typographic and pictographic design that can speak to broad audiences often made up of an international population (see Visual 6–7).

Enhansive design embellishes the look of a design venue. Enhansive graphics also can add a measure of entertainment value to a design application. Theme parks, retail industry, games, advertising, editorial, and electronic media all rely on enhansive graphics to present a more visually interesting and compelling product (see Visual 6–8).

It is important to realize that these functions are interrelated. In fact, many design applications incorporate several of these categories in their concept and design. For instance, a packaging design needs to persuade consumers to choose the product from the shelf and, at the same time, give them information about the package's contents. A magazine or book needs to compel an interested consumer to pick it up for examination and offer entertainment value in the design and graphics.

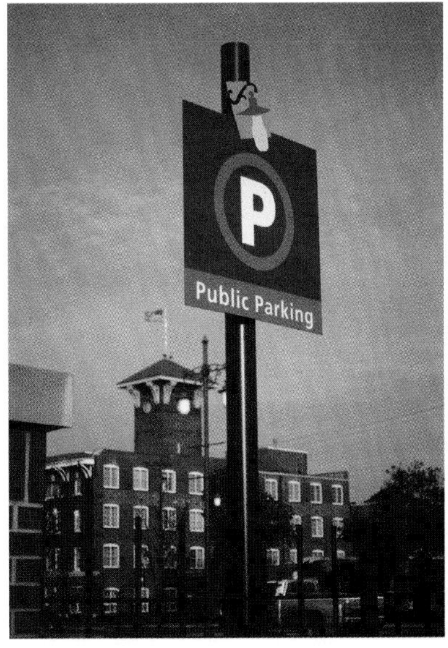

visual |6–7|

Sign systems in urban environments aid people in navigating from one place to another. These systems rely on a combination of pictographic and verbal languages. By doing so, they communicate to people who are of a broader range of nationality and background. The purpose of the systems is to direct and identify destinations in the interest of orderly interaction of individuals in their environment. *(Signage system for Wichita, Kansas, by Hunt Design Associates)*

visual 6–8

A bright color scheme and a set of playful illustrations are used to enhance the function of this board game design. *(Game design by Morris Creative)*

KNOWLEDGE AND DESIGN

Knowledge is the fact or condition of knowing something as acquired through experience, or you can think of it as the range of a person's information or understanding of truth or fact arrived at through reasoning. At the center of personal knowledge about any subject are experience and reasoning. The process of design requires knowledge from many sources and disciplines. It is impossible to know everything about every subject you will encounter as a designer. You will not be successful trying to solve every design problem directly from your acquired experience. Most design content will be unfamiliar. Therefore, you must develop research skills that will help you intelligently and systematically solve the problem. In effect, you are learning to teach yourself. The best way to begin is to gain a thorough understanding of the nature of the problem you are trying to solve.

PROBLEM SOLVING

Solving visual problems requires a range of knowledge and skills—facility with a variety of media; the ability to present ideas, develop ideas, and identify the right idea; technical knowledge; developed hand skills; verbal language skills; research skills; a working knowledge of history and math; and a general knowledge of contemporary culture. If you run your own business, you will need to make business decisions. That is an impressive and probably partial list of the scope of knowledge and skills needed to be an effective designer. But the process of learning all of these skills is accumulative as you acquire and master them over time. Most of them require practice and maintenance.

Wolfgang Kohler (1887–1967), a psychologist and cofounder of Gestalt psychology, conducted an important research study by observing apes to explain the nature of problem solving. Kohler's study involved hanging a bunch of bananas just outside the reach of a caged ape. Inside the cage were two poles that fit together. After trying to reach the bananas and failing, the ape attempted to hook the bananas with one of the poles. It was too short. Motivated, the ape eventually figured out how to assemble the two short poles to make one long pole and was successful in reaching the bananas.

Once the ape solved the problem, he was able to repeat his actions on subsequent tries. Kohler demonstrated creative problem solving with this simple study the first time the ape assembled the two poles to reach the bananas. Kohler referred to the subsequent learned attempts to retrieve the bananas as routine problem solving.

You can apply this lesson to your own attempts at solving problems. You tend to get creative when a problem is presented that is unfamiliar, complex, or intellectually challenging. Creative problem solving relies on invention. Invention is simply the imaginative combining of existing things resulting in something new. When you find a way to combine things creatively that are not normally associated together or that are disparate, the result can be intriguing, surprising, and sometimes brilliant (see Visual 6–10 and Visual 6–11).

visual | 6-9 |

One of the basic tools for researching visual ideas is a sketchbook. Artists and designers have relied on sketchbooks for centuries to observe the world and test and record ideas. Sketchbooks offer a personal, safe place to explore and manage ideas. This is a page from Leonardo da Vinci's sketchbook. He was working out an idea for a water-powered machine. (library.thinkquest.org)

visual | 6-10 |

This design firm Web page employs a creative and inventive arrangement of the two words that make up the firm's name. The words literally pivot to share the inverted, common first letter. This is a wonderful example of the imaginative graphic "combining" of existing visual forms. *(Web page design by Pivot Design, Brock Haldeman, art director)*

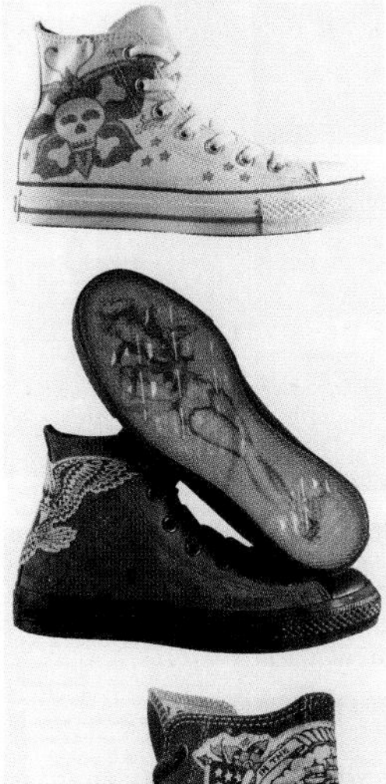

visual | 6-11 |

Combining the edginess of tattoo art with an American icon such as Converse shoes may not immediately present itself as a great match. The result, however, is a beautifully elegant fashion statement and design. The ultra-hip look is the creative problem solving of a young designer who is designing for a young adult market. A clever business arrangement nets the design firm royalties on each pair sold. *(GYRO Worldwide, Nick Paparone, art director)*

VISUAL INTELLIGENCE

Cognitive psychologist Jerome Bruner defined intelligence as "a person's ability to use the tools of a culture." That insightful view of intelligence recognizes that you can be intelligent in different ways—that there is no single standard for intelligence. What are the tools of a culture? Certainly, language (written, verbal, and visual) and technology (mechanical tools and machines) are two of the most basic tools of any culture. Whatever a person's gift, it involves the use of language and technology to some degree. Some people have an affinity for numbers and formulas; others, for working with things mechanical, organizing information, writing, managing, composing, or using languages. Those who are visually oriented tend to learn more through observation and perception than through knowledge found in books. The fact that you are studying visual art points to an intelligence that has prepared you as a visual learner. Visual learning requires an ability to think visually. Next, you will examine some aspects and strategies for visual thinking that can help you be more effective at solving visual problems.

VISUAL THINKING

Visual thinking is a problem-solving activity. Visual thinking is dependent on a relationship between mental and physical manipulation of an idea. A visual concept may begin as a mental idea, but there are limits to the degree to which you can develop and refine these ideas mentally. To solve a visual problem or work with a visual idea, you have to manage it visually; that is, you have to give it form in the real world. A common myth about artistic process is that the artist has an idea for an image, formulates the idea in her head, and then produces the image with a mysterious direct effort. That belief is impractical and rarely feasible. Most artists work their ideas through a rigorous process of research, practice, testing, and revision (see Visual 6–12). Visual thinking is a part of the process. Preliminary sketching, studies, and model building are ways artists externalize an idea from their mind to the real world. Brainstorming and group thinking sessions are effective in developing and testing ideas. Exploring media options and testing them to give form to an idea is visual thinking.

CREATIVE PROCESS

Many of the projects presented in this book include visual thinking strategies that help you mange the creative process of solving a visual problem. There are many models for the creative process. You can do an Internet search to study the models and adopt one that works for you. Most of the models have some common components or stages:

1. Identify the nature and scope of the problem.
2. Research all aspects of the problem and gather the facts.
3. Separate the big problem into smaller tasks, retaining useful information.
4. Develop and test potential ideas.
5. Allow for a gestation period, letting your ideas "live on their own."
6. Commit to one idea and execute it.
7. Evaluate the results.

Bradbury Thompson
WINK
Quick as a wink,
a typeface can express the
creative mood and spirit of a
graphic arts idea printed
on fine paper
WESTVACO

visual |6-12|

Once the idea of creating a face from typographic forms was established, Bradbury Thompson had to consider different fonts; make associations between facial features and letterforms; study arrangements; and in this case, take a creative risk to manage this experimental idea in a successful manner. The result is one of the most memorable and innovative uses of type in twentieth-century design. *(Brochure cover design for Westvaco by Bradbury Thompson)*

Creative process models are not developed exclusively for artists. They can be applied to many different kinds of activities and pursuits. Try using the previous model to plan a trip, rearranging a room, or plan a party. The steps in the models are not strictly linear. You will find that skipping a step, backtracking, or repeating steps is more the rule than the exception. But now you will take the essence of the seven steps presented here in conjunction with points made throughout this chapter and consider a design process model or guide that has practical application for student projects and professional projects. The process is based on a distillation of points commonly found in project models from a variety of professional sources.

DESIGN AS PROCESS

Beginning a design problem can be an overwhelming task that involves many decisions. Breaking down the problem into manageable tasks and points can be helpful but does not ensure that the design will be successful. Work and skill are required to arrive at a solution that solves the problem. Some key components must be carefully researched and developed. The Research Project Guide identifies the components and defines their role as they function in a design process.

Graphic Synthesis: A Comparative Case Study

This case study is a comparison of two design programs by Lance Wyman—the Minnesota Zoo and the American Museum of Natural History. Both designs use what Lance refers to as "a synthesis approach" of integrating form—in these cases, synthesizing animal forms with alphanumeric symbols. The typography of the Minnesota Zoo is designed as an extension of the animal images and became a custom typeface. The animal images of the Natural History Museum are designed as add-on shapes to an existing typeface, maintaining the original integrity of the typeface. The original reference for the zoo logotype is a moose combined with an *M*. This idea was expanded to design the numeric identifiers for various areas of the zoo.

The Natural History Museum begins with a graphic simplification of the building. Representative animals from each of the floors of the museum are combined with floor numbers. This imaginative and integrated design is an example of system design. System design is based on the development of a graphic device or structure upon which the parts of the larger design are based. While systems are defined and applied universally, they allow for variation to occur.

What is interesting about these two programs is that while the approaches to combining type and image are different, they accomplish the same objective.

The Minnesota Zoo

Finished identity symbol for the Minnesota Zoo.

Representative animal forms are combined with corresponding numeric figures.

Signage application with symbols. The flying bird is designed to function as a directional symbol. These types of symbols are referred to as pictographs.

A presentation of the pictographic program components including a photo reference of the moose, a selected font, applications of the symbols, and an article from *Time* magazine about the work.

The American Museum of Natural History

An exterior reference photograph of the American Museum of Natural History.

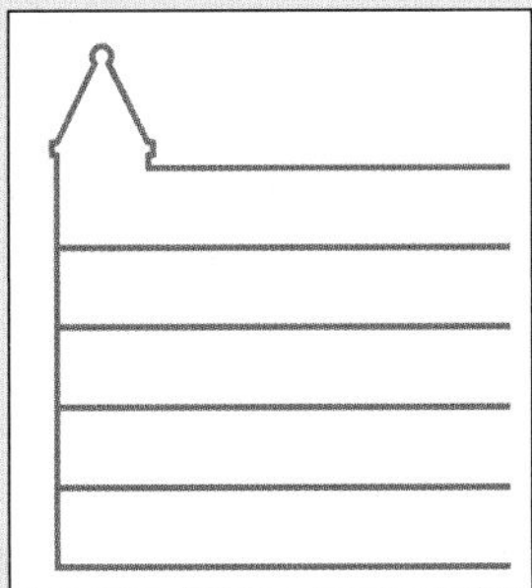

A graphic simplification of the building.

A photographic reference of *T. rex* is used as a source image for the floor and destination graphic symbol.

Graphic synthesis of the dinosaur form and numeric symbol.

Finished kiosk design with graphic elements. Floors 1–4 combine numeric symbols with a representative animal form. Notice the sensitivity and inventiveness that Wyman employs as he combines and "synthesizes" the animal with its corresponding numeric symbol to create a new figure. Wyman identifies the lower level of the museum, which contains the restaurant, with a zero, which is integrated with a table setting.

A presentation of program components includes source photography, symbol designs, and documentation.

Research Project Guide

Project Title: Give your project a name. While this item is first on the list, do it last.

Project Abstract: This is a brief one- or two-paragraph description of the thesis. It is a synopsis of the information presented below.

Project Goal: A goal is a big idea that is somewhat general in description. A goal serves as a conceptual umbrella. Goals are idealistic but attainable. However, goals may be achieved through a means that are different from the original plan. Sometimes goals are not achieved. This is not necessarily an indication of failure, but it can cause disappointment. Extraneous factors can change the quality and integrity of your realizing a planned goal. Resourcefulness and creative problem solving are critical skills when you must confront extraneous factors that impede your progress toward a goal.

Project Objectives: Objectives support the goal. They are linked to behavioral outcomes. They are specific to the task/project. They can be concrete and conceptual. The objectives provide a delineated outline of the project. They are the map that the facilitator uses to navigate her way through the project. Subobjectives contain further details of how the project will be realized.

Audience: This is the group toward whom you are directing the message/communication. The audience can be narrow or broad. The audience, referred to in marketing as the target audience, always has a profile. Even broader audiences are specially defined. Demographics are specific statistics that offer a profile about a given population. This data is critical information about human activity (i.e., individual and group behavior, attitudes, and beliefs). Attitudes and beliefs have their foundation in four distinct human activities: thinking, feeling, behaving, and interacting. To achieve the desired outcome of your objectives, you must research and know your audience.

Hard demographic research is compiled through the use of scientific surveys, focus group observation, and empirical research studies. Market-driven communications rely on this type of information.

Soft demographic research can be obtained by observing "what's out there"; applying existing research data to your situation; and making inferences about social and cultural trends from information media sources such as newspapers, television, the Internet, and periodicals.

Environment: Environment is a time/space relationship that affects the use and interaction of the user with the communication. In conventional terms, the environment is where the audience engages the message over a given time frame. Sometimes the environment is dictated by the user; sometimes the environment is dictated by the designer. Often it is determined by both. The visual impact of a good design often transforms the environment. The environment can be intangible, that is, cerebral or imagined. The environment can be the design/communication/message itself.

Media: There are two branches of media:

1. Vehicle: The materials used to physically produce the work—paint, digital prints, dry transfer type, paper, pastels, wood, etc.
2. Venue: Where the communication occurs; the form of the communication—a billboard, computer monitor, book, gallery wall, building lobby, etc.

Strategy: Strategy determines how you will manage the project and how you will produce the imagery.

Rationale: The rationale is why you think the project is worthwhile and what the subsequent reasoning is for pursuing your idea. Use the compiled research to support your decisions.

Budget: Budget includes the number of hours; the cost per hour; and the cost of incidentals, calls, transportation, correspondence, etc.

Four Components of Visual Communication

Purpose Need Benefit Expectation	Message Verbal Communication Visual Communication	Audience Demographics Psychological Foundations	Image Visual Language Visual Organization
Need of Client Want What clients think they need Need What research determines is the an appropriate direction Research provides a rationale Benefit to Client Improvement to current status Panda Express now serves 20 new countries Better communication City signage program for downtown Boulder Higher level of awareness Interactive Web site for the X-games Efficiency of use Color coding for pricing guide at an independant record shop Expectation Designer/Client Agreement This is important — Mutual Trust What I will do — Pledge Agreed outcome. — Deliver	Verbal Communcation What type of message will be sent? What will be received? Informational Jerry Springer is running for governor. Persuasive Vote for Jerry Springer. Directional Meet Jerry Springer at the town center. Visual Communcation Explore visual translations of the verbal message What venue (visual response) is appropriate? Research and test the response	Demographics Who is targeted? What is the audience profile? Gender Age Ethnicity Income Level Education Political Affiliations Cultural Preferences Psychological Foundations How a targeted audience Thinks Feels Behaves Interacts Psychological Foundations affect peoples attitudes and beliefs Attitudes Likes and dislikes Beliefs perceived relationships between two things	Visual Language How will the image function? Type Driven Image Driven What Semiotic meaning is associated with the image? Sign means what it says Symbol stands for something else Metaphor open-ended meaning Icon that which it represents Visual Organization What is the visual hierarchy of the composition? Which visual principles are appropriate for the composition? Does the image content support/address the Purpose Message and Audience?

Visual Thinking Is a Process

It may seem odd to suggest the idea of giving structure to creative thinking, but using thinking exercises or brainstorming models to guide the creative process can be very useful for generating ideas.

Ideas generally begin in the mind, manifested by our imaginations. Attempting to re-create an idea directly from our mind into visual form often brings disappointment.

Visual thinking is the process of working and managing an idea that begins in the mind into the visual word using drawing, paper cutting and folding, sources of color, and other studio media.

Determine a fixed time. Ten minute sessions to generate ideas.

Work quickly to generate as many ideas as possible.

Do not judge any ideas at this phase.

← EVALUATE

Review your ideas and choose two or three to pursue further.

← EVALUATE

Narrow to a single idea and produce a number of variations.

← EVALUATE

Refine and refine again.

← EVALUATE

Prepare the refined idea for final execution.

← EVALUATE

What Is Risk Taking?

Risk taking in your work can yield dynamic results. Think of risk taking as exploring outside the given parameters of a project or assignment.

Introducing the unusual use of media, an unexpected point of view, or novel use of color can turn an otherwise mediocre solution into a design gem.

However, time constraints limit the number of directions you can consider, and working an idea without a plan can make it difficult to reach a resolution.

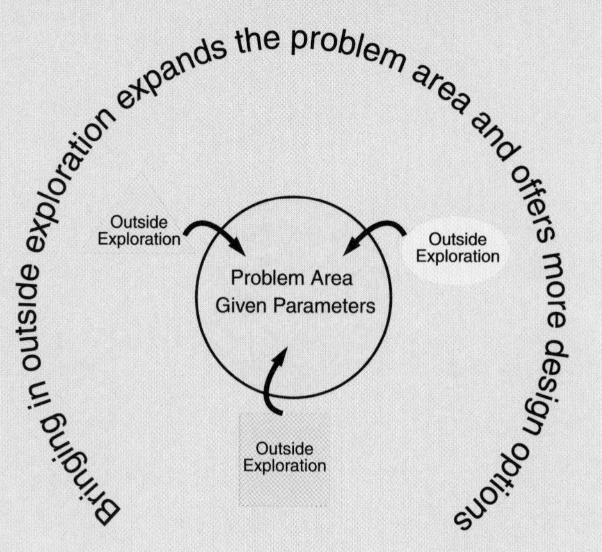

SUMMARY

Graphic design involves more than drawing skills, computer skills, and design acumen. A basic knowledge of academic disciplines, especially history and psychology, is significant. Most important is a thirst for lifelong learning. Proficient research skills are critical to producing informed and intelligent design solutions. Research skills also are critical to your growth and development as a professional designer. You must be able to defend your choices with meaningful and appropriate rationale to gain creative control. Evaluate your own strengths, weaknesses, learning style, and organizational skills. Strive to improve your research skills and depth of knowledge about fields of study related to graphic design. Work hard to expand your vocabulary and your presentation skills by practicing in class and with peer groups. Become intimately familiar with the field of visual communication. To generate innovative ideas, you need to know if they have already been done.

projects

Project Title Case Study Project

Objectives

Discuss the creative process of a professional designer

Explain the inner workings of a design business

Conduct in-depth research on a graphic design project

Display oral and written communication skills

Prepare a formal oral, visual, and written presentation

Discuss the components of design process research

Description

Select an agency, a studio, a freelance designer, or an illustrator. Choose one that is aligned with your interests. Arrange to spend an hour interviewing your contact. The objective is to gather information focused on the research, process, and development of a single project.

Limitations and Materials

This case study should follow the project from beginning to end. Use the questions on this form as a guide for acquiring the information. Complete a word-processed paper that includes the information from each question. You will present your case study to the class. Photocopy any visuals that will help explain the project.

Critique Discussion Points

Present each point in the study.

Discuss the nature of the project using the visual examples.

What flaws did you see in the firm's process?

What would you change in the firm's approach to project management?

Vocabulary

target audience, strategy, rationale, objective, venue, behavioral outcomes

References and Resources

If possible, try to locate a design firm or an individual and conduct this case study in person. Otherwise, find a design or ad agency on the Web. Do some research using the information available there and conduct the interview portion via telephone with a representative designer listed on the site.

Evaluation Criteria

Completion of the Points in the Study

Organization of Materials Presented

Depth of Research on the Chosen Case

Quality of the Oral Presentation

Case Study Inventory

Name of Contact/Individual:

Position:

Phone Number:

E-mail Address:

Business Profile:

Project Title:

Project Dates:

Client:

Project Team:

Art Director:

Designer:

Production:

Copywriter:

Artist:

Other:

Project Objective:

Target Audience Profile:

Describe the intended behavioral outcomes.

Project Strategy:

How is the project researched?

How is it executed?

Discuss the production process.

Describe the venue.

Discuss the rationale for the client's need

What is the amount of the general budget?

How is the success of the project measured?

Other Insights:

Project Title Destination Motif Board

Objectives

Complete the research and production of a destination motif board

Provide research for the motive, message, audience, and imagery/elements

Prepare a proposal that includes information from each component in the Project Guide

Work as part of a team to brainstorm a concept

Produce a motif board of textures, type, color artifact, and motif that are driven by group research

Description

Begin by working as part of a team to share background information and possible directions. Prepare a project brief that defines the motive, message, audience profile, and image profile. Refer to the Four Components of Visual Communication sidebar for elaboration of these points. The image profile should address questions of type style, motif, color scheme, and content elements. Once you have addressed those concerns, begin a visual exploration. Gather resources and references from which to work. Complete visual studies of media, composition, color, and possible arrangements. Use the research to complete a collage motif board of the assigned destination.

Assemble the written and documented research into a folder. Include the following:

1. A word-processed research brief addressing each component of the research guide and a destination profile (Use subheads, 11pt Times Roman, double-spaced type, and a title.)

2. The visual reference materials (i.e., studies and photocopies of cultural and graphic references)

Your instructor may ask you to give a ten-minute presentation of your project to the class for the final critique.

Limitations and Materials

Each team will be assigned a travel destination and audience profile. You will work with your team to generate research on the destination. You will work as part of the team to produce the project brief and design.

The final size is 24 inches by 24 inches. Use a variety of materials, fabric, color aid, textures, graphic elements, natural material, objects, typography, etc., to create an arrangement that encapsulates the essence of the destination. Use Gator foam board or comparable board as the base board. The collage/assemblage must be flat.

Critique Discussion Points

Describe the elements on your board.

How do your choices of color, texture, type treatments, and graphics reflect the destination culture?

How do your choices address the audience profile?

Why is your board effective as a visual "map" for a creative team?

Vocabulary

target audience, strategy, rationale, objective, venue, behavioral outcomes

References and Resources

Creative sources for materials are key to this assignment. Collect color swatches and wallpaper samples from paint stores; look to fabric stores for material and novelties and to import stores for ethnic and cultural artifacts.

Evaluation Criteria

Presentation

Research Paper

Quality of Design

Overall Rating

Destination Suggestions

Ivory Coast

Finland

Turkey

Malaysia

Nepal

Costa Rica

Argentina

New Guinea

Demographic Profiles

Gen X	1961–1981, 20 million, spending power of $20 billion
Gen Y	1979–1994, 71–80 million, 3 times larger than Gen X
Baby Boomers	1946–1964, 76 million, 29% of U.S. population

In Review

1. Define research in your own terms and discuss the scope of research for graphic designers.
2. What are the four psychological foundations of human activity? Describe each one.
3. What are Blumer's three core principles of symbolic interaction? Define them in your own words.
4. Give an example of how design is dependent on any aspect of symbolic interaction.
5. What are the four Perry levels of intellectual maturity?
6. Name the branches of communication design and give an example of each one.
7. Define *knowledge*. What makes up knowledge?
8. What is visual thinking? What does it involve for designers?
9. Describe the seven stages of the creative process.
10. What is the difference between a goal and an objective?
11. What are the two branches of media?

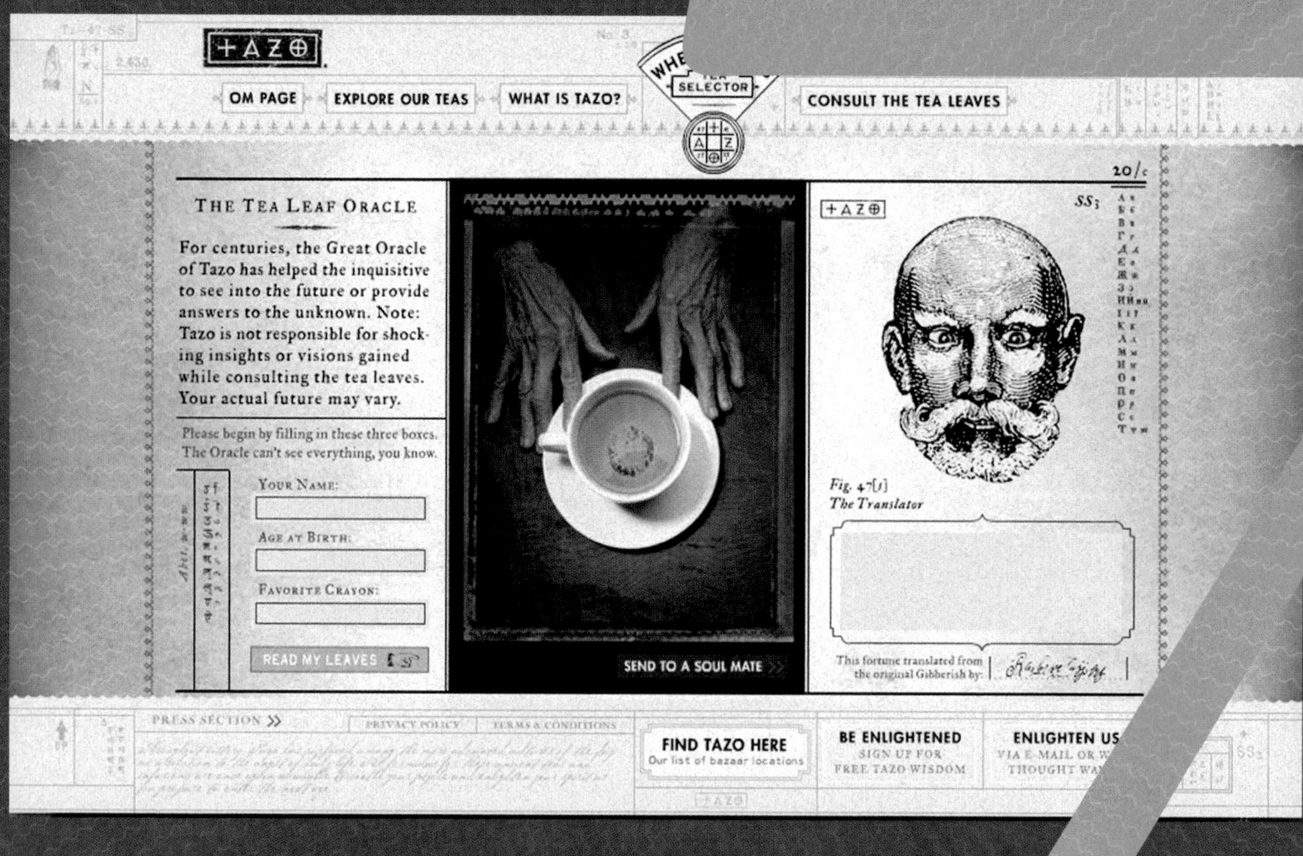

7 MEDIA *for* COMMUNICATION ARTISTS

objectives

Discuss the different media options available to graphic designers

Explain how graphic communication and media are interrelated

Explain how media can affect the delivery and perception of graphic content

Develop a historical awareness of the evolution of graphic communication and media

Explain how technological advancements have affected media development

Discuss how new and traditional media are combined in graphic communication

introduction

This book includes many visual examples of how graphic design works effectively in the environment. In some instances, you have seen how design works in magazines, books, newspapers, and other print media. Other visual examples presented have included how design is used in electronic media such as television commercials and Web sites. Other types of design examples have included signage, posters, billboards, and packaging.

In all instances, this book discussed how design elements and principles work to communicate verbal and pictorial content effectively. Although these principles and guidelines are important aspects to developing a better understanding of how to present a communication message in a way that attracts and engages an audience, nothing has been said about the delivery of this content.

Delivery of design content involves media. In addition to understanding how to design for different types of media, graphic designers also are involved in determining the best media for delivery of a graphic message. This chapter is devoted to media and the ways media affect graphic design and communication.

MEDIA THEN AND NOW

To better understand how media functions in the contemporary world, it helps to have an overview of the kinds of visual media that are used and the way they have evolved in Western culture.

The discussion will begin with what media is and does. A medium is the delivery means or channel for communicating a written, verbal, or visual message. A medium (or media if you are referring to more than one type of medium) can take any form. Examples of print media include magazines, books, billboards, newspapers, annual reports, brochures, and newsletters. Electronic media includes all broadcast media such as television, radio, film, and the Web. You experience some media, such as TV and radio, as passive participants, meaning that you are unable to respond directly or control how you perceive or interact with the medium or its message. On the other hand, interactive media refers to Web sites, CDs, and other means where the receiver of the message can respond to or interact with the media. Other types of media include posters, point-of-purchase displays, signage, and other situations where the message is posted in the receiver's environment. Later this chapter will discuss in more detail how these different types of visual media are most effectively used in design and communication.

Media is composed of the materials and tools involved in delivering a message. In contemporary culture, people continue to use media that has been in use for centuries, such as paper and pen. However, other materials and tools used today reflect the technological advances that have taken place over time. In addition to traditional forms, media today also includes a blend of sophisticated machinery and digital technology.

To better understand the various ways media functions in design and communication, it is helpful to know how media and visual communication have evolved.

Early Media Forms

As a graphic designer and communication artist, you will work with media that gives visual form to verbal content, a process called *graphic communication*, or communication through words and pictures. People have made use of graphic communication since prehistoric times, when pictorial representations of animals, human forms, and symbolic shapes were painted on the walls of caves. In fact, the earliest form of media that have been discovered are these crude paintings that provide some insight into how these ancient cave dwellers lived (see Visual 7–1).

Over time, these crude images evolved into more simplified pictorial representations called symbols or hieroglyphics. As primitive cultures developed more sophisticated means of communication, these primitive symbols evolved into pictograms or more abstract symbols. The ancient Egyptians were one of the first cultures to communicate with a combination of imagery and hieroglyphic symbols that they painted on papyrus, a type of paper. These ancient manuscripts also could be described as an early form of media (see Visual 7–2).

Ancient Near Eastern civilizations also developed their own written language, which they inscribed on clay, stone, metal, and other hard materials. The early pictograms that were used in this language, called cuneiform, evolved over time to a more abstract series of symbols in a linear style that were better suited to inscription on clay. These clay tablets, another primitive form of media, were then sun-dried or baked in kilns (see Visual 7–3).

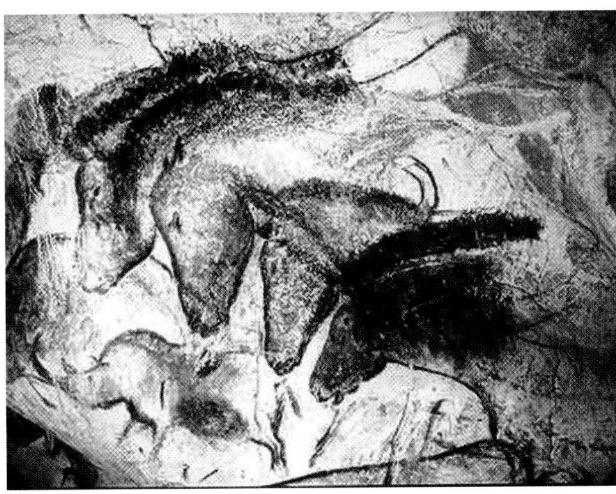

visual |7-1|

The crude imagery painted by ancient cave dwellers gives people an awareness of the lives of their primitive ancestors.

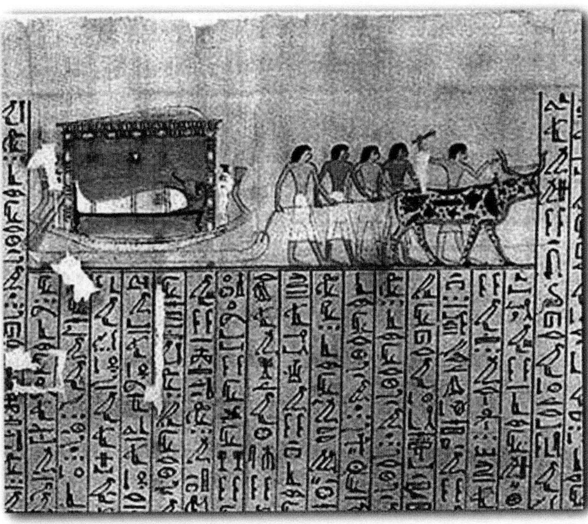

visual |7-2|

Early manuscripts were created by the ancient Egyptians, who painted imagery and hieroglyphic symbols on papyrus, a form of paper.

visual |7-3|

Early pictograms that served as the basis for today's alphabet were used to depict objects such as an ox (left) and a house (right).

The Phoenicians reduced the cuneiform script used by the Assyrians to a collection of twenty-two characters that came closer to today's alphabet. These ancient characters were adopted first by the Greeks and later by the Romans to an alphabet very similar to the one used today. (see Visual 7–4).

During the Middle Ages, the written word was available only to the ruling class, bishops, and religious scribes. However, during this period, early forms of today's media began to take form. Bibles and psalm books were hand-assembled for wealthy merchants, the nobility, and the monasteries. These early Christian doctrines, called illuminated manuscripts, were meticulously penned by religious scribes with a feather quill on vellum, a very thin sheet of calf or sheep skin (see Visual 7–5).

Letter	Unicode	Name	Meaning	Sound	Corresponding letter in				
					Hebrew	Arabic	Greek	Latin	Cyrillic
𐤀	□	ʾāleph	ox	ʾ	א	ا	Αα	Aa	Аа

visual 7-4

The alphabet used in written communication today evolved from the ancient Phoenician alphabet.

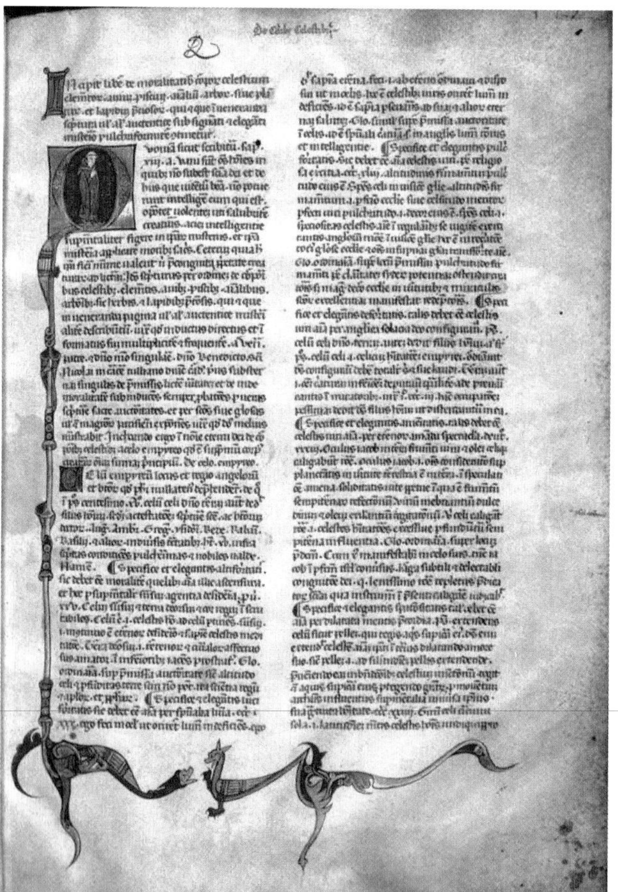

visual 7-5

Illuminated manuscripts were highly detailed religious books written by hand in gold, silver, and vivid color pigments.

During the Renaissance, mass production of the printed word became possible as a result of the efforts of Johannes Gutenberg, who is credited with the invention of movable type. Gutenberg developed a process of crafting single letters from brass and casting them in molten metal. Words were created by assembling these letters onto a flat printing surface that was then inked. Gutenberg used a crude press to transfer the inked text onto paper. His knowledge of typography and ability to design a printed page is evident in a Bible he printed in the mid-fifteenth century (see Visual 7–6).

Gutenberg's invention of movable type and the printing press was the first time mass communication was established through the printed word. After his death in 1468, publishing flourished in Europe and Great Britain. The printing method he invented, called letterpress, was widely used for printing up until the early twentieth century and is still in use today.

From the Renaissance through the industrial revolution, printing was the most common form of media. Newspapers, books, handbills, and posters were used to educate, entertain, and keep the public informed of current events and opportunities. During this period, visual communication as it is known today began to evolve in a way that integrated graphic and fine arts to further serve communication. Lithography, a means of printing from inked stones, was developed during this period of time and allowed artists such as Henri de Toulouse-Lautrec to reproduce colored imagery (see Visual 7–7).

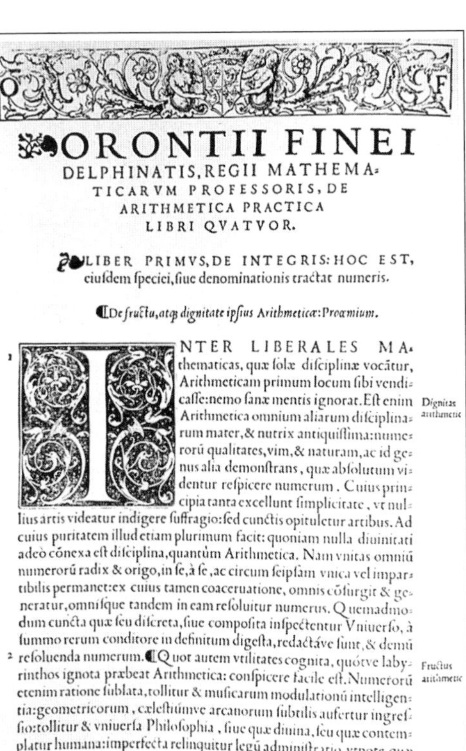

visual 7-6

The classic beauty of this page from Gutenberg's 42-line Bible is timeless in its skillful handling of layout, typography, and imagery.

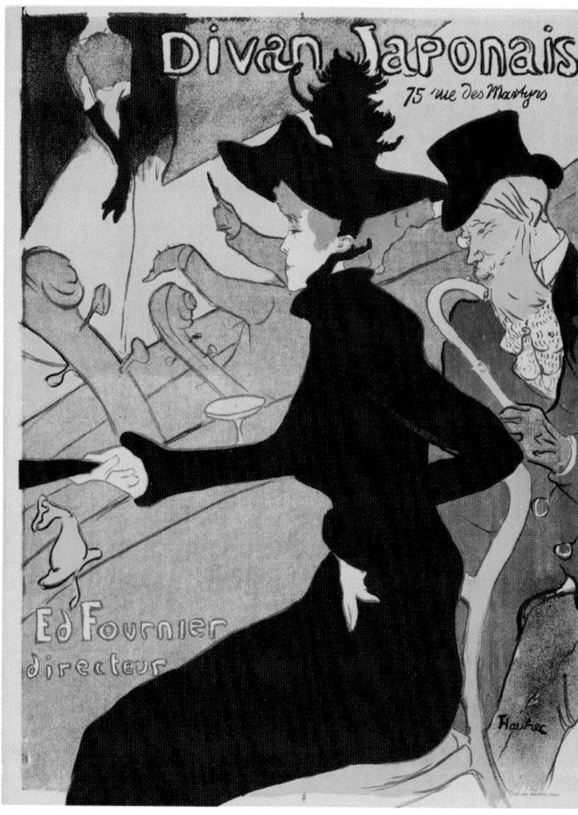

visual 7–7

Lithography was a printing medium that French artists such as Henri de Toulouse-Lautrec used to print color posters. *(Image of* Divan Japonis *courtesy of Digital Image The Museum of Modern Art (Licensed by SCALA/Art Resource, New York))*

Media's Coming of Age

Mass media began to shift to electronic media with the invention of motion pictures at the end of the nineteenth century. Going to the cinema became a popular form of entertainment in the early twentieth century, initially with silent movies. The introduction of sound technology in the late 1920s ensured that motion pictures would continue to evolve as a popular form of entertainment.

Early forms of animation incorporating stop motion also began to evolve in the early 1900s. Character animation was introduced by early cartoonists such as Winsor McCay, Pat Sullivan, and Max Fleischer. These animated features were offered as "shorts" in theaters along with featured motion pictures (see Visual 7–8).

In the 1920s, the Disney empire began when its founder, Walt Disney, developed his own animated cartoon characters. Disney initially created a character called Oswald Rabbit who appeared in silent animated shorts. However, Disney made history when he introduced the first successful sound animated film, *Steamboat Willie*. The animated cartoon featured a new Disney-designed character, Mickey Mouse. Disney also was one of the first animators to incorporate Technicolor in animation with his *Flowers and Trees*, an award-winning animated feature released in 1932.

In addition to entertainment, broadcasting began to take hold as a news and advertising medium when the radio came into common use in the early 1900s. As its popularity and accessibility to the public increased, radio began to replace newspapers and other print media as a means of communicating news and entertainment (see Visual 7–9).

visual |7-8|

Gertie the Dinosaur was the first animated cartoon distributed for public viewing. Released in 1914 and conceived and produced by *New York Times* cartoonist Winsor McCay, the silent animation lasted seven minutes and incorporated 10,000 inked drawings similar to the one shown here.

visual |7-9|

Radio became a popular form of electronic/broadcast media in the 1900s. Early radios called crystal sets were much larger than today's radios and required headsets for listening.

However, one of the most important advances in media technology came into being when television was introduced in the 1930s. Television blended sound with visual impact and began to replace radio as the broadcast media of choice for news and entertainment. Although the technology for television existed in the 1930s, broadcasting was experimental in those early years. After World War II, returning GIs and their families began to spend the savings they had accumulated during the war years, purchasing homes, cars, and luxuries denied to them during the war. In the late 1940s, an explosion of television sets occurred in the U.S. marketplace, with a sales boom occurring in England a few years later. By 1950, more than 8 million televisions existed in U.S. homes and 107 television stations were broadcasting. By the mid 1950s, color television was introduced.

Graphic design for motion pictures and television began to develop during this period. The popularity of these media and the attention they drew from consumers resulted in some noteworthy design achievements. William Golden, art director for Columbia Broadcasting System (CBS) for almost two decades, designed one of the most successful trademarks of the century for CBS. The CBS pictographic eye is such a classic icon that it still remains in use today, looking just as fresh as more contemporary logos and trademarks (see Visual 7–10).

The work of Saul Bass, another influential designer of the midtwentieth century, also featured prominently in broadcast and entertainment media. Bass worked as a designer for the movie industry, designing posters and titles for motion pictures (see Visual 7–11).

visual |7-10|

The iconic CBS logo was designed by William Golden in 1951. When it first appeared on television, it was featured as a translucent icon hovering in the sky. *(Logo design by William Golden)*

visual |7-11|

Saul Bass designed titles and posters for more than fifty films during the course of his career. One of his most well-known designs was for *The Man with the Golden Arm*, released in 1955.

As technology evolved over the latter half of the twentieth century, the computer gave designers more creative options in electronic media. Graphic communication became more sophisticated as designers incorporated computer animation into their designs (see Visual 7–12).

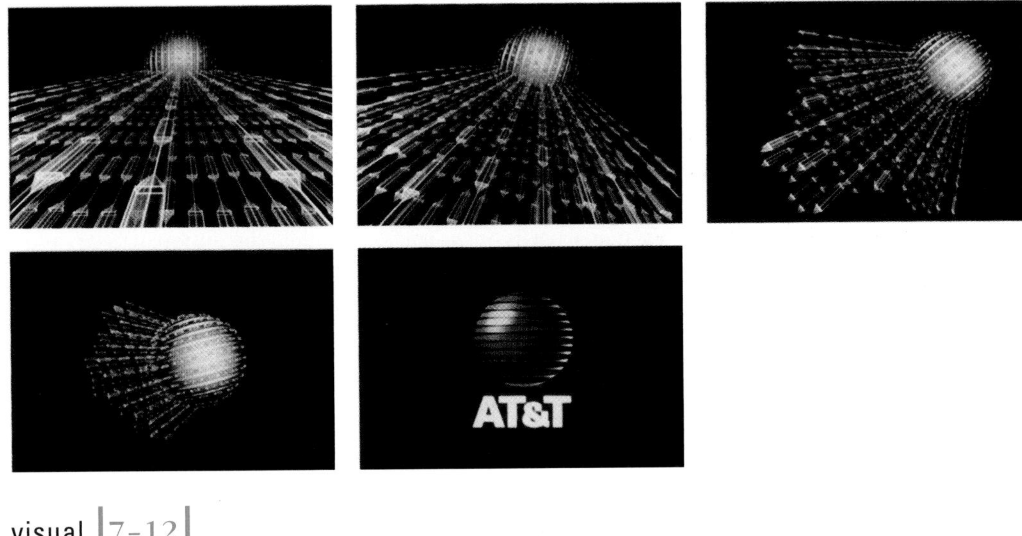

visual |7–12|

Saul Bass's AT&T logo design was featured as part of the corporation's television commercials. The computer animation starts with a spinning globe. As the globe gathers electronic bits of information, it gradually transforms into the AT&T logo. *(Design by Saul Bass & Associates)*

The Form of Media

When describing various kinds of media, it is helpful to distinguish between the media that the designer uses in the design process versus the media that is used to distribute the design product. To avoid confusion, the industry uses terminology to make this distinction:

- *Vehicle* refers to the materials used to physically produce the work. Examples include the computer, paint, pen and ink, and charcoal.
- *Venue* refers to the form the design assumes. Examples include electronic, print, environmental, and consumer product.

AN OVERVIEW OF NEW MEDIA

The end of the twentieth century heralded the digital revolution—a technological advancement that is comparable to the industrial revolution in terms of its impact on the way people live and work. As the industrial revolution moved people into the age of machines, the digital revolution pitched them into the age of computers.

The computer not only impacted the way designers work with and perceive typography, imagery, and two-dimensional design, but also profoundly affected the way designers react and interact with graphic communication. The result has been the invention of an assortment of media options the industry has dubbed "new media." Although that term is commonly used and accepted, *new media* is somewhat misleading in the sense that what is "new" now will likely be antiquated, or "old," tomorrow. But in this book, the term will be used to describe computer-generated media that goes beyond the two-dimensional realm, including interactive media, the Web, and multimedia.

New media presents different challenges for designers than conventional media. Interactivity, globalization, and blending of graphic design with audio and cinematic media are among the many aspects that designers need to consider when approaching new media. Later, this chapter will discuss in greater detail how the design principles presented earlier in this book can be applied to new media. For now, it is helpful to have an awareness of what the differences are between interactive media, the Web, and multimedia and where those media technologies overlap and how they have evolved.

Interactive

Interactive media allows the user to respond to, or control his or her media experience. Unlike books or film that require a viewer to process information in linear sequences, interactivity is nonlinear. It allows the viewer to access information on an individual basis according to his or her preference.

In its most basic form, interactivity is the ability to activate a link by placing a cursor over a keyword or an icon and clicking the mouse. This aspect, called hypertext, was one of the earliest forms of interactivity offered by Apple in the early days of computer graphics; hypertext was part of the software set (it was a collection of programs—set seems to describe this better) that came with Apple's personal computers. This technology has been adapted to the World Wide Web using *hyperlinks*, highlighted or underlined words, phrases, images, or icons that are coded to link to another part of a Web site or to a different Web site.

Before the Internet came into wide use, interactive programs were available on diskette. Some of the earliest applications were offered as educational programs and games. As technology evolved, CD-ROMs (compact disc read-only memory) allowed more digital information to be stored: animation, illustration, photography, sound, text, and video.

Since then, interactive media has become far more complex, combining audio, visual, and cinematic communications to form a body of information. In addition to the Internet, interactive technology is now available on DVDs, as electronic games, on cell phones, and as part of other evolving technologies.

The Web

The Internet was originally developed in the 1960s by the U.S. government as a covert system that would facilitate communication in the event of a nuclear attack. During the Internet's experimental stages, the government allowed access only to private users. In 1982, the National Science Foundation refined the system and made it accessible to computer research labs and institutions of higher learning. Legislation in the early 1990s made Internet technology available to public schools, two-year colleges, and businesses. That legislation encouraged digital pioneers to develop the technology necessary to transmit words, graphics, sound, photography, and video, furthering the Internet's growth. By 1997, more than 30 million users in more than 100 countries were linked via the Internet. This figure increased to 120 million in 1999. By 2002, 580 million people were using the Internet. At the time of this writing, it is estimated that more than a billion people are connected to the Web.

The popularity of the Internet has resulted in an increasingly global marketplace. As a consequence, designers who design for the Web must be aware of how they are communicating in a cross-cultural environment. In addition to developing a visual approach that will connect with a multicultural audience, Web site designers have been challenged by globalization to adapt their sites to include multiple languages (see Visuals 7–13a, 7–13b, and 7–13c).

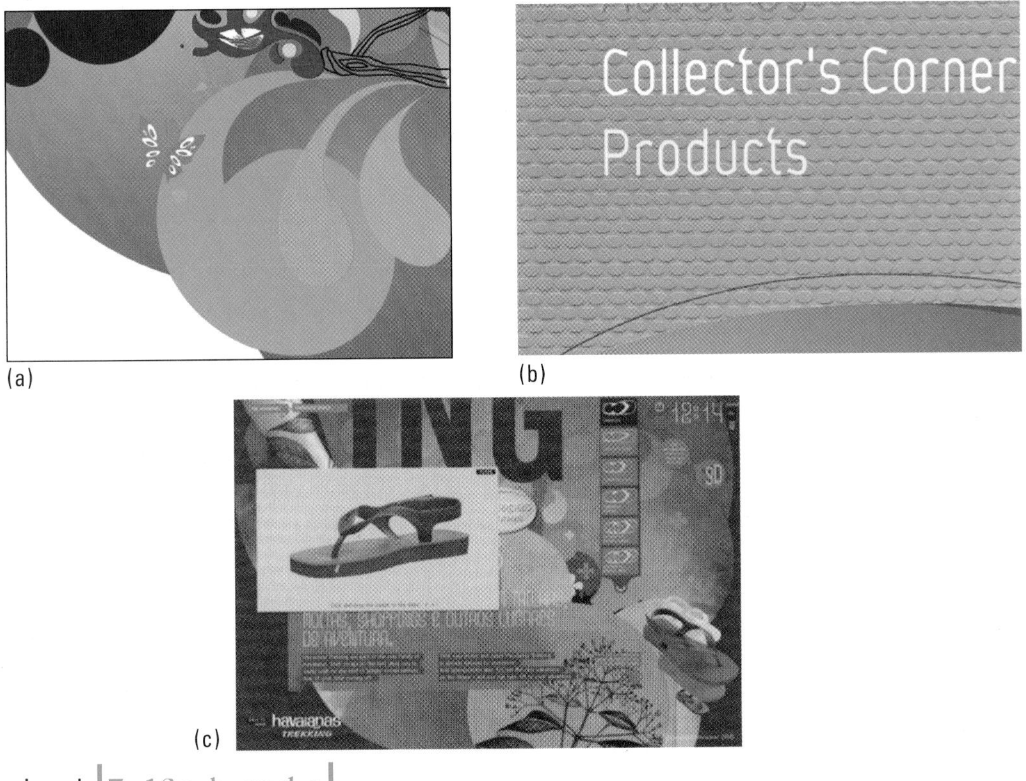

visual | 7-13a, b, and c |

Havaianas, a Brazilian manufacturer of sandals, has adapted its Web site to three languages. The site features elaborate animation and a fashion sensibility with broad appeal for its multicultural audience. *(Web site design by Sergio Mugnaini, Marcello Serpa, and Adhemas Batista)*

The Internet also has blurred the lines of media as they are known today. Until recently, media had fallen into two camps: mass media (such as broadcasting), and personal media (such as books), where communication takes place on a more intimate level. The Internet can do both. It lets anyone broadcast content to millions of users, but also facilitates interactivity, allowing users to respond to the communication they are receiving by navigating, providing feedback, and even making purchases.

Multimedia

The term *multimedia* is most often used to describe the integrated interactive formats that have evolved as a consequence of sophisticated digital technology. Multimedia technology blends animation, streaming audio, and video with text, imagery, and interactivity.

Multimedia has become an important component of today's Web and interactive technology. Today's Web sites come alive with animated graphics and audio/video technology (see Visual 7–14).

Beyond Web sites, multimedia applications include video and computer games. It is important to clarify that not all interactive media is multimedia. Web sites, DVDs, and other interactive technologies that are limited to text and imagery are not regarded as multimedia.

(a)

(b)

(c)

visual 7–14a, b, and c

Multimedia is an important component of this Web site offering high school football players instructional tips from top players, trainers, and college coaches. Visitors to the site can watch videos of training camps and learn from exclusive interviews with NCAA football coaches. A 3-D video game adds even more appeal for the site's youthful audience. *(Nikegridiron.com Web site design by Matt Howell, Winston Binch, Can Misirlioglu, and David Hyung)*

Making an audio, video, or animated sequence used to require a huge production crew with special expertise and skills. However, today's technology has made it possible for a designer to work alone in the creation of a multimedia project. Although a designer may be tempted to do it all, designing for multimedia requires an understanding of the technology involved as well as knowledge of time-based media. Graphic designers often collaborate with other media specialists in the production of audio, video, and animated sequences. In addition to graphic design, multimedia often requires script writing, animation, illustration, photography, live-action production, special effects, music creation, and video/audio editing.

ELEMENTS, PRINCIPLES, AND NEW MEDIA

The design strategies discussed earlier in this book apply to the Web, interactive media, and multimedia in the same way they apply to print. Design that supports the communication goal and is directed in a way that is appropriate to the intended audience is just as important in new media as it is in any two-dimensional design application.

The guiding principles of design also apply to multimedia, the Web, and interactive media. Pages that are part of a Web site are similar to brochure pages in that they involve a balanced arrangement of graphic elements. Web pages require designers to pay attention to typography and to use an underlying organizational grid to help unify the pages and make them reader friendly. Color has the same emotive and aesthetic possibilities on a Web site and for a multimedia application as it has in print media (see Visual 7–15a, Visual 7–15b, Visual 7–15c, and Visual 7–15d). Likewise, imagery that is compelling in an ad is likely to be just as arresting on a Web site.

However, new media design and communication differs from print in that it is time-based. Print designers often do not consider time as a factor; but on the Internet, every minute counts. Content needs to be streamlined and presented in a way that makes it easily accessible. The excessive time involved in navigating or waiting for a series of Web pages to load can alienate potential browsers or cause them to lose interest in a Web site.

Let's look at other design considerations that are unique to new media.

Motion

Motion graphics are a major factor in new media. Motion involves composition over time and space; individual frames are not as important as the cumulative effect of these images over a period of time.

Although type on a printed page is not inherently dynamic, computer technology lets designers animate type and give it movement. Instead of formatting type so that it is read in a linear format, designers have the ability to configure type so that it moves across the screen in a way that supports a verbal message.

Motion design involves a story or a sequence of events and requires prior planning. Sequences that last less than a minute still need to be sketched out in storyboard format, viewed, and then revised and refined before they are actually developed. Storyboards are typically hand-drawn so they are clearly seen as being developmental (see Visual 7–16).

(a)

(b)

(c)

(d)

visual | 7-15a, b, c, and d |

The Corzo Tequila Web site uses many of the design principles mentioned in Chapter 1 of this book. A grid is used to organize information on each page. A consistent color palette, typography, and graphic approach helps unify the pages. *(Web site design by Firstborn)*

Audio/video productions involve even more elaborate planning. Before production can begin, an outline is prepared; then a script is written. Character developers and illustrators are brought in when animation needs to be developed. Actors need to be hired and briefed when a video is developed. Sequences need to be storyboarded and revised. Music and sound effects also need to be planned and developed.

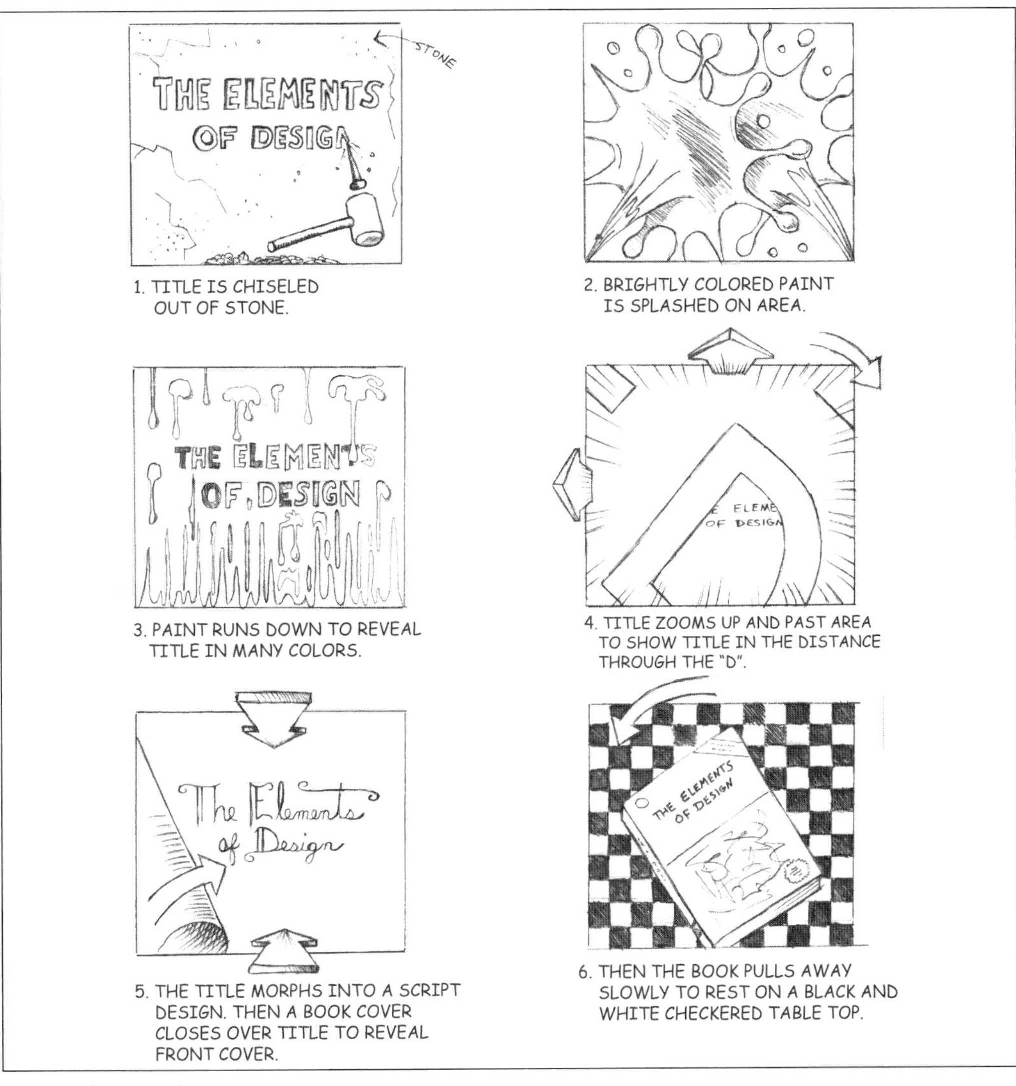
STONE
THE ELEMENTS OF DESIGN
1. TITLE IS CHISELED OUT OF STONE.
2. BRIGHTLY COLORED PAINT IS SPLASHED ON AREA.
THE ELEMENTS OF DESIGN
3. PAINT RUNS DOWN TO REVEAL TITLE IN MANY COLORS.
4. TITLE ZOOMS UP AND PAST AREA TO SHOW TITLE IN THE DISTANCE THROUGH THE "D".
The Elements of Design
5. THE TITLE MORPHS INTO A SCRIPT DESIGN. THEN A BOOK COVER CLOSES OVER TITLE TO REVEAL FRONT COVER.
THE ELEMENTS OF DESIGN
6. THEN THE BOOK PULLS AWAY SLOWLY TO REST ON A BLACK AND WHITE CHECKERED TABLE TOP.

visual | 7-16 |

Storyboards are typically hand-drawn to distinguish them from a completed project. In the case of this animated sequence, movement is given to type and imagery.

Web Site Design

Like print design, Web site design must support the communication goal and the purpose of the site. Web sites exist for many reasons. Some sites serve as sources for information, while others provide entertainment. Web sites also promote services, products, organizations, and events. In addition to advertising and promotion, many Web sites allow users to make online purchases of the products they are promoting. The design of a Web site should support and facilitate its purpose.

Web site design requires developing an information architecture, or an underlying structure for the site. Users must be directed to the portions of the site that are pertinent to their needs and guided through a sequence of pages. Before they begin to design, Web site designers usually establish a site map that serves as a blueprint for the site's logistics. Site maps usually start as rough sketches; then they are fleshed out into more comprehensive studies that show where type and images will fall.

Web sites challenge designers to make the most of theme and variation. Web pages must be unified and visually connected in a way that makes them work together as a cohesive whole. However, each page also must be able to stand alone and work effectively by itself (see Visual 7–17a, Visual 7–17b, Visual 7–17c, and Visual 7–17d).

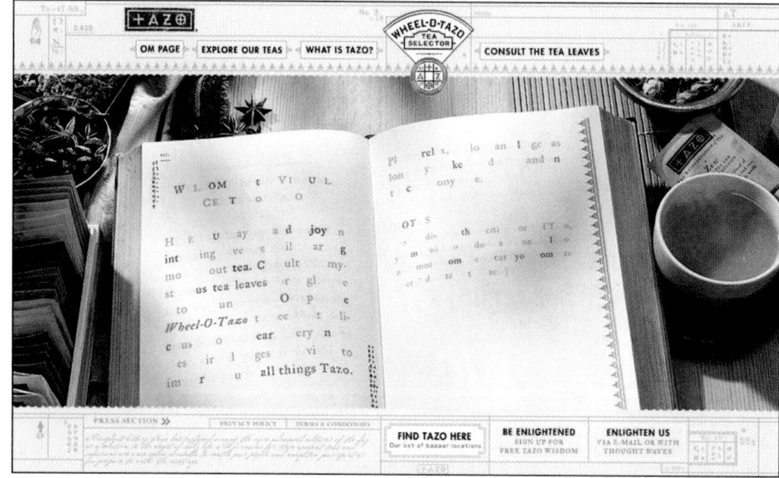

(a)

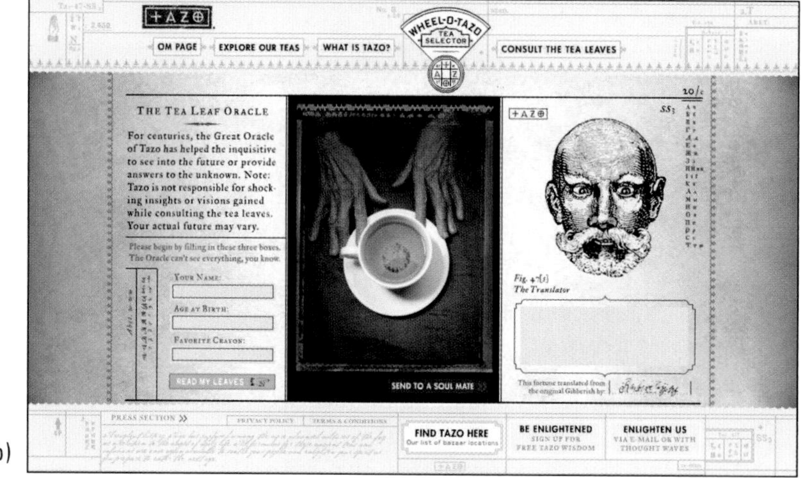

(b)

visual | 7-17a, b, c, and d |

TAZO Tea creates an online brand experience for visitors to its Web site. The site's opening pages take readers through a tea leaf reading. Other portions of the site get users acquainted with a variety of tea-related products. Although the various parts of the site are different, they appear unified as a result of a consistent graphic palette. The various arrangements of these graphic elements on each page add theme and variation to the site. *(Web site design by Steve Sandstrom, Jon McVey, Sandstrom Design)*

Many technical considerations are involved in Web site design. Web site designers need to be conscious of how type will read on a screen. Small type is not as difficult to read in print as it is on a computer screen. Style sheets need to be developed to ensure that type and layouts will look the same on all computers. Designers need to make sure that a Web site will work on all types of platforms and browsers, including older versions, as well as a range of screen resolutions. There also is an increasing need to adapt Web site design to evolving technologies. Today's Web sites need to look just as good on a cell phone or a Palm handheld as they do on a computer monitor.

(c)

(d)

THE RIGHT MEDIA CHOICES

Not too long ago marketing and communication specialists took a shotgun approach to their use of media. Mass media such as newspapers and broadcasting were more commonly used with the assumption that sending a message to the largest number of people would be the best way to elicit a response.

However, today's communicators realize that choice of media is an important consideration in the delivery of a message. In his books, *The Gutenberg Galaxy, Culture is Our Business*, and *The Mechanical Bride*, writer and sociocultural guru Marshall McLuhan asserted that the medium is the message. The various media options available today provide different experiences for their audiences. Some media are more specialized or provide a more intimate experience for the intended recipients than others. These differences need to be considered when making a decision on which medium or media to choose.

New Media vs. Traditional Media

As was mentioned earlier, some media, such as newspapers and broadcasting, reach a wide range of people. These media also are appropriate channels for disseminating large bodies of information. In a newspaper, this information would take the form of an article; on television, a program.

Magazine articles and books are similar in that they are content-heavy; however, they differ from newspapers in that they are usually directed at smaller audiences. Magazines are especially effective at targeting a specific demographic. Browsing the magazine racks at any store will yield a range of publications addressing a variety of interest areas, from kayaking to wedding planning. The industry uses the term *narrowcasting* to describe communicating through media that focuses on a narrow audience with a specialized interest.

Magazines and books also are intimate media in that that they provide a one-on-one experience with their audience. This experience is substantially different from the shared experience of viewing a television program or a movie as part of a group of people.

Today's media planners know when to take advantage of broadcasting and narrowcasting in their media campaigns. In fact, the best media campaigns use a combination of media to deliver a message. Because too much information can overwhelm an audience, media campaigns often use advertising in magazines, in newspapers, or on billboards, as well as broadcast media such as TV to communicate a simple message. When an ad captures a viewer's attention, the message may include a Web site address so interested individuals can follow up and find more information by going online.

Communication specialists are beginning to realize that advertising and promotion are occurring more frequently on the Web, particularly to target a youthful demographic. Online marketing is more of a grassroots approach. Online marketing is especially effective when the site becomes a venue for entertainment and information, in addition to product promotion and facilitation of online purchases. Savvy communicators realize the importance of developing a promotional strategy that ties in with online marketing (see Visual 7–18a, Visual 7–18b, and Visual 7–18c).

(a)

(b)

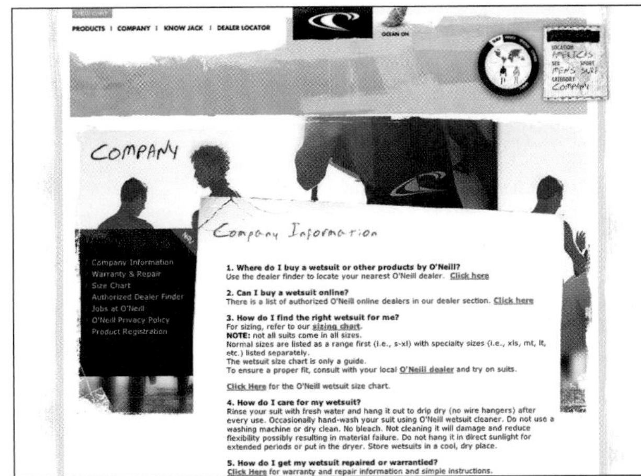

(c)

visual | 7-18a, b, and c |

The O'Neill surfing gear Web site combines a raw, grunge aesthetic with action shots of surfers. In addition to promoting surfing gear and the surfing lifestyle, the site also serves as a source of information about upcoming events. It facilitates purchases in that its deep links to specific product pages allow users to e-mail the pages to others with whom they want to share their preferences. *(Web site design by 2Advanced Studios)*

My Family "Census" Site

Accessing the U.S. Census Bureau's extensive database became much easier, thanks to the efforts of Ancestry.com. The Web site gives prospective members a taste of the rich family history that can be built using census data by allowing visitors to subscribe to Ancestry.com for a two-week trial period. During that time, subscribers can link with the U.S. Census Bureau's database to retrieve more than 140 years' worth of information based on their family history. Hornall Anderson Design Works, the firm involved in the site's design, was challenged to create a site with links to the U.S. Census Bureau's microsite, as well as to develop a look that would appeal to a broad audience ranging from children to seniors. The design team used vintage imagery and typography to project an aesthetic that communicates the site's historical theme with a color palette that combines dark brown and rich sepia tones with contemporary color accents.

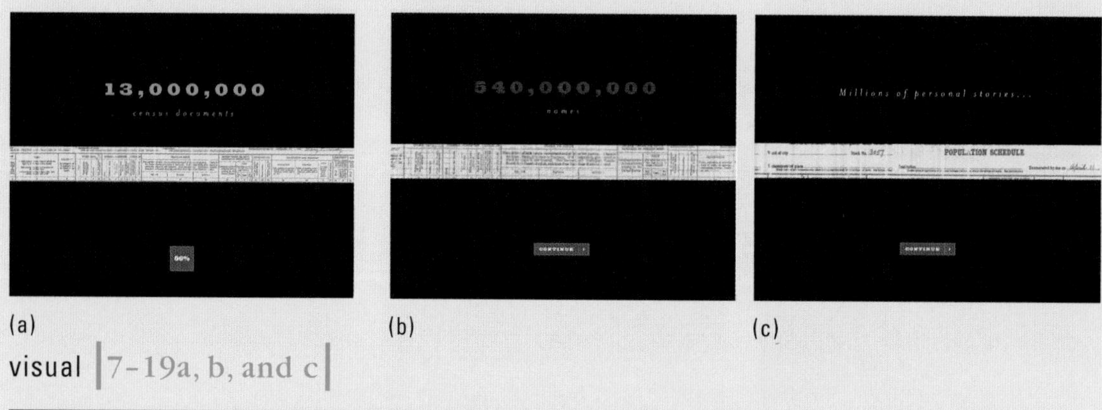

(a) (b) (c)

visual | 7-19a, b, and c |

An animated sequence plays while the Ancestry.com Web site loads onto the viewer's computer. The opening sequence reminds visitors of the enormous amount of information available in the U.S. Census databank. The site's color palette and typography are established with this splash sequence.

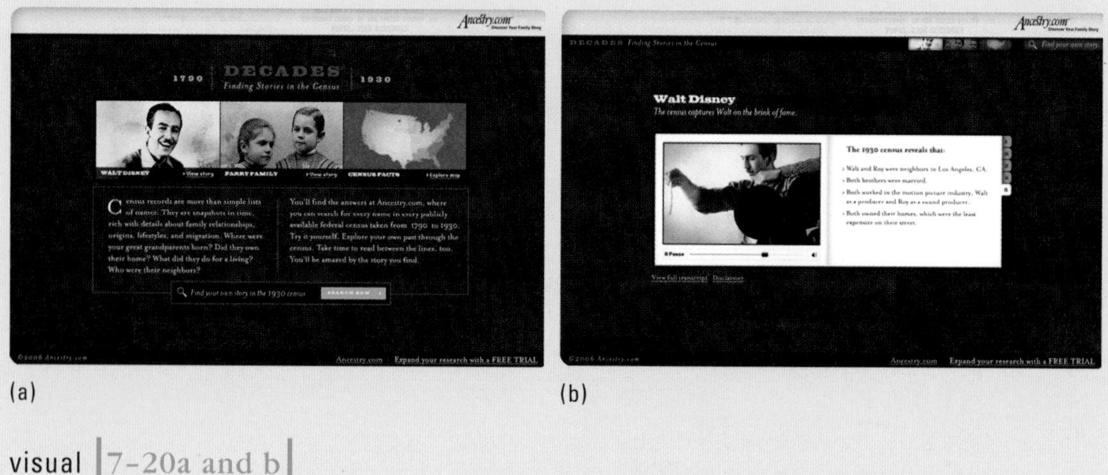

(a) (b)

visual | 7-20a and b |

Example stories draw the visitor in to learn how the data can be used to research a particular family or a person's life, while historical facts give a sense of the larger context.

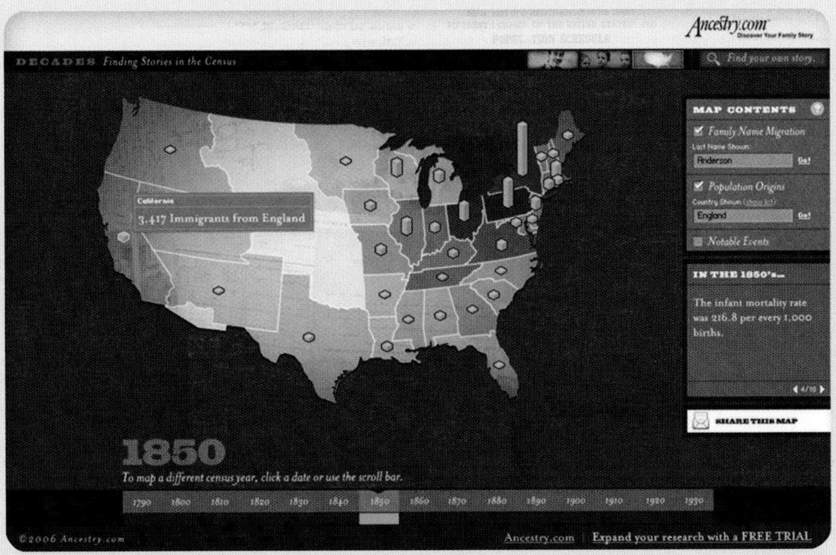

visual |7-21|

Visitors also can see population and immigration trends and trace the migration of a family name with a series of interactive maps of the United States. All of the pages of the site are unified by the consistent treatment of color and type.

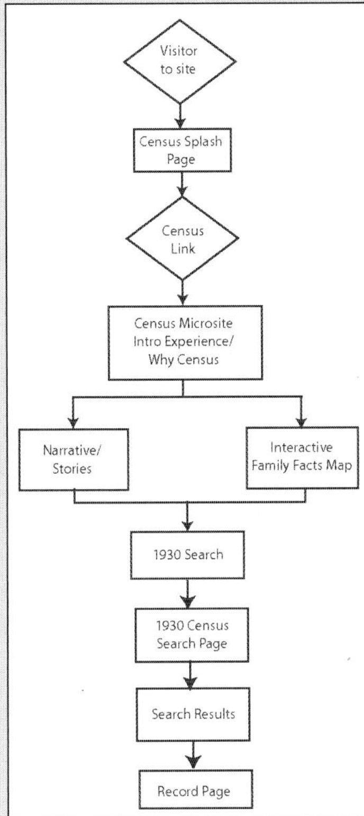

visual |7-22|

The Web site's map serves as a blueprint for how the site is structured and shows how visitors are linked with its various pages.

THE DESIGNER AT WORK

It's important to draw inspiration from outside of the field. There seems to be this fascination with speed and technology which leads to an incestuous cycle of everything looking the same because everyone has the same tools and is easily seduce by them. As a designer/director try to experience new things, new cultures and travel. Explore the analog world as well as the digital. Don't lose sight of your own voice. There will always be a new plug-in or software package to learn. The question is what ideas to do you have to contribute?

—Tuesday McGowan

tuesday mcgowan

Motion graphics designer Tuesday McGowan is one of a new breed of designers who started in traditional media and expanded into new media as technology evolved and became more advanced. McGowan is a 1986 graduate of the University of Cincinnati, where she initially majored in industrial design and later in communications. After graduating, McGowan worked as an assistant in a photography studio where she was able to get a taste of filmmaking.

McGowan moved to San Francisco in 1994, where she found opportunities to meld her experience in design, communication, filmmaking, and photography into the newly developing field of motion graphics. She was one of the founding members and the creative director of WIG, the graphics arm of Western Images SF. At WIG, McGowan started taking advantage of developing digital technologies by incorporating computer graphics and live action into her design work. Her career path in San Francisco eventually landed her a position as director of design at Radium, an award-winning broadcast, film, television, live-action, and design studio. While working at Radium, McGowan also directed live-action projects through Los Angeles production company Picture Park.

In 2002, McGowan returned to Cincinnati to work for Lightborne, a motion design and production studio composed of designers, directors, animators, editors, illustrators, sound designers, and effect artists. As co-creative director for Lightborne, McGowan is involved in music videos, television commercials, and other entertainment and promotional venues that involve motion graphics. She has received many awards for her directional work. Clients and projects she has been involved with include ESPN, MTV, VH1, Comedy Central, Fuel TV, Lifetime, Adidas, Levi's, Discover Card, and Compaq, as well as music videos for Sheryl Crow and Soundgarden.

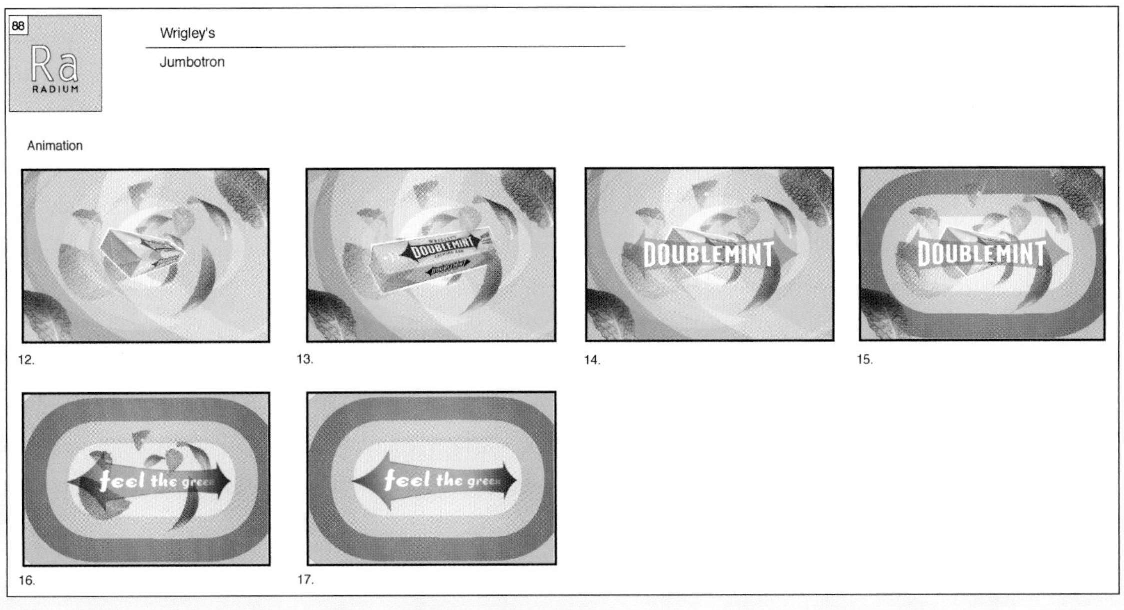

McGowan's work involves animated promotions such as this one for Wrigley's Doublemint gum. The animated sequence appeared on the Times Square Jumbotron in New York City.

This series of stills represent frames from "Pattern Skies," a music video for the Greenhornes.

SUMMARY

A medium is the delivery means or channel for communicating a written, verbal, or visual message. Electronic media can take the form of broadcast media such as TV, film, and the Web. Print media includes magazines, books, newspapers, and brochures. In addition, media falls into categories where the recipients are passive participants or where the recipients can interact with the media experience.

Media involves materials and tools and, in its simplest form, consists of pen and paper. Media has evolved over time to encompass a broad range of sophisticated tools. In ancient civilizations, media took the form of clay tablets or crude pigments applied to paperlike substances. Media as it is known today began to develop with Gutenberg's invention of movable type and the printing press around the time of the Renaissance. Electronic and broadcast media evolved during the twentieth century into the realm of technologies used today. Contemporary digital media are called new media and include interactive media, the Web, and multimedia.

New media differs from print media in that new media is time-based and involves motion, or a sequence of events. However, the elements and principles of design have application in new media just as they do in more traditional types of media. Designers and communication specialists understand the advantages of the various types of media available and know how to choose and combine them to make the biggest impact on a message or campaign.

projects

Project Title Forms in Motion

Objectives

Work with moving elements in a sequential series of compositions

Produce a short story using a consistent and limited number of elements

Create a storyboard or digital video pitch

Description

Work with (1) a circular form or object, (2) a facial feature, (3) a word, and (4) a line or linear element to develop a series of five black-and-white compositions. Control the visual relationship of the elements so they work together in a harmonious manner and create a sequence. You will be managing the four compositional elements and directing their movement through the series. Essentially, this series of five compositions will function like a storyboard. To achieve movement, manipulate size, scale, direction, proximity, orientation, and value.

Limitations and Materials

Begin by exploring the potential "character" you will be creating with the four composition elements. Work with flat shapes painted with acrylic paint or gouache and magazine clips. If you are working on a computer, use digital imagery and a photo editing or digital drawing program to generate ideas for composition elements. Once you have generated a library of compositional elements and imagery, sort and edit them and choose the four with which you will work.

Next, explore the movement and relationship of the four elements in the five compositions. You can work this stage at a scale of 4 inches by 4 inches. Use a combination ofdrawing, photocopying, and collage to explore solutions at this preliminary stage. Determine how much movement or change will occur through the series by studying and making incremental changes in the relationship of the elements. Use a grid of 9 or 16 units to help you make decisions about placement. Mount the five finished compositions in sequence on gray matt board.

Critique Discussion Points

How effectively does continuity of movement work in the series?

Does the series have aesthetic continuity?

Describe the narrative quality or theme of the sequence.

Does the sequence tell a story?

Vocabulary

narrative, sequential, theme, visual movement

References and Resources

South Park, Steamboat Willie

Project Title Hierarchal Progression

Objectives

Work with a hierarchal progression of graphic elements

Create a logical progression to communicate a visual theme

Manage theme and variation with a series of compositions

Description

Develop a series of five compositions in three colors working with (1) a single statement and (2) a line or linear element. Start by exploring statements that communicate an idea or a theme that can be visually supported with the design principles you have learned about in the earlier chapters of this book. Your statement must consist of at least eight and no more than twenty words. When you have developed your statement, research different typefaces to find several that support the statement's meaning. Break the statement down into five parts to develop a logical sequence of words and phrases. Each of these five parts of your original statement will be formatted and arranged in a 4-inch by 5-inch horizontal composition. Narrow your selection of typefaces to one or two fonts and explore visual possibilities by experimenting with the scale and placement of the words in each composition. Develop arrangements that support the meaning of your statement or add emphasis where needed. Apply your knowledge of balance, proximity, and proportion to develop interesting and/or aesthetically pleasing compositions.

You also must include a linear element in each of your compositions. Explore possibilities that support the meaning of your statement. Your linear element may be curved or straight and of any thickness. It can be repeated in each composition and throughout all five, or it can appear as a single element in any of the compositions and as multiple elements in another. When you are pleased with the compositions you have developed, select a color palette consisting of three colors that support the theme or meaning of your statement. Apply these colors to the type, background, and linear elements in your five compositions. Use your knowledge of theme and variation to create a cohesive series.

Limitations and Materials

Work on the computer to find typefaces or fonts for your statement. Work in a drawing program such as Adobe Illustrator or CorelDRAW to play with typographic arrangements in a 4-inch by 5-inch format. When you are satisfied with your arrangements, print them and use a pencil and pens and tracing paper to experiment with linear and color applications. Use the computer to add linear elements and color and to finalize your compositions as computer-generated color prints. Mount the prints in sequence on gray matt board.

Critique Discussion Points

How does the arrangement of type and/or the typeface support the statement's message?

How do color and the treatment of the linear element support the message?

What design principles are used to create emphasis?

What aspects of the compositions help to unify the sequence?

Vocabulary

triadic palette, figure-ground ambiguity

Resources and References

Avenue A/Razorfish, Mobium

In Review

1. How do television and the Web differ from each other in the ways in which they engage a viewer?
2. With what is Johannes Gutenberg credited?
3. How has media evolved during the twentieth century?
4. With regard to media, what are the differences between vehicle and venue?
5. How do interactive media, the Web, and multimedia differ from one another? What do they have in common?
6. How has the Internet affected communication?
7. What is a site map? How does it function in Web site design?

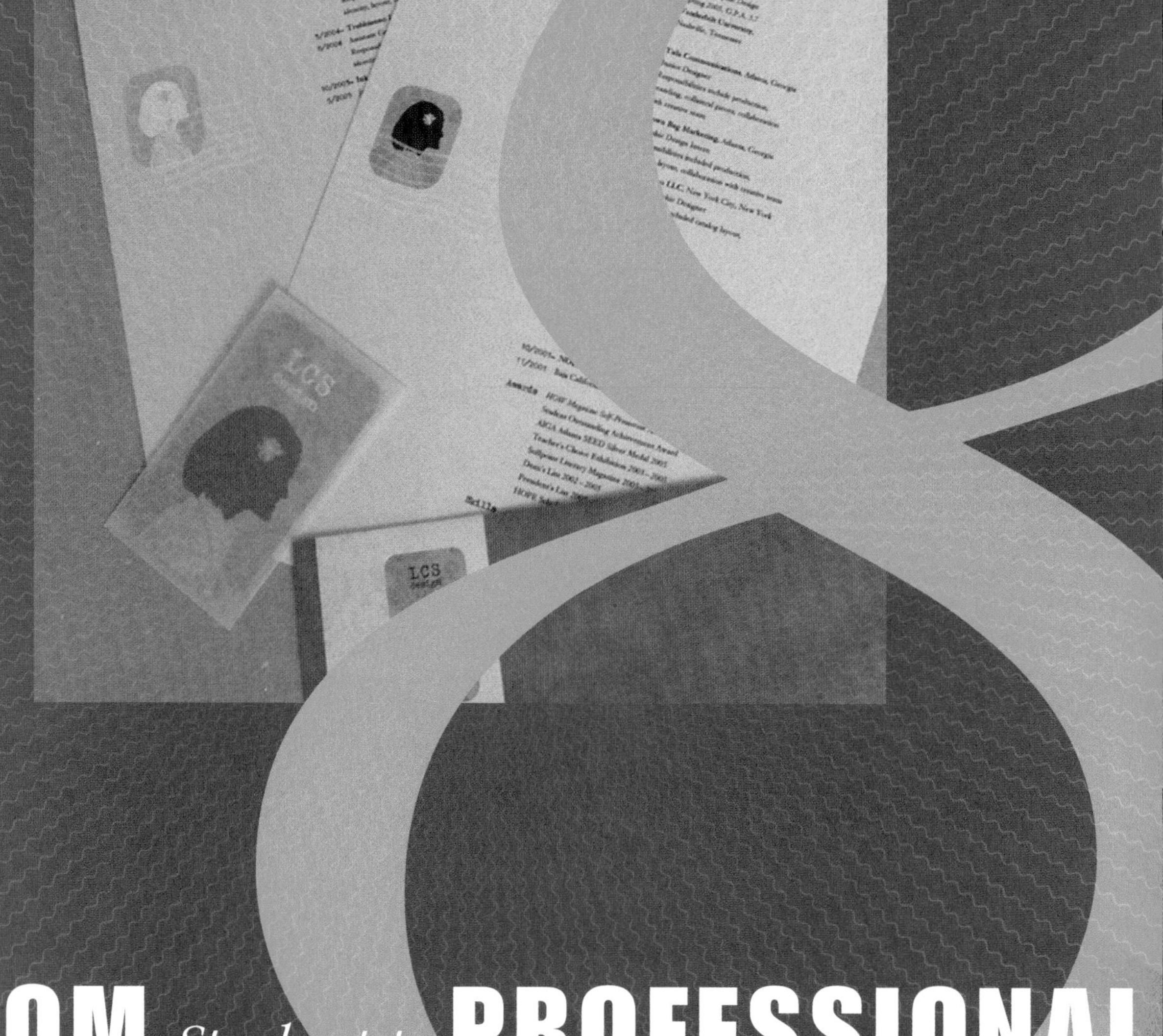

8 FROM *Student to* PROFESSIONAL

objectives

Explain how the field of graphic design developed and what it encompasses today.

Discuss career options in the graphic design industry.

Discover what will pique the interest of a prospective employer and help land a job interview.

Prepare a suite of promotional materials, including a résumé and letterhead.

Prepare and present a portfolio of your design samples.

introduction

Students of graphic design are often in the dark about what lies ahead after they receive their degree.

Those of you right out of school may be tempted to take the first design job that comes your way. But because so many professional opportunities exist in the design industry, you should consider getting involved in an area of design that speaks to your personal interests and can make the best use of your capabilities. To help you determine where your best fit may be, this chapter explores specialized areas of design, the places they are practiced, and the kinds of skills these design disciplines require.

In addition to having a career direction in mind, you also will want to develop a portfolio and strategy for finding a job. The design industry is very competitive. Unlike some professions where prospective employers come to campus to recruit graduates, employers looking for designers traditionally have relied on recent or soon-to-be graduates to come to them. A portfolio plays an important role in the recruiting process by demonstrating what you have learned and how that expertise has manifested itself in prototypical design solutions. By looking at your portfolio, prospective employers can determine if and how their organization can use your design capabilities.

In this chapter, you also will discover what employers look for in a portfolio and learn how to present your work in a way that demonstrates your problem-solving and communication skills—assets for anybody seeking a salaried position, but especially important for someone who wants to be a successful designer.

HOW GRAPHIC DESIGN FUNCTIONS IN BUSINESS AND COMMERCE

The field of graphic design initially grew out of the need for businesses to promote their goods and services. In the early part of the twentieth century, this promotion was fairly straightforward and limited to newspaper ads, billboards, posters, handbills, packaging, and signage. Designers also were hired by publishers of books, newspapers, magazines, and sheet music.

Over the years, as marketing and communication became more sophisticated and media options expanded, design grew to encompass an ever-widening range of venues. Today graphic design touches people in so many ways that it is almost impossible to avoid. When you pay a bill, the invoice to which you are responding and the postage stamp you use to mail your payment involved a designer. Turn on the TV, and you will find many design applications: commercials, the opening credits for a film, or a network logo, to name just a few. The interface of your computer software, search engines, and Web sites involved designers. At the supermarket, the product packaging, store signage, and magazines at the checkout counter all required design expertise. Even the currency and coins you use to pay for your purchases involved a designer.

Design Firms

When individuals or organizations need design expertise, they usually seek the services of a design firm. Design firms provide graphic design services to all types of businesses. They are hired by other providers of creative services, such as advertising agencies, financial institutions, manufacturers, retailers, and service providers.

A design firm can consist of one person or many individuals, and the services a design firm provides can be far-ranging or specialized. For instance, some design firms may limit their practice to environmental graphics or focus exclusively on brand development and package design. Design firms offering specialized services frequently serve a clientele that extends beyond the firm's regional area. Other design firms provide a broad range of services to local clients.

In addition to doing different types of design, design firms sometimes differ from one another in the aesthetic approach they take. In fact, it is not unusual for clients to select a design firm based on a look they know is a specialty of that firm. When adding to their staff, design firms sometimes seek designers whose aesthetic sense is in tune with the firms' standards.

Other design firms seek to diversify, looking to add employees who bring design sensibilities and areas of expertise the firms may not currently have on staff.

In-House Design Departments

Because of the large volume of design they need to produce, publishing houses, retailers, and large corporations often hire their own designers. An in-house design department may consist of one designer or a staff of designers who work with other company personnel to develop and implement design concepts.

Graphic Design: An Evolving Discipline

The activity of design has evolved over many centuries. The wall paintings in the caves of Lascaux, ancient writing systems such as the Sumerian pictographic writing and cuneiforms, and the Belleville Breviary illuminated manuscript are examples of visual communication through the millennia. These and many other forms of communication throughout history have played a profound role in defining the contemporary notion of design.

But the idea of graphic design as a discipline, driven by process and problem solving, was born in the twentieth century.

The industrial revolution spawned the need for market-driven communication, and the Bauhaus school provided a model. Since then, education, industry, society, culture, and technology have helped shape the field of design. Those forces also contributed to the nomenclature or designations that have been used to describe the areas in the field. It seems that the field is continually defining what it does by defining the various functions within it.

The field of design is a hierarchy composed of a group of disciplines that include graphic, fashion, industrial, and interior design. Each of those disciplines, in turn, is composed of specialty niches that constitute service to specific markets or industries. Graphic design encompasses work produced for print and digital communication.

Some niches are exclusively in the domain of one or the other type of communication, whereas other niches can be served by both print and digital communication.

For example, package, poster, catalog, and most publication design is exclusive to print production, whereas Web design, e-zines, and television graphics obviously function in the electronic realm. But other design categories function in both. Advertising, mail order, magazines, corporate identity, information, and promotional design rely on both print and electronic media.

Environmental, display, and exhibition design depend on a variety of fabrications; and they are three-dimensional in nature. Signage systems, theme parks, trade shows, transportation systems, events, and educational exhibits are included in the three-dimensional design arena. Industrial or product design is dependent on graphic design where surface graphics and product identification are concerned.

In the advent of technological advances at the end of the twentieth century (namely, electronic media) and the move toward a service-dominated economy rather than an industrial-based economy, graphic design became driven more by information and communication. New professional titles such as information architect and communication designer place special emphasis on the conceptual nature of the work.

The term *visual communication* is used interchangeably with *graphic design* but is, in a sense, more comprehensive.

Visual communication and communication arts encompass a full range of graphic arts that includes graphic design, illustration, multimedia, photography, television, film, video, and a variety of hybrid media. It is difficult to pinpoint the origin of the terminology, but it likely has evolved from the advertising industry and design education.

In-house design departments offer designers a chance to work in an area of special interest.

For instance, a designer who is drawn to fashion may want to work for a clothing retailer.

Other businesses needing in-house designers include manufacturers of sports equipment; record companies; and a wide range of nonprofit organizations such as museums, charities, and political groups.

Because their size allows them to put together health and profit-sharing plans that may be unavailable to smaller firms, corporations frequently can offer their in-house designers generous benefits packages and other perks.

SPECIFIC AREAS OF DESIGN

Now you will examine some specific areas of design, the kinds of expertise required, and the way a designer functions in these venues.

Advertising

Advertising agencies typically handle all aspects of marketing and promotion for their clients, developing a strategy and then implementing a plan that involves a variety of media applications.

Ad agencies hire designers to work as part of a team that involves sales and marketing personnel, copywriters, production coordinators, and media specialists.

Advertising-related print design typically includes magazine and newspaper ads, point-of-purchase displays, billboards and transit ads, sales and promotional brochures, posters, fliers, direct mail, and coupons. Ad agencies also use designers to develop other media advertising, including Internet marketing, Web sites, and radio and television ads. Designers involved in television advertising often help brainstorm concepts, produce storyboards, and design graphics for television commercials. Good verbal skills and the ability to come up with creative and innovative concepts are important to designers in this field.

Although advertising agencies hire designers to work as part of their staff, they also hire other creative personnel and firms to help them in their work, often subcontracting copywriters, photographers, illustrators, design firms, and other suppliers in implementing their projects.

Brand Design and Development

Branding is the consistent application of a brand's logo or trademark and visual identity on all of the brand's products and services. Brand designers are contracted by a client to conceive an overall look for its product line or services and to implement the scheme on all packaging and promotional venues. Branding may include a variety of media as well as vehicle, building, and uniform applications. In addition to designing a look that will work in a range of situations, brand designers often are involved in the early stages of a brand's inception, helping to develop a name as well as a logo and visual scheme. The ability to develop a flexible design scheme that works in two- and three-dimensional applications as well as packaging is important to being successful in this field.

Design firms specializing in brand design and development are sometimes called brand consultancies and are often larger than most design firms, staffing anywhere from 20 to 200 people.

In addition to designers, writers, and administrative personnel, design firms hire production experts who understand the materials and processes unique to packaging. Clients are typically large corporations needing to promote and market their products across a broad constituency.

Interactive and Web Design

Firms specializing in interactive and Web design typically get involved in CD design as well as Web site and Web banner ad design. In addition to design personnel, firms specializing in this type of design often staff marketing and promotional personnel as well as technology experts who are responsible for doing intricate coding and staying on top of current technologies.

Firms involved in this type of high-tech work often create motion graphics and other special effects for television and film.

Because interactive multimedia involves animation and sound, designers specializing in this field need to have technical aptitude and an understanding of animation, interactive design software, and Web design software as well as the ability to think beyond visual terms. Understanding how to organize information and visualize it in terms of flowcharts or navigational maps also is an asset.

Editorial Design

Editorial designers work with editors and publishers in the design of books, magazines, and newsletters. These designers range from independent freelancers or design firms contracted to do newsletter or cover designs to in-house designers employed by publishers.

Book and magazine design requires designing covers as well as working with text and imagery within a design theme that involves many pages. However, magazine and book design differs in that books represent a one-time design challenge; that is, when a book design is completed, a designer can move onto a new project. Because they are periodicals, magazines require a designer to work within an established design structure over many issues.

A knowledge of typography, an aptitude for organizing information, a love of the written word, and enthusiasm for a specialized area that a magazine addresses can be assets for designers considering this field.

THE DESIGNER AT WORK

"You realize how much there is to learn after you graduate."

—Lindsay Salet

lindsay salet

Like many high school seniors who enter college with an interest in but limited exposure to visual and communication art, Lindsay Salet was not aware of graphic design as an educational or career option when she started her freshman year at Vanderbilt College. During her first two years of college, Salet fed her interest in art by taking several fine arts studio classes along with her academic requirements. When she realized that Vanderbilt would not allow her to declare a major in studio arts, she decided to transfer to a college that would enable her to explore her interest in visual arts.

Salet initially enrolled in the University of Georgia (UGA) in Atlanta with the idea of majoring in printmaking. However, she came into contact with a graphic design major there who introduced her to the field of graphic design and the program at the school. Salet decided to apply to the school's graphic design program, which has stringent requirements. Although she had fulfilled all of the program's prerequisites, Salet was not accepted the first time she applied. Unwilling to give up, she took additional courses and reapplied the following year with a positive outcome.

Salet graduated from UGA in 2005 with a BFA in graphic design. While working on her degree, she benefited greatly from experience she received working at several internships, including one with a fashion-related firm in

New York City. Although she was offered a job with this company upon graduation, Salet decided to stay in Atlanta, where she took advantage of another design internship at a business-to-business marketing firm. Building on her experience (and adding pieces to her portfolio with each internship) put Salet in a position where she was able to find a salaried position as a junior designer six months after graduation. She advises recent graduates to look for positions that provide an opportunity to learn from others. "The worst situation you can be in is to be dropped into a firm where you're the only designer or you're just working with junior designers," she states. Salet found her job by networking and following job leads in the Atlanta area.

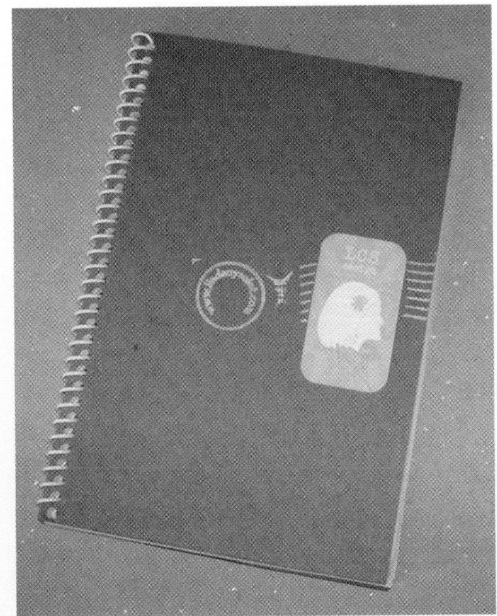

Salet's "mini-book" self-promotion won an Outstanding Achievement award in *HOW* magazine's Self-Promotion annual. Each translucent vellum sleeve bound within the book contains a postcard-size sample from Salet's portfolio. Her logo, which appears as a custom emblem on the cover of the mini-book, also appears on her letterhead, business card, and résumé. In addition to her logo, Salet's suite of promotional materials are tied together by a postal theme, including rubber-stamped lines that simulate the USPS cancellation mark.

Environmental Graphics

Environmental graphic designers design and develop systems of words and iconography that help guide others in identifying and finding what they need in unfamiliar surroundings. Firms offering this expertise understand how to organize information and make it user friendly and accessible, as well as how to work with signage materials and sign fabricators. Environmental graphic designers generally work as part of a team with architects, interior designers, landscapers, and other professionals involved in creating indoor and outdoor spaces. Environmental graphic designers often are brought in at the inception of a project to help in the development of an overall look and visual theme for an environment.

Applications for environmental graphics may be institutional venues (such as universities or hospitals) or recreational venues (such as museums, sports facilities, and parks).

Environmental graphics are also an important component in all kinds of transportation terminals as well as business and retail complexes such as corporate centers and shopping malls.

Finding Work

Those involved in hiring designers say that proven capability is probably the most important factor in landing a job. Your letterhead, your résumé, and other self-promotional vehicles you have designed promote your capability when you contact a prospective employer for an interview. At an interview, your portfolio serves as additional proof of your design and production capability and the way you present your portfolio shows pride in your work and the ability to package and display it professionally.

Career Tips

- Subscribe to one or two industry publications to stay current with design trends and directions in the field. If you cannot afford them, make a regular trip to the library periodicals section.
- Use a planner to help you manage time and projects. Establishing the practice of time management will keep you organized. Being liberated from having to remember dates and deadlines will allow you to use your brain for creative thinking.
- Visit design studios and firms in your city or plan to visit them when you travel. While you are a student, professionals tend to be very open to sharing their time, expertise, and work. Once you are a peer, you are perceived as competition and have fewer doors open to you.
- Join professional organizations or local groups of professionals in the graphic arts field. Some organizations have student chapters that offer events and services at a reduced cost. Membership is the best way to meet other young designers and professionals who can give you invaluable advice, direction about your work, and leads for jobs.

Getting Your Foot in the Door

Showing your portfolio to prospective employers is critical to landing a job. However, gaining access to those in a position to hire you is often difficult. Competition for design jobs is fierce; and sometimes a résumé sent with a cover letter requesting an interview is not enough to prompt someone to respond, especially when you are right out of school and your résumé shows little or no professional design experience.

To attract the interest of prospective employers, recent graduates and others new to the profession often create a self-promotional suite—something that demonstrates their design and conceptual capabilities in a single mailing. If it is successful, it will act as a lure by piquing the interest of its recipient and prompting her to want to see your portfolio. Even if you decide to develop a Web site on which prospective employers can view your work, a self-promotional suite that you mail to a firm is often necessary as a means of luring someone to your Web site. In addition, industry veterans like to see and experience how a student manages the paper choices and other considerations involved in developing a stationery system.

To develop a successful self-promotion piece, base your strategy and concept development on these considerations:

- Visual unity—A self-promotional suite typically has several components: an envelope or another shipping container, letterhead, a résumé, and possibly other materials that demonstrate your capabilities. Come up with a visual theme that works for all components.
- Intrigue—An effective self-promotion piece needs to be packaged in a way that will engage and prompt a response from your recipient. Think about what is most likely to catch her attention. It is probably something that deviates from the usual business mail—something large or colorful or three-dimensional (see Visual 8–1).
- Surprise—Something that surprises or makes an impact is more likely to leave a memorable impression than something that meets your recipient's expectations (see Visual 8–2).
- Staying power—A self-promotion that remains on a recipient's desk or gets used is more likely to serve as a reminder of your design capability. That is why coffee mugs and calendars are popular self-promotional vehicles.

Your self-promotion piece also should reflect the type of work you want to do. For instance, if you are interested in Web design, your piece should be an interactive CD or another device that leads

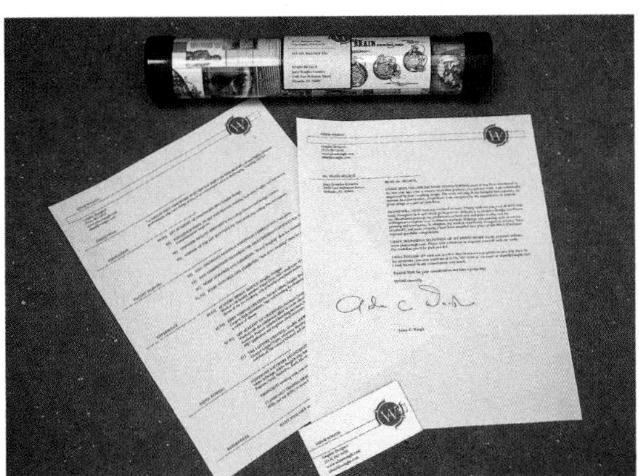

visual 8-1

This student self-promotion consists of a clear plastic mailing tube retrofitted with a printed representation of samples from the student's portfolio. The recipient gets an immediate impression of the student's work, and the mailing tube is more likely to attract attention than a standard envelope. Inside the tube is a letter requesting an interview, a business card, and a résumé. All materials are unified with a distinctive logo, the first initial of the student's last name. *(Self-promotion design by Adam Waugh)*

recipients to your Web site. If you want to do packaging, your self-promotion piece should involve a three-dimensional container.

Preparing a Portfolio

You need to begin by determining what size and type of portfolio case you want. Portfolio cases come in sizes ranging from 8 ½ inches by 11 inches to 34 inches by 42 inches. Although the trend in recent years has been toward smaller portfolios, you should pick a size that is large enough to accommodate your biggest piece and that is an appropriate size for carrying or shipping.

Portfolio styles can be broken down into three basic categories: clamshell boxes, binders, and attaché cases. Clamshell boxes are most suitable for shipping. But for one-on-one interviews, binders with acetate sleeves or attaché cases are your best options for portability. Which type you choose depends on your need for flexibility (see Visual 8–3).

visual 8-2

Memorable self-promotions sometimes incorporate a visual theme that plays on the individual's name. This self-promotion for recent graduate Craig Bell is a case in point. The promotional mailer features a series of cards that combine vintage imagery and typography to form "bell" words. *(Self-promotion design by Craig Bell)*

visual 8-3

Binders that display design samples within acetate sleeves and attaché cases containing samples mounted on boards generally work best for one-on-one interviews. They come in a variety of materials including vinyl, leather, cloth, and the leather and metal finishes shown here. (*Portfolio photos furnished courtesy of Pina Zangaro)*

If you want to be able to customize or rearrange your portfolio, samples mounted on illustration or matt board are far easier to shuffle and rearrange than sleeves in a binder. Mounted samples should be displayed on neutral-colored mount board with a 2-inch to 3-inch margin. Gray is usually better than black or white because it works equally as well as a backdrop for light- or dark-colored work. It is important to keep the board size and color consistent. Nothing can detract more from your work than samples mounted on boards that are of varying color and size.

Limit your boards to one or two sizes. It is best to start with the largest board that will fit within the dimensions of your attaché case. From there, come up with a smaller size that is proportioned to fit within this area so you can stack the smaller boards to fill the same area. (For instance, if your largest boards measure 12 inches by 16 inches, your smaller samples could be mounted on boards half that size or on boards 8 inches by 12 inches.) Although mounted samples offer flexibility, their downside is that they tend to show wear and tear. You can protect samples by covering them with a flap or protect samples and boards by wrapping them in acetate or inserting them in vinyl sleeves.

Presenting Your Portfolio

Before you contact a firm for an interview, you should know something about the organization's work. Prospective employers want to feel as though you are interested in what they do. But more importantly, you will want to know about a prospective employer's clients and the types of projects the firm takes on so you can determine whether the situation is a good fit for your skills and career goals. Most companies have a Web site that you can find through online search engines.

When you arrive at your interview, try to position yourself at the corner of a conference table or desk so you and the viewer are looking at the portfolio together, with you sharing rather than showing your work. You want to create an environment that is conducive to establishing rapport.

Prepare a list of questions about the position and the company's policies, such as performance evaluations, areas of growth for the firm, and its expectations of employees. Remember that you, in a sense, are interviewing the firm as much as it is interviewing you. Taking that mind-set to the interview can give you a measure of confidence that will show in your presentation.

At the onset of your interviewing, a good strategy is to secure one or two interviews at companies in which you are not as interested. You will have had these experiences as practice for that benchmark job you really want.

The Student Portfolio: An In-Depth Look

Student portfolios should show the breadth of experience and include samples that demonstrate capability across a broad range of disciplines: logo and letterhead design, brochures, packaging, ads, and one- and two-color work as well as four-color work. Including work that demonstrates capability in other areas, including Web or interactive design and illustration, also is advised. Visual 8–4 and Visual 8–5 provide a portfolio of a graduating senior in graphic design, Lindsey Salet, and some of the key components of her portfolio.

Salet's portfolio consists of mounted 8½- by 11-inch samples that she transports in an attaché case. Each of her samples is labeled so that those who view them know what types of projects they are. Salet's portfolio samples also are available as a PDF file, which she attaches along with her résumé (see Visual 8–4) to the e-mails she sends to prospective employers.

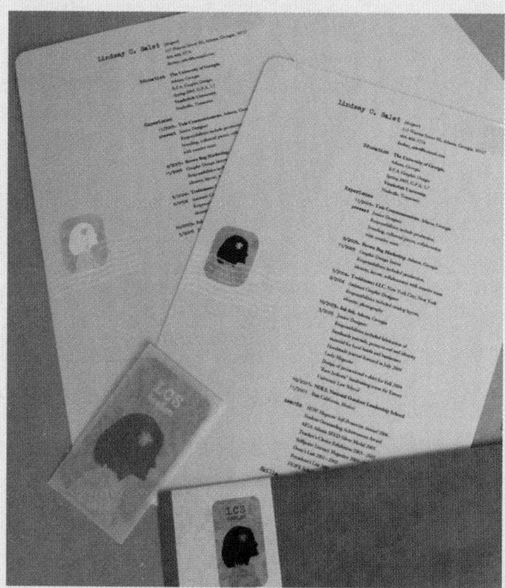

visual |8-4|

Salet's résumé includes all of the information a prospective employer would need to consider her for a design position. In addition to its professional look, the résumé design is stylistically consistent with her stationery system and other self promotion materials.

Avoid the temptation to include in your portfolio everything you have ever done. Instead, narrow down your selection to ten to fifteen samples of your best work. Beginners tend to want to include many projects in the belief that prospective employers will be impressed with the volume of work produced. In the process, beginners include some mediocre work, which tends to water down the overall impression or create a sense of inconsistency. It is far better to limit your portfolio to just eight or nine high-quality samples, as opposed to including pieces that fall below the level of the rest.

Because viewers tend to remember what they saw first and last, begin and end your portfolio presentation with your strongest and most vivid samples. Bold, colorful work tends to make the most lasting impression. Balance the rest of your portfolio by mixing four-color work with limited-color pieces.

(a)

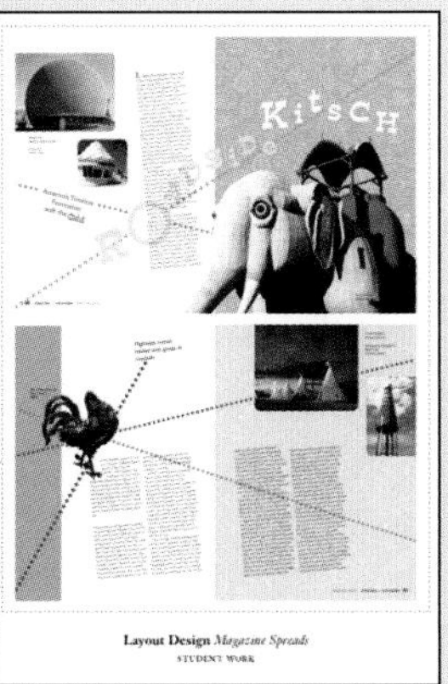

(b)

(c)

(d)

(e)

(f)

visual |8-5a, b, c, d, e, f|

Salet's portfolio demonstrates her breadth of experience as a student by showing that she has done projects in packaging, editorial, identity, and direct mail design.

(a)

(b)

(c)

visual |8-6a, b, c|

In addition to student work, Salet's portfolio includes examples from her internships and projects she did on her own time. Pieces that were produced in a professional setting are especially important to students who want to show they have experience carrying a project through all phases of production.

Students often have difficulty thinking of their work beyond the realm of a class project. But in a portfolio interview, you need to describe your work in real-world terms. When you talk about each piece, describe the communication goal and your design strategy—how the imagery, color, or typography you chose—work in support of this goal. Mention what restrictions, if any, were imposed and what they were. It is important to let a prospective employer know how you solved a communications problem in spite of outside constraints.

Supplement your presentation with a loose-leaf binder that shows some of your process sketches. Prospective employers want to understand how your design concepts develop and see what kind of alternative solutions you may have come up with.

Before you leave, give the person with whom you met your business card and/or résumé. And perhaps most important of all, within forty-eight hours of the interview, send a letter or an e-mail thanking your interviewer for her time.

If you are interested in learning more about the business aspects involved in freelancing, consult the *Graphic Artists Guild Handbook*. You can find information about that book and the Graphic Artists Guild in the Resource section of this chapter.

Pro Bono Work

Donating your creative services (called pro bono work) is a great way for fledging designers and illustrators to gain experience and visibility. Unlike paid projects, where a client's priorities often override or restrict the creative process, pro bono work usually allows creative professionals more freedom to develop a piece that showcases their talents and capabilities. In exchange for their donated time, they have a published piece with a credit line.

Young designers and illustrators often have a chance to showcase their skills by developing Web sites, posters, and other promotional vehicles for art and theater groups. Other possibilities for pro bono work include charity fund-raisers such as walkathons, dinners, and other events. Individuals involved with these causes often have a degree of prominence in the local community and may be in a good position to circulate your name or send more business your way. At the very least, you have a chance to do work with real value that impacts your community.

Is Freelancing For You?

Many students make money doing freelance work while they are in school and build on this income after graduating to establish a successful business of their own making. Freelancing offers many advantages to communication and visual artists, including plenty of flexibility and the chance to choose projects. It may be a viable alternative to being employed elsewhere if you have a great deal of drive and self-discipline and are willing to take on some of the business-related tasks involved in being self-employed. However, not everyone is suited to freelancing. If you think you might like to freelance, here are some important considerations to keep in mind:

- You should be a self-starter who is disciplined enough to get the job done from beginning to end. You also need to be able to work independently. If you have a tendency to procrastinate or need to have others involved to keep you on task, freelancing may not be a good option.
- Unlike a salaried job where sick days are paid for, sick days are lost time and money when you are self employed. At times, you will be responsible for fulfilling your obligations on a project even when you are not are up to the task. Good health, emotional stability, and the fortitude to get the job done even when you are not feeling well are important attributes for working independently.
- In addition to doing the creative work, you are taking on many administrative tasks that include organizing your time and your work environment. You also need to be involved in basic bookkeeping, such as keeping track of income and expenses.
- You need to develop proposals and contracts. Other business-related tasks involved in freelancing include pricing your services and billing clients, as well as collecting on delinquent accounts.
- Marketing skills are essential to maintaining a successful freelance business. You need to be able sell your concepts and communicate your personal vision to those with whom you will be working. If you are not skilled at selling yourself or your ideas, consider partnering with someone who has these capabilities.
- In addition to marketing skills, you need to develop promotional materials. An online portfolio or a Web site, a conventional portfolio, business cards, and stationery are essential to establishing and maintaining a business.
- You have to pay for or go without some of the fringe benefits associated with working elsewhere, such as paid health insurance, pregnancy/sick leave, and vacation time.
- You are responsible for paying Social Security as well as federal, state, and local income tax on the money you make as a freelancer. In addition to filing the forms associated with these taxes, you may have other tax obligations that are specific to where your freelance business is located.
- Many designers and artists prefer the convenience and comfort of working from home as freelancers, while others go on-site to work on a temporary basis for other businesses. If you are working on-site, the government still considers you a self-employed individual operating a business. Your tax obligations and many of the bookkeeping and administrative tasks associated with running your own business remain the same as if you were working from home.

Resources

GRAPHIC ARTS ORGANIZATIONS

ACMSIGGRAPH

www.siggraph.org This organization is made up of a diverse group of researchers, artists, developers, filmmakers, scientists, and other professionals who share an interest in computer graphics and interactive techniques. It sponsors the annual SIGGRAPH conference, focused symposia, chapters in cities throughout the world, awards, grants, educational resources, online resources, a traveling art show, and the SIGGRAPH Video Review.

American Center for Design

www.ac4d.org This national association for design professionals, educators, and students supports design education and promotes the value of design in the business community.

The American Institute of Graphic Arts (AIGA)

www.aiga.org Founded in 1914, the AIGA is a nonprofit organization that promotes excellence in graphic design. With more than thirty local chapters, the AIGA holds a national conference and sponsors annual competitions.

Graphic Artists Guild

www.gag.org This national advocacy organization represents designers, art directors, illustrators, photographers, and others in the industry. It publishes *The GAG Handbook: Pricing and Ethical Guidelines*, a valuable resource for professionals and students.

Society of Illustrators

www.societyillustrators.org The New York headquarters houses the Museum of American Illustration, which promotes monthly exhibits and traveling exhibits of premier illustration. The group also sponsors an annual student and professional competition that recognizes the best in illustration in the United States.

The Society of Publication Designers

www.spd.org This organization offers a monthly newsletter and an annual design competition, and it sponsors a biennial conference that alternates between new media and convention publishing.

DESIGN PUBLICATIONS

CMYK

www.cmykmag.com This quarterly publication is a showcase of the freshest design, illustration, photography, and advertising, featuring work by students from across the United States. Students can have their work submitted by instructors.

Communication Arts

www.commarts.com Published eight times per year, this quality journal features the best of the year's graphic communication. Student subscription discounts make it an affordable publication.

Émigré

www.emigre.com This quarterly magazine showcases work by type designers, illustrators, and others whose work is on the cutting edge of creative graphic communication. Émigré also produces typefaces that it sells from a directory and from its Web site.

Graphis

www.graphis.com This bimonthly graphic design magazine showcases premier design from around the world in a lavish publication.

HOW

www.howdesign.com This bimonthly graphic design magazine covers ideas, techniques, and other aspects of the trade.

HOW sponsors an annual conference and competition.

Print

www.printmag.com This magazine covers the graphic design industry and sponsors annual competitions and national seminars.

STEP Inside Design

www.dgusa.com This bimonthly magazine focuses on how designers, illustrators, photographers, and other graphic professionals create projects from beginning to end.

Wired

www.wired.com This monthly magazine promotes and reports on technological innovation in digital communication, computer publishing, multimedia, and graphics. Social commentary and trendy graphics reflect current pop culture.

U&lc Magazine

www.itcfonts.com/ulc This online magazine is dedicated to typography and the graphic arts. Published by the International Typeface Corporation, U&lc's Web site offers valuable information on type, type history, and use. Fonts can be purchased from the Web site.

WEB SITES

In addition to the Web sites connected with the organizations listed previously, the following sites contain a great deal of information and links to other relevant Web sites:

www.thedesignencyclopedia.org

This online resource includes book reviews, articles, and links to other design organization Web sites.

www.designwritingresearch.org

Produced by design scholar Ellen Lupton, this Web site includes books, products, essays, and teaching materials for design educators. The links portion of this site connects with type foundries, design blogs, and sources for materials and supplies.

SUMMARY

Most of this book has been devoted to presenting design essentials, theories, and strategies. This chapter on preparation for a career in the field focuses on practical information that you may or may not need in the future. However, the goal of your study of design is to become a professional in the field. Visualizing yourself as a working designer can be challenging at the beginning of your studies, but there are things you can do now to help you assume the role of a professional. The portfolios in the professional profiles presented throughout the book and the student portfolio and self-promotion in Chapter 6 are meant to provide a window into the profession and some real inspiration and motivation.

Continue to work on developing your design sensibilities; but also study the work of designers, photographers, illustrators, and artists. Study art and design history to gain an understanding of the world of visual communication in which you are working.

projects

Project Title: Self-Promotion

Objectives

Evaluate your career interests in the field

Research design firms and agencies

Research strategies for self-promotion

Produce a written plan proposal for your promotion project

Produce the visual components to use in pursuing a job

Description

Produce a self-promotion/communication initiative that includes the following:

A written project plan proposal that address the following questions:

What is the project goal for promotion?

What are the specific objectives of the project (tasks to complete, message)?

What is your design strategy?

How do you expect the recipient of the promotional design to respond?

What is your budget?

Personal identity

Logotype, symbol, image, graphic element, stamp, personal look

Apply it to all aspects of self-promotion, including letterhead, envelope, and/or shipping label and business card.

Letterhead/envelope/business card

Portfolio venue

Web site, video, CD, conventional case, cards, unique package tearsheets

Optional ancillary pieces

Giveaways such as stickers, mouse pads, or other novelties

Design the promotion as a suite of related components. Apply the design motif or look to all aspects of the promotion, including the résumé, portfolio venue, and print material.

Limitations and Materials

Materials to produce the self-promotion should be responsive to the strategy and objectives of your proposal.

Complete the written plan proposal before beginning the design of visual components. Word-process and double-space the proposal. Each section must include the necessary explanation and detailing to convey your intentions.

Critique Discussion Points

How does the promotion reflect your professional interest?

Discuss the how the communication message works.

What was the most challenging aspect of the project?

Vocabulary

design strategy, ancillary pieces, tear sheet

Evaluation Criteria

Project Fulfills Proposed Plan

Complete Project Inventory

Quality of Concept

Technical Consistency and Craft

Project Title Résumé

Description

Your résumé presents an opportunity for you to give prospective employers a sense of how well-qualified you are for a position. In addition to stating your qualifications, the design of the résumé gives a sense of your knowledge of typography and design capabilities. Prepare a résumé that gives prospective employers an overview of your education, employment history, and professional capabilities. Design it so that it is visually in sync with your letterhead, business card, or other promotional materials. Résumé areas should be clearly differentiated from one another so they can be found easily at a glance. Use subheads to set these areas apart. Information should be listed chronologically so that the most recent experience comes first. Consult the model included with this project as a guide for structuring your résumé (see Visual 8–6) as well as the other sample shown on page 259.

The information that you feature on your résumé is standard for all types of businesses and includes the following components:

1. Your name, address, and other contact information should be prominently placed near the top of the page.
2. After your name and contact information, you typically list your postsecondary educational background, including your degree or anticipated date of graduation. State the name of the school and your degree and area of concentration, as well as the year the degree was or will be awarded.
3. Experience or employment history is where you list your job experience. This is where you show a prospective employer that you have a history as an employee. List all meaningful employment, not necessarily just the design positions you have held. State the dates you were employed, the name of the firm, the city and state where the firm is located, and the position title. Include a brief description of your duties and responsibilities.
4. List other qualifications or skills you would like to bring to the attention of a prospective employer. These items can fall under a heading such as "Qualifications" or "Achievements." You can include computer skills under this category as well as professional organizations and/or activities. This area also is where you want to include information that will set you apart from other prospects, such as bilingual capability, managerial experience, and/or military service. You also can include academic awards in this category. If you have a long list of significant achievements and awards, you may want to make a separate listing under the category of "Awards."

Limitations and Materials

Your résumé should fit on a single 8 ½- by 11-inch page and be formatted so it is easy to read. Explore format options with rough sketches. Design and produce the final version on the computer and print it on the same type of paper stock that you are using for your letterhead and business card. Produce a PDF version of your résumé if you want to submit it online or post it on a Web site.

Critique Discussion Points

Is anything missing? Does the résumé represent your experience in the best possible way?

Is the résumé easy to read and aesthetically pleasing?

Does the résumé tie in visually with letterhead, business cards, or other promotional materials?

Vocabulary

PDF, paper stock

Name
Contact Information

Education	School Name City, State Degree, Major, Year of Graduation
Employment History	Firm Name, Dates of Employment City, State Job Title Job Duties
	Firm Name, Dates of Employment City, State Job Title Job Duties
	Firm Name, Dates of Employment City, State Job Title Job Duties
Achievements	Proficient in Adobe CS2Quark XPress, PC and Mac Deans List 2003-2007 President, AIGA student chapter Fluent in Japanese

In Review

1. What is pro bono work? What advantages does it offer new designers?
2. What are some important considerations for freelancers with regard to taxes?
3. How many pieces should comprise a student portfolio?
4. Which pieces should go in the front of a portfolio?
5. Why is it important to know about a firm's work before interviewing with that firm?
6. Why is designing a self-promotion piece important to landing an interview?

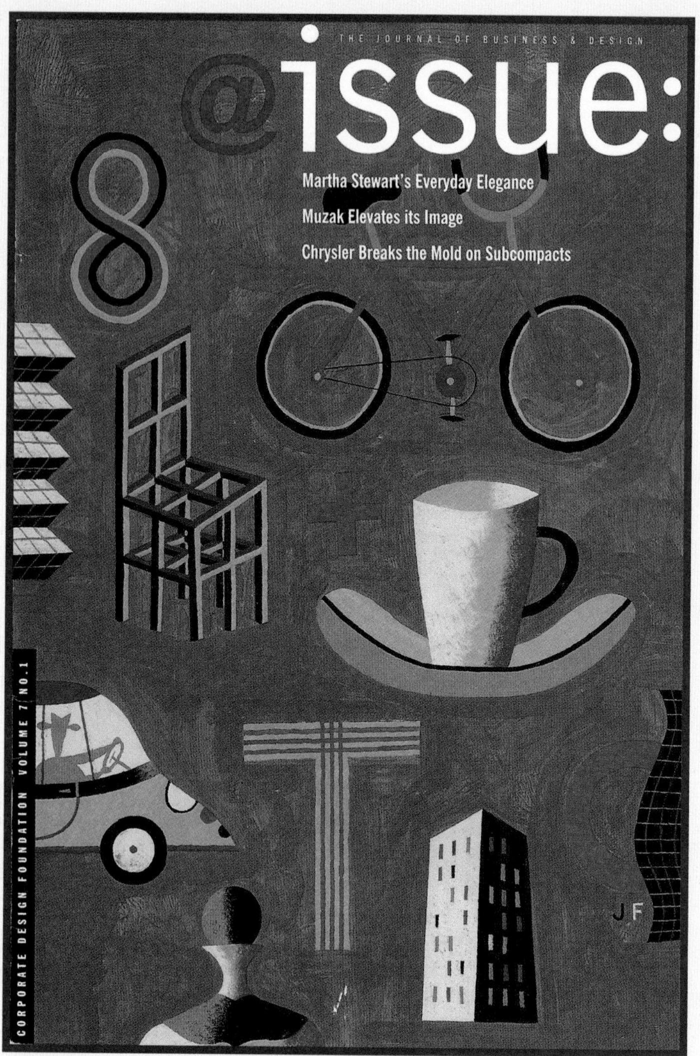
THE JOURNAL OF BUSINESS & DESIGN
@issue:
Martha Stewart's Everyday Elegance
Muzak Elevates its Image
Chrysler Breaks the Mold on Subcompacts
CORPORATE DESIGN FOUNDATION VOLUME 7 NO.1
JF

glossary

abstract Images that resemble the physical world but are a simplification or distortion of the things in it.

achromatic gray A mix of black and white.

additive color system Color system of white light.

ambiguous figure/ground An arrangement that presents an uncertain relationship between shape and space.

analogous hues Color found adjacent to others on a color wheel.

analysis A level of visual inquiry involving the examination of compositional form and its function.

anomaly The presence of an element or visual relationship that is unlike others that dominate a composition.

asymmetric balance Sometimes referred to as dynamic symmetry, the art of creating balance using uneven numbers, sizes, or kinds of elements.

audience The group toward whom you are directing the message/communication.

balance The visual distribution of elements in a composition.

behavior To the actions or reactions of a person, usually in response to environmental factors.

chroma The amount of colorant present in a pigment.

closure The condition of being closed, a dependent relationship of relative position or the relational distance from one object or shape to another.

CMYK Cyan (blue), magenta (red), yellow, and black.

cognition Thinking, a person's mental processes, the processing of information and intellectual understanding or comprehension.

color Inherent hues found in light and pigment.

commitment Level three of William Perry's levels of intellectual maturity; knowledge is constructed from experience, from interaction with others, and from reflective thinking, There are potentially many solutions to a problem but aren't equally valid.

complementary hues Any two hues found directly opposed on the color wheel.

continuous tone Gradations of a series of values or grays blending from one to another.

contrast A juxtaposition, a relational, comparative placement of two or more similar or unlike elements.

description A level of visual inquiry involving the identification of facts.

directional design Visual communication intended to help people find their way through architectural, virtual, or environmental spaces.

dominance The prevailing influence of one element over another, and a function of hierarchy.

dualism Level one of William Perry's levels of intellectual maturity; concrete thinking, thinking in terms of right and wrong.

dynamic symmetry Managing the relationships between negative and positive space and form and counter form.

economy The efficient or concise use of elements.

elements of design Shape, space, line, size, color, texture, and typography.

emphasis Stressing the importance of one element over another.

enhansive design Visual communication intended to add a measure of entertainment value to a design application or embellish the look of a design venue.

environment A time/space relationship that affects the use and interaction of the user with the communication, and where the audience engages the message over a given time frame.

feeling Emotional expression that produces psychological change.

figure/ground reversal A graphic affect where figure can function as ground and ground as figure.

focal point A single feature or mark in a composition that attracts the viewer's eye.

format The surface area that contains the design composition; the arrangement of the design components as they will be printed, cut, scored, and assembled.

gestalt Translated from German to mean "form" or "the way things come together."

graphic design The art of arranging pictographic and typographic elements to create a communication message.

grid A device used as a means of scaling smaller images to larger works; to break down the observed world into smaller, more manageable sections.

halftone Conversion of continuous tones into a dot pattern.

helix A 3-dimension spiral form.

hierarchy An arranged order. Hierarchy is the established order, importance, emphasis, and movement given to visual elements, from the dominant ones to those that are subordinate.

hue The same as color, it is the inherent color referred to by a name or formula.

hyperlinks Highlighted or underlined words, phrases, images, or icons that are coded to link with another part of a website or a different website.

icon An image that possesses similar traits or qualities to the referent.

index An image that shows evidence of something observed or inferred.

information design Visual communication intended to educate an audience.

intelligence A person's ability to use the tools of a culture (Jerome Brunner).

interactive media Media that allows the user or viewer to respond to or control the media experience.

interpretation A level of visual inquiry involving finding meaning in the image.

levels of intellectual maturity A hierarchy developed by William Perry that identifies stages of learning development and readiness to engage in the learning process.

line The moving path of a point.

line art Black and white art that has no continuous tones.

logo A symbol that represents an organization or institution.

media The vehicle—materials used to physically produce the work; the venue—where the communication occurs, the form of the communication.

monochromatic A single color mixed with tints, shades, or tones.

motif The appearance of the overall image in a design; there are three general kinds of overall images—non-objective, abstract, and realistic.

multimedia Interactive digital format that blends animation, streaming audio and video with text, and imagery.

multiplicity Level two of William Perry's levels of intellectual maturity; recognition that thinking can be diverse, more than one solution can be possible.

new media Computer-generated media that goes beyond the two-dimensional realm, including interactive media, the Web and multimedia.

non-objective/non-representational Images having no resemblance to anything recognizable in the real world.

orientation The point of view determined by the designer; the way the viewer is meant to visually relate to a design or image.

persuasive design Visual communication intended to persuade an audience to think or behave in a deliberate, sometimes different, way from what they are accustomed.

polygon A flat sided shape comprised of three or more sides.

primary principles Affect the design as a whole and include unity, variety, hierarchy, and proportion.

problem solving The process or method of managing higher order thinking aimed at achieving a goal, it involves understanding the problem and shaping possible ways to solve it.

project goal A big idea described in a general description; a conceptual umbrella, which is idealistic but attainable.

project objectives Intentions that support the goal, linked to behavioral outcomes and are specific to the task/project.

proportion Size relationships in a composition that serve as the image area and "surface" design.

proximity The position and space given to the placement of elements in a composition.

rationale The reasoning for pursuing an idea.

realism/representation Imagery that replicates the real world in a descriptive manner using objects that have defined and namable referents to the real world.

relativism Level three of William Perry's levels of intellectual maturity; knowledge is relative, knowledge is not universal, but a matter of context and situation.

repetition A pattern of related or juxtaposed elements.

research Intellectual inquiry or examination, the collecting of information on a subject.

rhythm An alternating repetition of shape and space, or a planned movement of elements in a composition.

routine problem solving Applying previously established methods or sets of known procedures.

saturation The purity of a color.

scale Size comparisons of the internal parts of a composition—the visible elements that can be seen on the surface; scale is the relationship of size or a comparison of size from one element to another.

semiotics The study of signs and symbols.

shade The mix of black with a color.

shape A figure or mass.

sign symbol An image that conveys a one to one correspondence to its reference

simple figure/ground The coherent, independent presence of a shape juxtaposed in a space that serves as the ground.

simultaneous contrast An illusory effect where the eye provides a complement based on a sensory response.

size The physical dimensions of an element or format.

strategy How a project is managed or how you plan to produce the design.

subtractive color system System based on mixing color pigments.

support principles Affect internal relationships of the design and include scale, balance, repetition, rhythm, and proximity.

symbol An image that stands for or represents something else.

symbolic interaction The process of forming meaning in support of the formation of personal identity and human socialization.

symmetric balance Elements that are arranged the same or very similar on either side of a central axis.

target audience The group toward whom you are directing your message/communication.

tertiary hues Colors found between primary and secondary.

texture The tactile quality and characteristic of a surface.

theme A subject or topic being represented; the quality or character of a represented idea.

tint Adding white to a pure hue.

tones Grays, also referred to as mid-tones.

typography The arrangement and aesthetics of letterforms. (See the expanded list of terms for typography in Chapter 4.)

unity Overriding principle that is served by all others; unity is the control of variety.

value Lightness or darkness.

variety Visual contrast.

vehicle Materials used to physically produce the work. Examples include the computer, paint, pen-and-ink, charcoal, etc.

venue The place where the communication occurs or the place where the user engages the communication. Examples include electronic, print, and environmental design.

visual communication Conveying meaning through the use and management of images.

visual metaphor An image that can be observed from a variety of viewpoints.

visual thinking A visual problem solving activity dependent on a relationship between mental and physical manipulation of an idea.

index

INDEX